Doing without
Adam and Eve

THEOLOGY AND THE SCIENCES
Kevin J. Sharpe, Series Editor

BOARD OF ADVISORS

TITLES IN THE SERIES

Doing without Adam and Eve

Sociobiology and Original Sin

Patricia A. Williams

FORTRESS PRESS
MINNEAPOLIS

DOING WITHOUT ADAM AND EVE
Sociobiology and Original Sin

Cover art: *Adam et Eve*, 1935–39, by Fernand Léger (1881–1955). Copyright © ARS, N.Y. Used by permission.
Cover design: David Meyer
Book design: Michelle L. Norstad

Library of Congress Cataloging-in-Publication Data

Williams, Patricia A.
    Doing without Adam and Eve : sociobiology and original sin / Patricia A. Williams.
        p. cm. — (Theology and the sciences)
        Includes bibliographical references and index.
        ISBN 0-8006-3285-0 (alk. paper)
    1. Sin, Original. 2. Evolution—Religious aspects—Christianity.
3. Bible. O.T. Genesis—Criticism, interpretation, etc. I. Title. II. Series.

BT720 .W55 2001
233'.14—dc21

2001023794

The paper used in this publication meets the minimum requirements for American National Standard for Information Sciences—Permanence of Paper for Printed Library Materials, ANSI Z329.48–1984.

Manufactured in the U.S.A.

AF 1-3285

05   04   03   02   01   1   2   3   4   5   6   7   8   9   10

To the Episcopal Church:
Without having participated in its liturgy and ambiguity
I would not be who I am

Contents

Preface

Who are Adam and Eve? Christians everywhere know them as the primordial pair who ate the forbidden fruit and caused the corruption of human nature from which we all suffer, even though Jesus redeemed us. Adam and Eve brought evil into the world.

But suppose, as many Christians now do, that Adam and Eve are irrelevant symbolic figures in an imaginary garden rather than the cause of all our woe. Suppose further that the idea of "the fall" from grace is not in Scripture? Does this destroy Christian theology? This book says no. This book says that doing without Adam and Eve while drawing on sociobiology improves Christian theology and helps us understand the origin and persistence of our own sinfulness.

My curiosity about Christianity and sin began early. By the age of five, I had reached the confused conclusion that the members of the church I attended hated people, and I was afraid of them. Why I thought so is a mystery, although my fears probably had something to do with my parents' unhappiness with the church. Soon, my religious life brightened, for my parents joined the Episcopal Church. The Episcopal *Book of Common Prayer* is filled with human humility and joy and God's forgiveness and charity. The church also has a lot of music and pageantry. I fell in love.

I entered high school at eighth grade, with a new library to explore. Almost immediately, I read up on world religions. Right then I decided I would never know which religion was the true one, if there were a true one. Conservatively I decided to remain an Episcopalian unless I saw reason to change. I continued as an Episcopalian for another thirty years.

Two or three years after my decision, I became convinced that, because plants, animals, and people have evolved, the Genesis creation narratives are myths. My religious faith was unmoved by my new insight. My earlier skepticism about true religion served me well. Later, as a graduate student in philosophy, I fell in love with the theory of evolution and became a philosopher of science, specializing in philosophy of biology. That is, I became an expert on the theory of evolution. I concentrated on evolutionary ethics and sociobiology. I published academic articles on sociobiology and ethics and coedited a book with Robert Wesson entitled *Evolution and Human Values* (1995).

Before entering graduate school in philosophy, I had explored everything the Episcopal Church offers. I participated in its services; read its history, poetry, and mystical traditions; studied its liturgy, theology, and creeds; engaged in critical examination of the Bible; attended Episcopal seminary; and investigated joining an Episcopal convent. At one time, I thought I had lost my belief in God. Later, I discovered I had not lost what was central: my experience of God's continuing presence and my belief in God's goodness and forgiveness.

Shortly before *Evolution and Human Values* appeared, the academic quarterly *Zygon: Journal of Religion and Science* published an article by Michael Ruse entitled "Evolutionary Theory and Christian Ethics" (Ruse 1994). Various essays accompanied his, mostly supporting his position. His claim was that Christianity and evolutionary ethics are irreconcilable. His article and those accompanying it seemed so wrongheaded I had to respond. Two years later *Zygon* published my reply as "Christianity and Evolutionary Ethics: Sketch toward a Reconciliation" (Williams 1996a). I considered turning my article into a book uniting Christianity and science, and I developed a proposal. Just as I completed it, I received a letter from Rem B. Edwards, Lindsay Young Professor of Philosophy at the University of Tennessee, Knoxville, with whom I was unacquainted, praising my article, saying his graduate students found it fruitful, and encouraging me to write a book. This is the book.

Because this book is the product of a lifetime, I would like to begin my thanks with the College of William and Mary, where I received my undergraduate degree in English literature. The English department taught me to read carefully, write clearly, analyze texts closely, and understand metaphor and symbol.

Peter Heath of the philosophy department at the University of Virginia introduced me to philosophy of biology in an individual study course in graduate school. He is the most articulate person I have ever met. I learned much from him about how to do philosophy.

Tom Settle taught me philosophy of science at the University of Guelph, Ontario, where I received my doctorate. Guelph combined an excellent graduate program with the most benevolent, friendly, helpful graduate philosophy department anywhere. It also had a physics department that invited major physicists to speak, then insisted they give their talks without the aid of mathematics, so undergraduates could understand them. Through these speakers, the physics department kept me in touch with the physical sciences and cosmology while I pursued philosophy. I am grateful to both departments.

In their very different ways, Michael Ruse and Rem Edwards inspired me to write this book.

Annual Biblical Archaeology Society seminars in Greensboro, North Carolina, sparked and maintained my interest in the historical Jesus.

The librarians at Alderman Library, Clemons Library, and the Science and Engineering Library at the University of Virginia have been unfailingly pleasant and eager to help with research materials. As the library system went from card catalogue to computer, then to computer with Internet, the librarians also saved me from being baffled by more than one unfamiliar library search engine.

I also want to thank all who read and commented on the manuscript, especially Jay Worrall, whose constant encouragement and innumerable editorial suggestions were welcome companions after I composed each chapter. Rem Edwards and I have stayed in touch since his unexpected letter, and he kindly read and commented on the entire manuscript, as did Beth S. Neman, an English professor at Wilmington College in Ohio; Maggie Potts, on whose judgment I rely for many things; and Carol Blair. Charles R. Tolbert and Mark Whittle of the astronomy department at the University of Virginia read the section on cosmology, cheered me on, and saved me from error. Michael West, editor-in-chief at Fortress Press, made several suggestions, all helpful. His request that I present more scholarship on the Hebrew Scriptures resulted in the present chapter 6, without which the book would have been incomplete. I gratefully thank everyone. Any remaining mistakes, omissions, and infelicities are my own. Finally, I would like to confess that working on this book has been personally rewarding and a great deal of fun!

I can be contacted through my Web site at http://hometown.aol.com/theologyauthor/myhomepage/index.html, which has links to information on the books I have authored or edited. I can also be contacted by e-mail at theologyauthor@aol.com.

Introduction

The purpose of this book is to unite Christianity with science. By *Christianity*, I mean classical, orthodox Christian doctrine. The book assumes that six beliefs are essential to classical Christianity. First is the existence of one God. Second is the resurrection of Jesus, without which Paul says Christian faith is vain (1 Cor. 15:17a). Third is the fullness of God in Jesus, classically expressed in the doctrine of the two natures of Christ, fully divine, fully human, without which Christ's atonement is impossible. The fourth doctrine is the Trinity, emphasizing the sovereignty of God, the exaltation and living presence of Jesus, and the continuous action of God in the world through the Holy Spirit. The fifth lists God's attributes of omniscience, omnipotence, omnibenevolence, and creativity, by which we know that there can be nothing greater than God and there is no other creator of the universe. Sixth is the moral law Jesus summarizes in commending love of neighbor.

By *science*, I mean mainstream, standard science, all of it. This book defends the theory of evolution and the evolution of modern human beings from nonhuman ancestors. In doing so, it embraces modern geology. It also describes sociobiology and its application to human psychology. Therefore, it accepts modern genetics. Finally, it explains modern cosmology, the theory that the universe began some 12 billion years ago in the Big Bang and evolved through time to become the universe we now inhabit. Along with modern cosmology, the book accepts modern physics and chemistry.

To unite classical Christianity and modern science, I focus on the Christian doctrine of original sin, because it is amenable to scientific analysis. In its classical formulation, original sin is a doctrine about human origins and human nature, both now subjects of science. Bringing science into Christianity through the doctrine of original sin effects a natural union between science and Christianity. Science offers Christianity a new way to reformulate ancient Christian doctrines—original sin, the atonement, and an answer to the problem of evil.

To my knowledge, no one has done this before. Most books dealing with science and religion fall into four categories. First are books seeking to replace religion with science. Second are those trying to replace science with religion. Third are books that separate science and religion into different fields, speaking different languages. Fourth are books seeking to unite science and religion. This book is in the last category.

Books in this category by creationists often claim to present science fairly and accurately, but they fail to do so. This book is different. It presents science accurately. True consolidation requires an accurate grasp of science.

Books in this category by scientists are typically interested in proving the existence of God through science using a version of the argument from design. But to prove the existence of God through science is to give science priority. This book is unlike those, for its Christian assumptions rest on faith and Scripture. It does not give science hegemony by using science to prove the existence of God or the truth of Christian doctrines. In this book, science and Christianity are equal partners.

This book unites Christianity and science, not theism and science. This is unusual. To do so, it focuses on the theological doctrine of original sin and the scientific theory of sociobiology. This is unprecedented.

The classical doctrine of original sin has two separable parts. One is the historical claim that the first human beings, Adam and Eve, sinned by eating fruit God had forbidden them to eat. The second is the psychological claim that human nature was once virtuous, but the first sin corrupted it. Part One of this book argues that both claims are false. The alleged corruption of human nature is not found in Genesis 3. It is not scriptural. Moreover, science tells us that Adam and Eve are not historical figures. Therefore, the narrative about them cannot explain our inclination to sin or the origin of evil.

Part Two uses science to provide a new theory of human nature. The new theory retains a central place for sin. Because sin remains central, science and Christianity can be united. Furthermore, as this book demonstrates, the scientific theory of human nature is richer and more complex than the theological one and so reflects human nature more accurately. Science provides a new perspective on the origin of sin, a perspective crucial to reconceiving the doctrine of original sin, solving the problem of evil, and understanding the atonement.

Thus, the argument of the book has two parts, negative and positive. Part One gives the negative argument in six chapters. Chapter 1 introduces the scientific, scriptural, and doctrinal issues. Chapter 2 offers reasons for us to be skeptical of our own explanations, then presents ways to test them for truth. Chapter 3 uses the tests of truth to demonstrate that the change in human nature alleged to have occurred when Adam and Eve disobeyed God is not in Scripture. Chapter 4 employs the tests of truth to evaluate the three main Christian doctrines of original sin. Chapter 5 tests the broader creation narratives of Genesis 1–9 for truth and ends by testing the contrasting scientific account. Chapter 6 applies the tests of truth to Scripture in general, including the New Testament.

Part Two presents the positive argument by developing a new theory of human nature based on the evolutionary science of sociobiology, then applying it to the doctrines of original sin, the problem of evil, and the atonement. Chapter 7 explains the theory of evolution, and chapter 8 extends that explanation to sociobiology, the part of the theory of evolution applicable to human nature. Chapter 9 is the culmination of the previous chapters. It shows how the sociobiological model of human nature reformulates the theological doctrines of original sin while retaining the centrality of sin. With the new concepts of human nature and sin in hand, chapter 10 addresses the problem of evil. Chapter 11 shows that current atonement doctrines fail to pass the tests of truth, then employs modern scholarship on the historical Jesus to show that Jesus demonstrates how to deal with our complex, evolved nature, our culture, and our relationship to God.

This book takes on a radical task, a new interpretation of the Christian doctrines of original sin and atonement and a new solution to the problem of evil. Yet, it stands by the orthodox and catholic in classical Christianity and questions only controversial and divisive doctrines. Current controversies about original sin provide a serious obstacle to reconciliation among the three major branches of the Christian church: Roman Catholic, Eastern Orthodox, and Protestant. The historical proliferation of conflicting atonement doctrines is a scandal to any thoughtful Christian. Finally, with the demise of Adam and Eve, the problem of evil in Christianity needs a new solution. Rewriting controversial and divisive doctrines and offering a new solution to the problem of evil should support orthodoxy and lend stability to classical Christianity.

This book also stands by science. It does not rewrite science to suit Christianity. Philosophically, it assumes science and theology are searches for truth. Because it makes this assumption, it freely applies tests of truth to science, theology, and Scripture.

Almost anything can be tested for truth, from everyday statements and concepts to narratives, theological doctrines, and scientific laws. In order to avoid a proliferation of technical terms and lengthy discussions of what constitutes a concept, a doctrine, or a law, I subsume anything that can be tested for truth under the term *theory*.

To avoid an unsightly number of capitalized words, I do not capitalize the religious doctrines that are discussed at length in this book: the fall, original sin, the atonement, and the resurrection.

In quoting from Scripture, I use the New Revised Standard Version of the Bible. It seems to be the translation most acceptable to the majority of Christian churches. I use standard references to biblical verses. For example, the First Letter to the Corinthians, chapter 15, verse 17, is 1 Cor. 15:17. Reference to half verses uses *a* and *b*; that is, 1 Cor. 15:17a refers to the first half of verse 17, 17b to the second half.

In ordinary usage, the term *orthodox* is ambiguous. It refers to Christians who believe the central doctrines of Christianity, but it also refers to one of the three branches of the Christian church. *Catholic* suffers much the same ambiguity. It refers to the universal church, but also to another of the three branches of Christianity. (The third branch is Protestant.) To avoid confusion, I will capitalize *Orthodox* and *Catholic* when referring to their respective branches of the Christian church. If confusion still seems possible, I will add the adjectives *Eastern* Orthodox and *Roman* Catholic to refer to the entire branches of Orthodox and Catholic Christianity, although this usage is not, strictly speaking, correct. (There are Catholic churches not attached to Rome and Orthodox churches that do not think of themselves as Eastern.)

With these details clarified, let us together explore whether Christianity can be united with science by doing without Adam and Eve.

PART ONE
THE DEMISE OF ADAM AND EVE

Chapter 1

Science, Scripture, and Doctrine

According to Christianity, God created the material universe and gave it order. Science investigates the material universe and affirms its order. Logically, then, Christianity should embrace science as the discipline that examines God's creation and shows us God's works and plans. Yet, Christianity's reaction to science has been largely negative, even violent. A few conflicts have been over theological doctrines, but most have centered on certain passages of Scripture.

Prominent among these passages is the creation narrative at the beginning of Genesis. In Genesis, God forms the universe in brief, decisive steps, and when God rests, the work of creation is finished. From that moment on, little changes. The universe is essentially static. According to biblical chronology, the universe and Earth are barely six thousand years old. God created each biological species separately and fashioned humankind as a single pair, Adam and Eve. Soon, they disobeyed God and were cast out of Eden, their garden paradise. God punished Adam with hardship in farming, Eve with pain in childbirth, and both with mortality.

Science tells a different story. According to science, the cosmos has developed for some 12 billion years, Earth for 4.5 billion, and organisms for approximately 3 billion. The universe is always in a dynamic process of change. Biological species evolved from one another. Humankind is simply another species, evolved like other species and from other species. All creatures are mortal, and garnering resources and reproducing are the tasks of all living things.

The three branches of the Christian church have had three different reactions to this collision between science and Scripture.

Science and Scripture

Conservative Protestant churches have asserted that the Bible is a scientific and historical document, to be read literally and treated as inerrant or infallible. Where science and Scripture disagree, science is wrong, even demonic.

The modern Roman Catholic Church has taken a second, more moderate position. Having learned from its mistake over Galileo, it recognizes the claims of science. It says the Genesis creation narratives contain figurative language. However, where questions arise about the historicity of Adam, Eve, and the fall, the church insists that the narrative in Genesis is historical: "The account of the fall in *Genesis* 3 . . . affirms a primeval event, a deed that took place *at the beginning of the history of man*" (*Catechism* 1994, 98; emphasis in original).

Taking a third position, the liberal Protestant churches say the Bible is not a scientific or historical document. They treat the creation and fall as metaphor and myth that tell us about ourselves and our relationship to God, but not about science or history. These churches are willing to accept the scientific story in its entirety.

Each of these positions has its difficulties. The position that the Bible is infallible is challenged not only by science, but also by evidence internal to Scripture. Claims to inerrancy are not logically tenable because the Bible has internal inconsistencies. Doublets of narratives, events, and even genealogies contradict each other so that both cannot be true. Genesis 1 and 2 provide an example. In Genesis 1:11-27, God creates vegetation, then sea dwellers, then birds, then land creatures, then humankind, male and female together. In Genesis 2:5-22, God creates a male human being first, then plants, animals, and a female human being. Both these accounts cannot be historically, inerrantly true. Either human beings were created together or separately; either plants and/or animals were created before or after the first human being.

Such contradictions are not limited to the Hebrew Scriptures. The infancy narratives in Matthew and Luke also contradict each other. In Matthew 1:18—2:23, Joseph and Mary travel from Bethlehem to Egypt to Nazareth. They are motivated by fear of a massacre, then by a desire to avoid settling in Herod's son's territory. In Luke 2:1-39, they travel from Nazareth to Bethlehem to Jerusalem and back to Nazareth. Their initial travels are motivated by a census/taxation by

Rome, their trip to Jerusalem by their desire to fulfill Jewish law, their return to Nazareth by their wish to go home. Matthew has a star leading astrologers to Joseph's house, Luke an angelic host pointing shepherds to a stable. Again, both these narratives cannot be historically, inerrantly true. Astrologers at Joseph's house or shepherds in a stable, massacre or census, Egypt or Jerusalem—only one story, if either, is true. To read the Bible literally and believe it infallible means rejecting the simple logic indispensable in daily life. The price is too high.

The liberal option also pays a high price. Liberal churches have tended to embrace the *God of the gaps.* The God of the gaps fills explanatory gaps left by incomplete scientific explanations. For example, the Middle Ages considered God to be directly active in every event. In 1687, Isaac Newton demonstrated that gravity, not the mighty hand of God, moved the planets in their courses. A gap closed.

The response was to find God's hand in the familiar, natural world. God might not move the planets, but God directly created each biological species. In 1859, Charles Darwin closed that gap. Since then, other gaps have closed, and God has continued to retreat. As the twentieth century ended, the God of the gaps was vanishing over the horizon. It is true that God is still seen as creator of the Big Bang and of laws governing the universe. However, this is not the personal God of Christianity but the distant God of Aristotle and of the eighteenth-century Deists; the God of the philosophers, not the God of Abraham and Isaac and Jacob; the unmoved mover, not the living God who meets, rescues, and frees us. This is the originator of everything, the sustainer and savior of nothing, the God whose creation we inhabit but whose presence we no longer need. From this perspective, Jesus becomes a great man, a sage or a prophet, but he is no longer divine.

As far as the fall is concerned, liberals insist it be retained as central because of its theological importance for the atonement, yet they consider it a myth. Logically, however, the living, historical Jesus can no more atone for the sins of fictive, mythological forebears than we can suffer the real consequences of their fabled sins. On a strictly logical level, treating the narrative as myth means it has no theological work to do. The liberal response is that it is a myth with a message. It tells us about human nature, about our condition of exile and alienation. Yet, as I will argue, we evolved here. Earth is our home. We are not exiles. If the myth is primarily about alienation, it misleads us about the human situation. Moreover, as Christians, we should look to Jesus for revelation about the human condition, not to an ancient Hebrew myth.

The Catholic Church seems unusually aware of the theological dangers of treating Adam, Eve, and the fall as myth. Although it does not assert the inerrancy of the Bible, it claims infallibility in its Pope. In spite of maintaining that the creation narratives use mythological language, the Pope insists on the historicity of the fall (Pius XII [1950] 1956, 287). Catholicism thinks the doctrine of the atonement will crumble if the fall is not a historical event creating original sin. As it notes, "We cannot tamper with the revelation of original sin without undermining the mystery of Christ" (*Catechism* 1994, 98). Without a historical fall, Catholicism thinks Christianity itself is in danger.

The difficulty with this middle position is that if Adam and Eve and/or the fall are not historical, Christianity will hardly be strengthened by closing its eyes and shouting, "No, no, no!" Integrity demands open eyes and honest efforts to see the truth and its consequences. In order to see the truth, it is necessary to examine central Christian doctrines. Christianity begins with doctrines explicitly found in Scripture.

Central Scriptural Doctrines

Traditional Christianity as it is recorded in the earliest canonical Christian documents, the letters of Paul, begins with the belief that Jesus Christ truly died and was raised from the dead (1 Cor. 15:1-4). As Paul notes, without belief in Jesus' resurrection, Christian faith is in vain (1 Cor. 15:12-19). Jesus' resurrection is the central tenet of Christianity, which shares its monotheism with Judaism and Islam.

Like other central doctrines of the Christian faith, Jesus' resurrection cannot be proved or disproved by science, for it is not open to empirical examination. Because it can be interpreted as a spiritual resurrection not entailing physical resuscitation, even finding the undisputed bones of Jesus would not disprove it. Nonetheless, it is open to a kind of psychological and sociological affirmation.

The Gospels tell of disciples who do not understand Jesus, who abandon him in his hour of need, who deny knowing him when assent might endanger their own lives. After Jesus' death, they either hide behind locked doors or scatter across Galilee, returning to their old homes and occupations. Yet, before long, they are speaking in the streets, forums, and synagogues, jailed, beaten, and stoned, but never dissuaded from preaching in the name of Jesus. Something happened. Something turned these once confused and frightened people into stalwart evangelists.

They preached Jesus raised from the dead. Quite what that meant to them or means to us in physical terms is unclear. Whatever exactly it meant physically, psychologically it meant these were changed men and women. Their explanation is that they encountered Jesus alive after his crucifixion, death, and burial. Because their lives were radically changed, their own explanation of that change is worth heeding.

A sociological perspective is also valuable. Because many other first-century messianic movements did not outlive the deaths of their founders, but this one did, its success deserves consideration. Several experts on the Jesus movement of the first century conclude that the best explanation of the movement's success after Jesus' death is that he really was raised from the dead (Sanders 1985, 240; Hurtado 1988, 121; Wright 1996, 29). Of course, neither the change in the disciples nor the success of Christianity constitutes empirical proof of the resurrection. However, they provide reasons not to limit our search for answers to what philosophers call *naturalistic explanations*.

Naturalistic explanations are explanations limited to science or common sense. To naturalize a miracle is to explain it in scientific or common sense terms, for example, that Jesus could walk on water because he knew where the sandbars were. Not only is the resurrection, like other fundamental Christian doctrines, a matter of faith and not of knowledge, its power for change suggests that naturalistic explanations of it fail to capture its psychological and historical import. A miracle might have occurred. And miracles, if they occur, will not be captured by naturalistic explanations.

Because the resurrection of Jesus is the central tenet of the Christian faith, we might assume that the major branches of the Christian church agree that Jesus was raised from the dead. They do. Nonetheless, Christians disagree about whether the resurrection entails the physical resuscitation of a dead body or whether the resurrected body is a different kind of entity.

Stating the issue in terms of the resuscitation of the old body versus the resurrection of a new one highlights the ambiguity in the relevant biblical material. On the one hand, on more than one occasion the disciples fail to recognize the resurrected Jesus (Luke 24:13-16; John 20:14-16). The resurrected Jesus passes through locked doors (John 20:19, 26). He appears and disappears (Luke 24:36, 51; Acts 1:9). The resurrected Jesus seems to be different in appearance and attributes from the Jesus the disciples knew before his death.

Furthermore, when Paul discusses the general resurrection of the dead, he comments that resurrected bodies will be different from our mortal ones: "We will not all die, but we will all be changed" (1 Cor. 15:51b). Further, he comments, "For this perishable body must put on imperishability, and this mortal body must put on immortality" (1 Cor. 15:53). It appears that Paul, our earliest canonical source, believes resurrected bodies differ from mortal ones.

On the other hand, all four Gospels tell of an empty tomb. Biblical scholars think that faith, evangelism, and arguments about authority in the early church lie behind these narratives (Crossan 1993, 123–26), and that the empty tomb was not one of the disciples' experiences (Spong 1994, 228). The empty tomb is certainly not found in Paul. However, for the noncritical biblical reader, the narratives of an empty tomb provide reason to believe in Jesus' resuscitation.

In the end, the scriptural evidence cuts both ways. The scriptural evidence does not compel those Christians who believe in Jesus' resurrection and postresurrection appearances to believe in his resuscitation. On the other hand, those Christians who read of an empty tomb have warrant for believing in it. Christians who hold either belief think Jesus was raised from the dead. Although the manner may be disputed among Christians, the resurrection itself is not.

The major branches of the Christian church also believe God inspired the Bible. They all believe the Holy Spirit breathes through the biblical authors in such a manner that the Bible is, in a unique sense, God's word to humanity. How this belief is interpreted is another matter, and one about which there is serious disagreement. Robert Gnuse (1985) provides a thorough discussion. I will simplify the issues.

Scriptural interpretation from earliest times to the late Middle Ages assumed that Scripture contains secret meanings hidden in its details (Kugel 1998, 15). Often interpreters employed allegory. Before his conversion in 386, Saint Augustine rejected Christianity partly because a literal reading of the Hebrew Scriptures shows God approving of immoral actions (Brown 1967, 42–44), and he later accepted Christianity partly because Saint Ambrose taught him to interpret Scripture figuratively and allegorically (Brown 1967, 83–87; also see Augustine [397] 1961, 108). In interpreting Scripture allegorically, not only were Christians following the lead of the rabbis, they were also following Paul, who explicitly employs allegory. Commenting on the birth of sons to Abram/Abraham by Hagar and Sarah (Genesis 16 and 21), Paul says, "One, the child of the slave, was born according to the flesh; the other, the child of the free woman, was born through the promise. Now this is an allegory: these women are two covenants" (Gal. 4:23-24a).

Faced with the esoteric readings and heavy allegorization practiced in the late Middle Ages, the Reformers rejected both, insisting on the plain sense of Scripture. Because Scripture contains internal contradictions, insisting on a literal, plain interpretation led the more systematically inclined Reformers to engage in some heady logical contortions. During the nineteenth and twentieth centuries, commitment to interpretation of the literal plain sense of Scripture has resulted in conflict with science, history, and literary criticism. This conflict has forced those who wish to read Scripture solely with a straightforward, plain-sense interpretation to employ what Marcus Borg refers to as *conscious literalism* (Borg 1994a, 174–78).

Reading with conscious literalism means interpreting Scripture literally or considering it inerrant or infallible while knowing that the results of this method of interpretation contravene received knowledge in disciplines as diverse and established as paleoanthropology, archaeology, sociology, chemistry, physics, cosmology, stratigraphy, radio carbon dating, biogeography, anatomy, embryology, DNA analysis, evolutionary biology, history, literary criticism, and biblical criticism. No educated person can discard the discoveries of these disciplines and maintain intellectual integrity.

Nonetheless, considering all this knowledge will not refute central scriptural doctrines. Using it, even the Jesus Seminar, so critical of the historicity of the Gospel accounts of the deeds and sayings of Jesus, thinks Jesus' commendation of love to neighbor represents his views (Funk, Hoover, and the Jesus Seminar 1993, 104).

Neither will taking these modern developments into account refute Christianity's central theological doctrines.

Central Theological Doctrines

The most central theological doctrine in Christianity is the Trinity. Both historically and logically, Trinitarianism begins with the scriptural doctrine that Jesus was raised from the dead. This being so, he was an extraordinary person. John's Gospel presents Jesus before his birth as the preexistent *Logos* (John 1:1-18). The Letter to the Hebrews speaks of the postcrucifixion Jesus as exalted above the angels (Heb. 1:3-4). Nonetheless, here on Earth, he was a person like us. As the same letter notes, "Therefore [Jesus] had to become like his brothers and sisters in every respect" (Heb. 2:17a). Here is laid the foundation for viewing Jesus as divine and human.

According to the Gospel of John, Jesus promises that, after his departure, the Holy Spirit will be with the disciples to comfort and teach them (John 14:15-17). Acts narrates the astounding event of the Spirit's descending en masse upon the disciples in Jerusalem where they speak in tongues (Acts 2:1-11). And Paul speaks of the "fruit of the Spirit" that comes to "those who belong to Christ" (Gal. 5:22-24a). Here is God as Holy Spirit in the world. While the third person of the Trinity, the Holy Spirit, has scriptural foundations, the doctrine of the Trinity is articulated in Greek philosophical language.

In 325, an ecumenical council of the Christian church met at Nicaea and formulated the Nicene Creed, the creed that is the classical, theological statement of Christian Trinitarianism. Roman Catholic, Eastern Orthodox, and many Protestant churches use this creed today as part of their regular liturgies, but other Protestant churches reject it and all formal creeds on the grounds that such creeds are not scriptural. Not only were the formal creeds developed after the New Testament was written, their terminology derives from Greek philosophy foreign to Scripture. On both of these points, the Protestant churches are correct. However, while rejecting the explicit formulation of Nicaea, these same Protestant churches would be the first to affirm that Jesus embodies the fullness of God, that he was raised from the dead, that he is Lord, that the Holy Spirit spoke through the prophets and the disciples, and that this same Spirit is with the church today.

Apparently, the argument over the philosophical formulation of the doctrine of the Trinity is not so much an argument over theological beliefs as it is over terminology. The Nicene Creed asserts that Jesus is "of one substance with the Father." The Protestants who reject the Nicene Creed reject the term *substance* as unbiblical. Yet, the authors of the creed were trying to assert that Jesus is completely united with God, and to make that assertion clear and explicit in the philosophical language available to them. In rejecting this language, the Protestant churches do not reject the concept of Jesus' divinity. The fact that the terminology is not scriptural should not obscure the conceptual continuity between the New Testament and the Nicene formula.

Another council met in Chalcedon in 451. This time the issue was not the Trinity but Christology. The council reaffirmed the formulation of Nicaea regarding the sameness of substance of Jesus and the Godhead. It then proceeded to more precise theological statements of the personhood of Christ, asserting that he has two natures (divine and human), but nonetheless is one person, one Christ, one Lord, without division or separation. Again, terms such as *person*, *nature*, and *substance* are all technical terms from Greek philosophy and foreign to Scripture. However, the concepts behind these terms are scriptural. *One person* refers to Jesus Christ as a single, undivided individual, an integrated man whom the disciples knew as a unique human being, and whom later Christians also know as one, although raised and glorified.

I join with the Protestants who object to the Greek philosophical terminology of the Nicene Creed and the statement of Chalcedon, but I join them from the other side of the historical and conceptual world. My objection to the Greek terms is not that they are not scriptural but that they are incommensurate with contemporary philosophical and scientific notions of how things are. For example, there is no way to translate *substance*—that which makes a thing what it is—into contemporary notions of atoms and their constituents. This is especially true where the Greek concept of substance arises most importantly in Christian theology, namely in Christology and in Eucharistic doctrine. Yet, I do not reject these Greek philosophical formulas of Christian doctrines.

Since they are so foreign, why not reject them? There are four reasons. First, the doctrines are traditional Christian responses to profound questions about the relationship of Jesus Christ to the

Godhead. No better responses to these questions exist, and I suspect that better responses could never be developed without recourse to Greek philosophy if only because the questions themselves are couched in Greek philosophical terms. Second, these formulas developed from New Testament statements, and rejecting them would entail denying the existence of a history of ideas that helps us understand both the New Testament and our own place in Christian history. Third, the major branches of the Christian church today accept these formulas. To reject them would be to invite further division among Christians. Finally, they are brief, carefully formulated statements about the fundamental beliefs of Christianity. Such statements remind Christians to distinguish between the fundamental and the peripheral. Having them helps Christians maintain perspective during controversies and assert that the identity of Jesus is central to Christianity, whereas being antiabortion or antiwar are ancillary. More open to analysis are today's controversial doctrines.

Controversial Doctrines

Christians have killed each other over many doctrines. Heretics have been burned at the stake for a variety of beliefs, some esoteric by modern standards, and the Protestant-Catholic rift of 1517 brought wars in Europe that lasted for three centuries. Which doctrines aroused the most ire and bloodshed depended on time and circumstance. Doctrines that once caused strife became accepted while others developed into sources of division. The early church deposed bishops over the Trinity. By the Reformation that doctrine was settled, whereas the Eucharist was controversial.

As divisive as the doctrine of original sin was in the early church, and as important as it was in both the Catholic-Orthodox rupture of 1054 and the Protestant-Catholic breach of 1517, as far as I know no one died for it. Yet, if we examine Christian doctrines today, the doctrine of original sin is the one fundamental Christian doctrine upon which each separate branch of the church holds disparate views. Protestants hold one doctrine of original sin, Roman Catholics another, and the Eastern Orthodox another. A doctrine so divisive cries out for reexamination.

Because the doctrine is so divisive, it is difficult to define. However, the basic idea is that human nature is corrupt. Ideally human beings should love and obey God and should also love each other. (Indeed, the ideal of loving God and others is contained in that of obeying God: to obey God would be to love God and others.) However, human beings are not disposed to love God and others. Ancient authors named this indisposition *pride*. Capturing the ancient rather than the modern meaning of pride, modern psychology calls it *egocentricity*, which is the term I will employ.

The idea that human nature is corrupt implies that it was corrupted, that once it was pure. The notion that human nature has been corrupted makes the question of the origin of sin compelling. If we were once virtuous but are now wicked, how did we come to be that way? The remainder of this book explores this question.

Closely connected to the doctrine of original sin is that of the atonement. They are related because understanding the origin and persistence of sin provides insight about the work atonement must accomplish. Unfortunately, more than a dozen conflicting doctrines of atonement had been articulated by the end of the Reformation. Which doctrines received the most emphasis shifted over the centuries as cultural pressures, intellectual customs, and interpretations of related doctrines changed.

The primary cause of this flux is the New Testament. The New Testament is rich in metaphors interpreting the atonement, metaphors borrowed from law, theology, ritual, and slavery. In the New Testament, Christ redeems us from slavery just as people literally purchased their relatives and friends from servitude; in ritual, he is sacrificed like an offering at pagan or Jewish temples; theologically, he is priest, the one who offers the sacrifice; in law, he mediates and advocates, a defender before the Godhead of those who trespass. All these usages are metaphorical and not to be taken literally. Taking one or more of them literally is a glaring defect in many atonement doctrines. All have in common a message of forgiveness and liberation that must be retained in any adequate interpretation of the atonement.

I think there is a second cause for the historical fluctuation of the doctrines. Jesus' crucifixion baffled early Christians. It should not have happened. The predicted messiah was to have been a victorious leader, a king restoring Israel to freedom and greatness. Recent examination of the Dead Sea Scrolls has confirmed this interpretation of first-century messianic expectations (Wise, Abegg, and Cook 1996, 229–33 and 291–94). In contrast, Jesus suffered and died as a criminal. As Paul says, the crucifixion was "a stumbling block to Jews and foolishness to Gentiles" (1 Cor. 1:23b). Because it baffled, the crucifixion demanded explanation, so explanation focused upon it. Most doctrines of the atonement developed to explain the crucifixion.

In a culture with different expectations, this might not have been so. In place of the cross, the resurrection might have received the most attention. Yet, a glance into almost any Christian church demonstrates that the cross is central. In sacramental churches, it holds the central place in the sanctuary. In nonsacramental churches, it is often the only symbol of Christianity in the building.

Or Jesus' teachings might have been emphasized. Yet they were not. Mark, the earliest canonical Gospel, records relatively few teachings; almost one-half of the Gospel focuses on the passion and crucifixion. Indeed, in comparison with most of the noncanonical Gospels, the four canonical ones all emphasize the passion and crucifixion.

In contrast, a noncanonical Gospel, the Gospel of Thomas, whose foundations might have been laid contemporaneously with the letters of Paul (Funk, Hoover, and the Jesus Seminar 1993, 18), consists only of sayings. This Gospel did not survive the winnowing of the early church, surely a commentary on where the church's interest in Jesus lay. Not only did this Gospel not become canonical; except for three small fragments, it entirely disappeared from history until a copy of it was discovered in a cache of ancient documents at Nag Hammadi in 1945.

Even among the canonical Gospels, accurate preservation of Jesus' authentic sayings is uncertain. The authenticity of each saying has become a matter of scholarly debate (Funk, Hoover, and the Jesus Seminar 1993). In contrast, there is almost no debate about the historicity of the crucifixion. It is mentioned in ancient historical works. It is attested throughout the New Testament. The early church preserved many records of it. Jesus' passion and crucifixion seem more central to emergent Christianity than his teachings.

Perhaps more interestingly, Jesus' lifestyle did not assume central place. Rather than being venerated or emulated, it was ignored and rejected. Jesus' festive attitude and his barrier-dismantling inclusiveness were replaced early on by asceticism and exclusion as a way of life among Christians (Borg 1994b, 53–56, 121–31; Crossan 1991, 360–67). Among theologians, only Peter Abelard (1079–1142) made the example of Jesus' life central to the atonement. Yet he, too, emphasized Jesus' suffering during his crucifixion, slighting his life in Galilee and his message. Chapter 11 makes Jesus' life, message, and resurrection central to the atonement, correcting Christianity's historic overemphasis on the crucifixion. However, this overemphasis cannot be corrected without further examination of science, Scripture, and doctrine. To delve into them more deeply requires evaluative tools. These tools are the standard philosophical tests of truth.

Chapter 2

Tests of Truth

———————

"What is truth?" Pilate asks Jesus (John 18:38), but Jesus offers no reply. Against the Gospel's silence, philosophers speak. They offer three answers to Pilate's question. True statements must be logically coherent. This is the *coherence* test of truth. True statements must also correspond to the way the world is. This is the *correspondence* test of truth. Philosophers of science present a third test, the *consilience* test of truth, which applies best to scientific theories, although sometimes it may be useful in other contexts. It says that scientific theories must eventually fit together to create a picture of the material world in which the coherence and correspondence tests are satisfied.

These tests of truth are important. In this chapter, I explain them in detail, then apply them in the remainder of the book. Their importance is partly explained by the existence in our brains of an *Interpreter* that insistently invents explanations whether it possesses the relevant information or not. The existence of the Interpreter makes all our explanations suspect. Moreover, some of our thinking is stereotyped, fitting simple patterns in our minds rather than complex, objective facts in the world. Other animals react in stereotyped ways, too. Biologists say these stereotyped reactions are *canalized*. If ideas fit a canalized pattern, we should be especially skeptical of them. Thus, canalization provides a weak and negative test of truth. This chapter begins by introducing the Interpreter and explaining the concept of canalization.

The Interpreter and Canalization

George examines a picture of a snow scene and another of a chicken claw. From an array of choices, he selects the appropriate matching pictures. He chooses a shovel and a chicken. When asked why he made these choices, he says, "Oh, that's simple. The chicken claw goes with the chicken, and you need a shovel to clean out the chicken shed."

Shown the word *walk*, Susan gets up from her seat and begins to walk across the room. When asked why, she says she is going for a Coke. Shown the word *laugh*, Margaret does so. When asked why she had laughed, she comments on the humor of the test situation (Gazzaniga 1992, 124–125, names created here for convenience).

These reactions illustrate typical responses of *split-brain* patients. The human brain has two hemispheres, each specialized for various functions. Surgically separating the two halves severs communication between them. For medical reasons, the brains of George, Susan, and Margaret had been surgically separated into left and right hemispheres. Given the information the test subjects see, they all act appropriately. Yet, when they explain their responses, they seem unaware of crucial information, information presented exclusively to the right side of their brains by limiting it to the left visual field, the field connected to the right brain. Ignorant of why they respond as they do, they invent plausible but false explanations for their own behavior.

Because split-brain patients continually invent spurious reasons for their behavior, ignoring what the right brain knows while responding to the information the left brain possesses, scientists have proposed that the left brain contains a specialized area dubbed the *Interpreter*. The Interpreter correlates information in meaningful ways. It tries to make sense of what it knows.

Of course, the Interpreter does not know that the explanations it gives in split-brain persons are false, for it has no contact with the right hemisphere of the brain, the side that knows the relevant, missing information. Only the onlooker knows the explanations are false, for only the onlooker has access to all the relevant data. Interestingly enough, even after undergoing many tests, the patients themselves remain oblivious to their condition. Although they understand something about their surgery, they never explain their behavior as the consequence of having a split brain that does not consciously record information presented to its right hemisphere (Gazzaniga 1992, 127–28). This suggests that the Interpreter makes judgments about the plausibility of its own explanations. It has a strong bias toward inventing explanations that fit the ordinary circumstances of human life. Having a split brain is not one of them.

Each human brain houses an Interpreter. In many ways, the Interpreter's situation in split-brain patients reflects the predicament of us all. We, too, try to make sense of the world around us by developing explanations based on the information we have, but we are not omniscient. We, too, have an Interpreter that almost incessantly produces explanations without caution or patience, explanations that seem plausible to us but may well be false. The Interpreter is not passive. It actively structures our experience. Immediate plausibility seems to be its fundamental criterion of truth, and thus it is our own as well.

The existence of the Interpreter suggests that we must be very cautious in accepting explanations at face value, whether they are our own explanations or those of other people, those of our own culture or those of other cultures. When we examine the explanation of human origins and the human condition offered in Genesis, we might ask how important a role the Interpreter played in generating the explanations offered. When we examine theologians' interpretations of the text, we will do well to keep the creativity of the Interpreter in mind.

Although highly illuminating, the artificial experiments on split-brain patients do not reveal the interpretative nuances of the natural, whole brain. Scientists have learned of further biases from studies both of other animals and of human beings. Much learning and interpretative behavior seems to follow fairly consistent patterns. Biologists call this tendency to respond in patterned ways *canalization*. Canalization produces simple, stereotyped behavior in many animals. In people, it produces simplistic, stereotyped thinking that misses the nuances of complex human behavior and situations. Canalized thinking can mislead us badly. Moreover, because it feels right, we are often extremely resistant to having it corrected.

One of the simplest and most familiar manifestations of canalization in animals is *imprinting*. Imprinting is the almost instant process in which an infant animal becomes attached to its immediate, primary caregiver. Konrad Lorenz brought imprinting to the attention of the general public when he mimicked a mother goose in the vicinity of goslings and made movies of himself being followed around by them as if he were their mother. Like many simple behavioral phenomena, imprinting occurs because of the interaction of the genetic makeup of the animal with environmental cues. In geese, the genetic makeup is "innate information that, if translated into words would read as follows: 'Whoever responds to your lost piping is your mother; take careful note of her appearance'" (Lorenz 1979, 146). Lorenz deliberately behaved like a mother goose, hovering over the hatchlings and making appropriate sounds. Because he was more or less the right size and made more or less the right vocalizations, the goslings imprinted on him. Their behavioral response is canalized, needing only broad environmental cues to become activated in a way that is rigid and stereotyped.

Recent experiments have brought Lorenz's investigations of behavior into the biological world of chemistry and neurons. The experiments have demonstrated both that chemical changes occur in specific locations in the brains of chickens coincident with the occurrence of imprinting (Sheu et al. 1993) and that some behaviors in birds are encoded in the very structures of their brains (Balaban et al. 1988).

Although not especially rigid, many human learning processes are also canalized. Language learning is a familiar example. No matter what their native language, children learn its elements in the same sequence the world over. Deaf children learn sign language in the same order that hearing children learn vocal language, making the same mistakes at the same age and correcting them in the same manner (Sacks 1989, 74–116).

Cognitive development is also canalized. Jean Piaget (1967) studied children's development and found four stages. Each child must master the earlier stages before proceeding to the later ones. Jerome Kagan writes of "a sequence of intellectual abilities that include recognition and retrieval of the past, the ability to compare past and present, and inhibition of primitive and automatic reflexes" and of attachment to the primary caregiver (Kagan 1984, 70–71).

Moral development also appears to be canalized. Kagan writes of moral development in very young children, of the sequenced emergence of standards of right and wrong. Lawrence Kohlberg's work (1981, 1984) shows similar results. He discovers three levels of moral development that he divides into six stages. Development is sequential. A person cannot start at stage six. In a refinement, Carol Gilligan (1982) finds that females develop a morality somewhat different from that of males. Canalization may separate men from women in the moral sphere.

Certain types of explanations also show signs of canalization. One of the most general and common of these canalized explanations is that agents cause events. Such agents, whether actual or fictional, are known as *personal causal agents*. We posit personal causal agents because we are social beings and therefore think of events as having social causes.

The canalized tendency to explain events in terms of personal causal agents rests on the fact that human sociality itself is canalized. We are social animals. Human infants respond immediately and predictably to their caregivers without having been taught how to respond. Moreover, their responses are reinforced because their dependency on the care of others makes their newborn world a social one. When children become old enough to think in terms of cause and effect, they readily assume that personal causal agents lie behind all events, whether social or natural.

In his discussion of this insight, psychiatrist Brant Wenegrat tells an illustrative story about a boy of two (1995, 143). The boy's mother was reading him stories when an earthquake shook their neighborhood. In fright at the trembling of the house and the rattling of the windows, his mother cradled him in her arms and took refuge in the nearest doorway. When the movement stopped, she explained to him that an earthquake had shaken the ground and, with it, the house. Later, the boy greeted his father with the perturbing story of an earthquake person that had come from the ground and shaken the house, then disappeared under the ground.

His father explained the event to him as a shaking of the ground rather than the act of a person. The boy found this incredible. He maintained that a person lived underground. He could clearly describe the person and the person's dwelling. For months afterward, he tried to keep the person away by shouting, "Go away!" as he ran toward the window. Wenegrat concludes,

> As far as this child was concerned, agents must cause events. If the windows shook, someone must have shaken them. If the house creaked and groaned, someone must have pushed on it. If someone was doing these things, then he must live somewhere and be capable

of fright or discouragement. It must be possible to persuade him not to return. (144)

This attribution of personal agency to natural forces came from a very young child, and he maintained it despite his parents' repeated efforts to explain the earthquake in natural terms. Interpreting the causes of natural events as personal causal agents is a tendency deeply canalized in young children and therefore in us all.

Adult language is filled with references to implicit personal causal agents. Every day we personify objects that we clearly know are not persons. We speak of angry clouds, threatening weather, and vicious storms. Diseases are cruel. Protracted illnesses are unrelenting. We make friends with teddy bears and stuffed dogs. We name our cars, shout at them when they fail to start, blame them for breaking down, and speak of their dysfunctional engines as "dead," even though we know they were never alive.

Almost everyone understands intuitively when someone else treats an inanimate object as a person. The friend who recently took my little laptop computer to fix wrapped it in his arms while thoughtfully informing me of visiting hours. Neither of us needed to clarify the personification he enacted. We understood intuitively. There are innumerable examples of the fact that we naturally think socially. Because we think socially, when we encounter problems, we seek social solutions for them. We look for personal causal agents. Even when we know the immediate causes are natural ones, we still ask why the earthquake happened now, and why it affected us rather than others.

Walter Burkert (1996), an expert in ancient religions, has made a careful, cross-cultural study of one form of canalization positing personal causal agents. He demonstrates that when we encounter events we construe as catastrophes, we react in a patterned way. We posit personal causal agents as the causes of these catastrophes, and we seek atonement from the agents. Here is my reconstruction of Burkert's discussion.

In ancient Greece, in the camp of the Achaeans, a plague rages. Death reigns and smoke rises from burning pyres. For the warriors, the plague is a catastrophe, an incredible evil. Everyone asks, "Why us? Why now?" Their leader suggests consulting a seer. The seer's diagnosis is that one of the warriors sinned in taking captive the daughter of a priest. The seer tells the assembled warriors what they must do to avert further catastrophe. They must return the girl and purify their camp by sacrifice and sacred song (Burkert 1996, 102–3).

The biblical Philistines defeat the Israelites. They capture the holy Ark and take it to the temple of their god. The statue of their god falls on its face and tumors fall upon the people of the town. They transport the Ark to another town and another, but tumors follow wherever the Ark goes. The plague of tumors is a terrible catastrophe. "Why us? Why now?" the people cry. They consult priests and diviners who say that the Ark must be returned and sacrifices offered. When these things are done, the plague ceases (Burkert 1996, 104, taken from 1 Samuel 5 and 6).

On every inhabited continent and in different epochs, far from the geographical or temporal reach of cultural transmission, a pattern recurs. A catastrophe strikes. The catastrophe may be a disease or a storm or an earthquake. It may be a defeat in war. The only requirement is that it be felt psychologically as a catastrophe, as a visitation of evil upon the individual or the community. If it takes this form, people's reactions to it are typically canalized.

The canalized reaction has four stages. First, people construe the event as a catastrophe; second, they consult a mediator; third, the mediator explains the catastrophe as the result of transgression; fourth, the people make atonement. If the transgression has been against a deity, the catastrophe is perceived as a justified response of the deity. If the suffering is universal, then "universal and unchangeable divine justice may be invoked. In this perspective, all the sufferings of humans are explained as divine punishment" (Burkert 1996, 121–22). In the face of catastrophe, this was the perspective of the Hebrew prophets (Burkert 1996, 122). They, the mediators, declared catastrophes had or would occur and demanded that the people repent and atone for their sins.

One interesting point about the canalization of our response to catastrophe and atonement is that there seems to be a kind of balance struck between the magnitude of the catastrophe, the sin causing it, and the degree of atonement. A small, local catastrophe brought on by modest transgressions seems to require only a limited atonement. In contrast, a catastrophe perceived as horrendous or ubiquitous leads us to posit awful transgressions and a universal atonement. As I shall show, the reverse also seems to be true. The belief that we have received a magnanimous or universal atonement leads us to search for comparably appalling transgressions and catastrophes.

When we recognize that explanations follow canalized patterns such as this one involving catastrophe and atonement, we need to be especially wary of accepting them as true, for rather than being reasoned responses to situations existing objectively in the world, canalized responses follow the structure of our minds. Moreover, because canalized explanations arise from the structure of our minds, they are liable to command our easy assent and be difficult to question. For all these reasons, we need to treat them with special skepticism.

Christian theology provides one canalized explanation on Burkert's pattern. The mediators are Christian theologians. They declare Jesus' death the atonement for the catastrophic transgression at the fall. Because this explanation is canalized, we should approach it with deep and careful skepticism. In future chapters, I test this explanation for truth. In order to do so, I apply to it the two philosophical tests of truth not restricted to science. One of these is the *coherence test* of truth.

The Coherence Test

The coherence test of truth depends on logic. It says that if a theory is logically coherent, it is true. Here, I use the term *theory* very loosely. It applies equally to statements, concepts, theological doctrines, and scientific laws.

For any theory to be logically coherent, it must follow the basic laws of thought. The most basic laws are intuitively obvious, for example, two statements that contradict each other cannot both be true. Traditional and modern logic have elaborated the basic laws into volumes. However, this book will only refer to intuitively obvious laws, laws that seem to be canalized in our species. Although our canalized logic sometimes leads us astray when we deal with complex problems, the logical issues in this book are simple. Knowing academic logic is not necessary for understanding them.

Science is concerned with the coherence of scientific theories. (Scientific laws are simply well established theories.) This is why science relies on mathematics, because mathematics is a form of logic. Ideally, all scientific theories would be expressed in mathematical form. If the mathematical expression of any given theory is correct, then the theory is logical, and in that sense, it is true. For theories that cannot be or have not been expressed in mathematical form, logical rules still apply, but there are fewer rules. Theories in the form of narratives have still fewer rules. Nevertheless, the logical rules that apply to narratives are fairly stringent. To relate that Jeff was eating dinner at home with his wife at 6:00 P.M. yet claim that he was at the bowling alley at 6:00 P.M. the same day disobeys the rule that something cannot be in two different places at the same time. Logically we cannot believe both these things regarding Jeff's location at 6:00 P.M. Either he was at home or at the bowling alley—or somewhere else altogether.

Rules that apply to narratives are the sorts of rules employed in courts of law. When we serve on juries, we are not given special training in the rules of logic. We are all intuitively familiar with the sorts of rules that apply to narratives because of our own natural, canalized abilities.

The same natural abilities allow us to read the creation account in Genesis and find its logical flaws ourselves, without having to depend on experts. The narrative says that Adam was created together with Eve, yet also was created before her creation. We know immediately that both descriptions cannot be true, not if Adam is one person, and it seems clear from the rest of the narrative that he is. We are faced with the logical problem that a single narrative claims one person was created on two different occasions. How to solve the problem is less intuitively obvious, so we turn to scholars.

When we ask scholars for a solution, they say Genesis contains two accounts of creation, one beginning at Genesis 1:1, the other at 2:4b. In the first, Adam and Eve are created simultaneously. In the second, Adam is created before Eve. Dividing the single account into two reveals two fairly coherent narratives. Of the two different orders of creation, one falls into the first narrative, the other into the second. God also told Adam both that the fruit of all the trees is good to eat, and that all but one tree has fruit good to eat. This difficulty, too, is solved if the narrative is divided into two accounts at Genesis 2:4b, because each statement occurs in a different narrative.

Finding a solution to coherency problems is not the sole reason for scholars to posit two narratives instead of one. If, like the scholars, we could read the original Hebrew, we would discover that each account calls God by a different name. Doing so is not incoherent. Perhaps God has two names. If we are merely seeking truth of the coherence sort, the only problems that disturb us are logical ones, and we need only logical solutions. The person who insists against logic that there is one, single account rather than two bears the burden of proof. This person must explain why the single narrative theory does not violate the rules of logic, or else how the rules of logic can be violated, yet the narrative be true.

Within its own parameters, the coherence test of truth is probably the best of the tests of truth. It is clear. Its simple, basic rules are intuitively obvious and its complex rules are highly developed. However, its parameters are narrow. When we ask for truth, we generally seek something beyond logical coherence. Scholars may have solved the incoherence problem of Genesis 1–3 by uncovering two narratives, but our questions about the truth of the narratives do not end here. We want to know which narrative really happened, if either did. The coherence test of truth will not help us answer this question. The coherence test of truth lays the foundation for truth, but other tests must construct the building. The other general philosophical test of truth is the *correspondence* test of truth.

The Correspondence Test

The correspondence test of truth is paradoxically the most intuitively obvious yet the most difficult to understand. It says that a statement is true if it corresponds to the way the world is. At the obvious level, if I tell you that the apple is in the cooler, and you look for an apple there and find one, then you will credit my statement with being true. I said that the apple is in the cooler, and you found the apple there.

Historical cases prove more difficult for the correspondence test. In the case of the apple, you saw and touched it. You were there. But historical cases must be reconstructed. Often they must be reconstructed from inadequate data. What sort of evidence do we have that Adam and Eve existed? Even strong biblical inerrantists do not claim that there were human eyewitnesses to their creation around six thousand years ago according to biblical dating, and even inerrantists agree that the narrative was not written down until Moses' lifetime, more than twenty-six hundred years later according to biblical dating. Many academic scholars date the writing of the creation narratives to the Babylonian exile, another eight hundred years from the biblically dated creation of the first couple. In a court of law, the reliability of an event unseen by eyewitnesses and recorded 2,600 to 3,400 years after the event would be highly suspect.

Worse, when closely examined the correspondence test suffers from a philosophical fever. It turns out to be extremely difficult to explain how a statement that is a linguistic entity ("Adam and Eve existed") corresponds to the way the world is (the historical existence of Adam and Eve). The linguistic entity and the first couple seem to have nothing in common. The linguistic entity is neither physical nor human. Adam and Eve are not statements composed of nouns and verbs. Nothing in one is similar to or corresponds with anything in the other. The problem of similarity arises acutely in science when we ask what the linguistic and mathematical theories of science refer to, for they often refer to unobserved and unobservable entities. They cannot refer to things in the world, as Nancy Cartwright demonstrates in a disturbing book aptly entitled *How the Laws of Physics Lie* (1983).

Despite the drubbing it has received at the hands of philosophers, the correspondence test of truth best captures what the average person wants when seeking truth that lies beyond coherence. As it stands and if used loosely, the test is useful. However, it can be improved by inserting a map or model between the linguistic statement and how the world is. When this is done, linguistic statements refer to models, and models represent the way the world is. This revision addresses the problem of similarity.

To change the correspondence test in this way places it in a category of philosophical theories known as *semantic theories.* The name arose for historical reasons obscure and tangled enough to frighten the most intrepid explorer. Such an explorer will find a brief history and a thorough exposition in Frederick Suppe's *The Semantic Conception of Theories and Scientific Realism* (1989) and a more accessible, naturalized version in Ronald Giere's *Explaining Science* (1988). Because I am discussing tests of truth, whereas Suppe and Giere are interpreting the relationship between scientific theories and realism, my discussion differs from theirs.

As Giere notes, when we use models to think about the world, we employ the human mind's natural predilections (1988, 4–7). The mind is canalized to make maps and models of the world. Not only is this canalization the basis of cognitive psychology, all of us know from our own daily experience that our minds readily make models and maps of the world. We know how to get from our kitchen to our bedroom, from our house to our car, and from there to work, to the grocery store, and to grandmother's house. We also know that the maps we make are not complete. Our maps do not include every thread in the rug between kitchen and bedroom, every blade of grass between door and driveway, or the colors and shapes of the houses between home and store. Notwithstanding their incompleteness, the maps we make are unquestionably adequate because, using them, we reach our destinations. Our maps are pragmatic. They work, and that is good enough for us.

In its emphasis on pragmatism, the revised correspondence test of truth incorporates within its parameters a test of truth often considered separate, the *pragmatic* test of truth. The pragmatic test has a familiar slogan, "If it works, it's true." The test developed after the rise of science and technology, and science and technology are the areas in which it is most clearly applicable and most free of philosophical criticisms. The test claims that when technology is based on a particular scientific theory and the technology works, then the scientific theory is true. If our airplane flies, then our aerodynamic theory is true. If we can make electrons flow where we want them, build lasers from photons, and use protons as research tools, our atomic theory is true.

The pragmatic test of truth has two difficulties, both mitigated when it is integrated into the correspondence test. First, its parameters are narrow. It originally developed in response to the rise of science, and its application outside science and technology has been highly criticized, especially in cases limited to individual experience. That a religion "works" for an individual by making the individual happier, for example, hardly proves the religion true; it merely proves its psychological effectiveness for that individual. The test is also plainly difficult to apply to historical cases like that of Adam and Eve. When the pragmatic test is incorporated into the correspondence test, the additional criteria of truth help widen its scope.

The second difficulty is that the pragmatic test of truth at best verifies approximate truth, as far as we can know. If our airplanes fly, if our photons stream coherently, then clearly our theories of aerodynamics and atoms are in the ballpark. They are good theories. This does not guarantee that they are correct descriptions of the physical world. All the pragmatic test tells us is that they are good enough to provide blueprints for technology. Because good science has been done based on false theories, the pragmatic test does not guarantee the kind of truth we ultimately seek. However, it does guarantee that the models constructed under the auspices of the correspondence theory capture significant aspects of the world.

Emphasis on the pragmatic test uncovers a secret about the models we construct with the correspondence test of truth. We do not want our models to correspond perfectly with the world. A perfectly correspondent model would be an exact replica of our house, kitchen to bedroom. As such, it would be useless. The model's details would confound its purpose, for its purpose is simplification. We want a schema of the world, not a replica of it.

The revised correspondence test of truth asserts that the linguistic and mathematical statements we use in our theories are not supposed to correspond to the way the world is, for they are not about the world but about the maps or models we make of the world. The maps or models we make, if they are adequate maps and models, correspond to the portions of the world that interest us in relevant respects and in sufficient degrees, and they succeed pragmatically.

Whether the respects are relevant and the degrees sufficient are questions we must raise anew for each separate model. We often answer pragmatically. The respects in which the map to grandmother's house corresponds to the roads along which we travel are few. Its roads are linear, as are the traveled roads. The length of its roads is proportional to the length of the traveled roads. Its roads have the same names and numbers as the traveled roads. The respects of correspondence are linearity, proportionate length, name, and number. The respects and degrees of correspondence between the map and the traveled roads are sufficient for us to reach grandmother's house. According to the pragmatic test of truth, the map is true, for we arrived at our destination. However, the map most certainly does not correspond perfectly with the traveled roads.

A more scientific example may further clarify how the correspondence test of truth works. Newton's gravitational theory says gravity decreases as the inverse square of the distance between two objects. When we apply this theory to the Earth and the moon, we first make a model of the Earth-moon system. In our model, the Earth and the moon are points in space. The moon has no craters, the Earth no mountains or seas or grassy plains. These details do not sufficiently affect the force of gravity between the Earth and the moon to be relevant in our model, so we leave them out. We might think of the Earth and moon as tiny particles. Then we say of our model something like this: "The positions and velocities of the Earth and the moon are modeled here to approximate closely a Newtonian system with two particles held together by a force obeying the inverse-square law." In this scientific case, the degree of resemblance is "approximates closely." The respects in which it does so are position and velocity (after Giere 1988, 81).

As both these examples show, interest has turned from issues about correspondence between statements and the world to issues about the model. The model needs to be relevant to the information sought and to resemble the world in ways that are pertinent. The model will never perfectly correspond to the world, but that is not a defect in the model. We do not want models that correspond perfectly to the world. Instead, we want models that radically reduce the complexity of the world. These we can think about, construct, deconstruct, and reconstruct. They are simple enough for us to understand.

In brief, scientific theories are about simplified models of the world. Nonetheless, they often predict events in the world with great accuracy.

The revised correspondence test of truth solves a once-intractable puzzle in the history of science. Good science has been done with false theories. For example, early work in electromagnetism depended on the theory that an undetected substance called the *ether* pervaded the universe. As it turns out, the ether does not exist. Yet in many ways, electromagnetism behaves as if it were a disturbance in the ether. The model of the world that includes the ether is not a completely false model. In some respects, it resembles the world. However, it is not a good model because its central term refers to something that does not exist (Giere 1988, 107). As a result, scientists ceased to use it.

Scientists continue to use theories they know are false but provide good models of the world. Albert Einstein showed that Newton's theory of gravity is, strictly speaking, false. Yet scientists use it daily. Mathematically it is far simpler than Einstein's theory and, for most purposes, it works. The model is sufficiently relevant to be retained for restricted purposes.

Thus far, I have discussed the application of the correspondence test of truth to the physical world. However, the correspondence test has another application. It also applies to written texts. In this application, statements are true of a given text if they correspond to statements in that text. The corresponding statements provide a model, which is similar to the text in relevant respects and sufficient degrees. One way to characterize such a model is to say that it *stays close to the text*. A model that stays close to the text is a good model. A more ordinary way to say the same thing would be to say that an interpretation of a text that stays close to the text is a good interpretation. One that strays far from the text by adding details to the text that are not there, or making extravagant claims about what the text says, is a poor interpretation.

The coherence test of truth is also applicable to texts. If a text is incoherent, an explanation is needed. With its many inconsistencies, the Bible has been a fascinating laboratory for explanations of inconsistent texts, a matter to which I return in chapter 6.

Applying the coherence and correspondence tests of truth to texts means not reading with conscious literalism, not seeking esoteric meanings, and not reading allegorically except where the text is obviously an allegory. Using them means approaching a text from a stance that might be termed *scientific* or *rational* rather than *religious* or *faith-based*. In chapters 3 and 4, I will apply both these tests of truth to the narrative of the fall in Genesis 2 and 3; in chapter 5, they are applied to Genesis 1–9. Applying them to the narrative will save grappling with the complexities and confusions of contemporary literary theory while capturing much that is best in it.

The coherence and correspondence tests of truth come from traditional philosophy. A third test of truth arises from the history and epistemology of science and assumes that we inhabit a *universe*—one unified world. If our world is unified, then we can expect our theories to coalesce eventually. The ultimate ideal of science is to develop one big, unified theory, the recently much touted *theory of everything*. For many reasons both practical and philosophical, the development of a theory of everything will probably remain forever an ideal. Still, science has discovered that many theories do coalesce, and this unification provides a final test of truth. Nineteenth-century philosopher of science William Whewell named this integration of scientific theories a *consilience of inductions* (Ruse 1989, 13). The integration of scientific theories provides the final test of truth, the *consilience test*.

The Consilience Test

Inductions are logical arguments that move from the particular to the general or, more broadly, from the observed to the unobserved. Whewell based his ideas on Newtonian induction, the example par excellence of good science in Whewell's time. *Consilience* comes from the same root as *conciliate* and *reconcile,* to bring together. A consilience of inductions unifies scientific theories that originally seemed to apply to separate fields, although the term *consilience* by itself can be used loosely to indicate the consolidation of evidence in any field. Newton formed a consilience of inductions by showing that gravity applies equally to the Earth-moon system, the solar planets, the tides, the precession of the equinoxes, the fall of an apple, and the trajectory of a cannon ball.

Darwin constructed a consilience of inductions when he showed that the theory of evolution by natural selection explains conundrums in geology, biogeography, paleontology, embryology, anatomy, and classification. Theodosius Dobzhansky, George Gaylord Simpson, Julian Huxley, Ernst Mayr, and others created a major consilience in biology when they unified the theory of evolution with modern genetics, producing *neo-Darwinism* or the *New Synthesis.* Another consilience in biology formed when the New Synthesis and observations on animal behavior combined to explain animal social behavior.

James Clerk Maxwell created a consilience in physics between the theories of electricity and magnetism. Steven Weinberg, Abdus Salam, and Sheldon Glashow fashioned another between the theories of electromagnetism and the weak force in atomic nuclei. Max Planck developed yet another when he formulated quantum theory, which originally united two disparate theories of radiation and later explained the behavior of atoms, electrons, and particles in atomic nuclei.

The history of science is filled with consiliences. Whewell argued that such consiliences provide confirmation of scientific theories. He seems to be right. Consilience is one of our best indicators of the truth of scientific theories (Ruse 1986, 2–4; 151–54). Consiliences in science are similar to having many witnesses provide corroborating evidence in a court of law. If several witnesses agree together about a fact or a story, the jury is likely to consider this sound evidence that the fact or story is true. On the other hand, if a theory stands alone, if it does not contribute to our understanding of the universe as unified, then we are apt to question its veracity. One thing that makes the scientific theory of the origin of human beings so powerful, so likely to provide a good model for how our species came into existence, is that it draws from many fields of science. It is a point of consilience for many theories separately corroborated elsewhere.

This chapter begins by warning us to be skeptical of our own explanations. It discloses the Interpreter who leads us to develop plausible-sounding but dubious interpretations of information. It shows that canalization is common in other animals and in us, leading us to believe certain types of stereotyped explanations and to resist changing them. We need ways to test our explanations for truth.

This being the case, the chapter presents three tests of truth. The coherence test looks for sound logic. The correspondence test seeks to build simplified models of the world in hopes that the models will resemble the world in sufficient respects and degrees to provide blueprints for knowing about and manipulating the world. The coherence and correspondence tests can be applied to interpretations of written texts. The consilience test applies to science, which assumes that the universe is unified and that therefore, when our theories fit together, they are likely to be true. In the next chapter, I apply the coherence and correspondence tests of truth to the event Christian theologians call *the fall*.

Chapter 3

The Fall

The last chapter argued that people caught in the middle of a catastrophe respond in a canalized way. We ask, "Why us? Why now?" and seek a diagnosis that will tell us why we are suffering, so that we may atone for our transgressions and end our pain. The early Christians responded to their situation in the same canalized way, but in reverse order. Rather than think they were caught in a catastrophe, they believed they had received an atonement. They thought Jesus had made an atonement when he was crucified, and they looked for a catastrophe to explain his death. What dire transgression had occurred that could account for Jesus' terrible crucifixion?

Mark's Gospel captures this reversal of the human response to catastrophe, this reconstructive strategy in Christian thought. In Mark's account, the disciples do not know what is happening or who Jesus is until after the resurrection. Only then do they look back and reconstruct their experience with Jesus. Paul's letters show the same strategy. Paul is converted by a personal encounter with the resurrected Jesus. After his conversion, he must reconstruct what he knows of Jesus, whose followers he had been persecuting. What he discovers is the crucifixion, "a stumbling-block to Jews and foolishness to Gentiles" (1 Cor. 1:23), making Jesus the "righteousness and sanctification and redemption" of humanity (1 Cor. 1:30). Jesus' crucifixion effects an atonement. But how?

No satisfactory answer to this question ever emerges. In two thousand years, the Christian church has never supplied an answer that the church as a whole accepts. Rather, the church has developed more than a dozen distinct and often-conflicting doctrines of Jesus' atonement. Apparently, the Interpreter has been working here on intractable material, a suspicion bolstered by the fact that this pro-liferation and irresolution stand in stark contrast to the settlement of more complex theological problems like those of the Trinity and Christology. I will address the problem of the atonement in chapter 11. Here it is sufficient to note that, regardless of how it works, Christians are certain that an atonement occurred with the death of Jesus.

This chapter is about Christianity's search for a catastrophe dreadful enough to account for Jesus' excruciating and humiliating crucifixion and death. I show how the canalized human response to atonement propelled the early church from one scriptural narrative to another in its search for an equally awful catastrophe. One of these narratives is Genesis 2 and 3, the story of Adam and Eve. Christians from different groups interpreted Genesis 2 and 3 from different perspectives. At least two groups of Christians arrived at opposite conclusions about the meaning of the text.

I assume the texts can be read intelligently without resort to the intricacies of modern biblical scholarship, which ancient, medieval, and Reformation interpreters did not have available. I test each interpretation for truth using two tests of truth from the last chapter, coherence and correspondence, to the text of Genesis. I also examine each for canalization. The canalization of the Christian response, the diversity of passages used, the variety of interpretations of Genesis 2 and 3, and the lack of correspondence between the most influential Christian interpretation and the text of Genesis 2 and 3 should make us wary of Christian doctrines of the fall. This exploration begins in the early church.

The Early Church

When the earliest Christians look for a catastrophe to account for Jesus' crucifixion and atonement, none turn to Genesis 2 and 3 except Paul (Tennant [1903] 1968, 249). Instead, they find their catastrophe in Genesis 6:1, "When people began to multiply on the face of the ground, and daughters were born to them, the sons of God saw that they were fair; and they took wives for themselves of all that they chose."

The early Christian interpretation of this passage follows that in the apocryphal Jewish *Book of Enoch*. According to the *Book of Enoch,* the sons of God are angels who lust after mortal women. The children of these unions are demons. These demons are everywhere, infecting people soul and body, causing people to sin (Kelly 1960, 167). The pervasive existence of demons constitutes a catastrophe for human beings because all people are subject to demonic power and corrupted by it, sinning and dying. The Gospels present Jesus as an exorcist, casting out demons. He exercised power over them during his lifetime, and his resurrection shows that he has power over them even in death. Jesus' resurrection marks his victory over the demons. Early Christians maintained that Jesus freed them from demonic powers, thus liberating them from sin and death.

However, as Christianity developed, it rejected this account of catastrophe and salvation. The history of this rejection is unclear. Perhaps later theologians objected that the interpretation did not correspond to the biblical text, because four verses further along is a clear statement that the children of women and angels are heroic warriors, not demons: "These were the heroes that were of old, warriors of renown" (Gen 6:4b). Or perhaps the interest in demons waned with the end of the Roman Empire and the demise of the pagan gods whom Christians thought of as demons. Alternatively, perhaps being beset by demons did not seem like a great enough catastrophe to warrant Jesus' crucifixion.

Everyone in the ancient world, whether Jewish or Gentile, worshiped divine beings by animal sacrifice (Young 1975, 9). It was thus natural for both Jewish and Gentile converts to Christianity to interpret Jesus' death as a sacrifice. This is the interpretation of Jesus' death by the author of Hebrews. Many of these sacrifices were offered as means of expiation and atonement for sin. Expiatory and atoning animal sacrifices in neither Jewish nor Gentile tradition evoked demons, but they did emphasize sin (Young 1975, 28–30). Perhaps these traditions led early Christians to reject the purported demonology of Genesis 6 and, instead, consider the sin of Adam and Eve in Genesis 2 and 3.

In any case, by the third century, Genesis 2:4b—3:24 had become the central text Christians accepted as describing the catastrophe they sought. (For simplicity, I refer hereafter to this narrative as Genesis 2 and 3.) It came to Christianity through Judaism as an already highly interpreted text. The interpretations rested on ideological applications of the coherence and correspondence tests of truth (although not by that name) and made four assumptions about the text (from Kugel 1998, 15–19).

First, interpreters assumed that the text is divinely inspired. Literally, the whole text is God's words. Therefore, every detail is inspired, and every detail is significant, for God would not use superfluous words. Many interpreters thought Scripture was first written down in heaven, then delivered directly to Moses, David, Solomon, and others believed to be its transcribers. Thus, these interpreters believed it meets the correspondence test of truth by corresponding precisely to God's words.

Second, the interpreters assumed that the Bible is a book of instruction, relevant now. What the text says corresponded to events in the interpreters' lives. For example, interpreters living under Roman rule might read a text about Babylon, but be certain that it really referred to Rome. Christian interpreters might read a text about David, certain it was a reference to Jesus.

Third, they assumed the entire text is harmonious, without error or contradiction. They were confident that it passed the coherence test of truth. Thus, they spent much time, effort, and ingenuity on contradictory passages, trying to make Scripture obey the test.

Finally, all the interpreters assumed that the Bible is cryptic, with esoteric messages hidden in its details. It is so cryptic in places that, when the surface of the text says one thing, the cryptic meaning is the opposite. This assumption helped interpreters make Scripture coherent and correspond to events in their daily lives, but it destroyed any possibility of reliable analysis. It also implied that expert interpreters were needed, that ordinary people, even literate ones, could not properly understand the text. Thus, experts held the biblical text under an enigmatic intellectual microscope.

The Reformation removed the microscope. Martin Luther (1483–1546) in Germany, John Calvin (1509–1564) in Switzerland, and Thomas Cranmer (1489–1556) in England thought Scripture had a plain sense that ordinary people could understand without esoteric training. The Reformers translated and printed the Bible, making it available throughout areas where the Reformation flourished, so the people could read it for themselves.

Yet the Reformers also assumed that the Bible is coherent and corresponds to the way the world is. The problem with these assumptions is that they are not merely literary conjectures about how to read a text. They constitute an ideology. Before such interpreters ever see the text, they know much about it. They are already certain it is the coherent, inspired words of God, relevant to their lives. When they arrive at the text, they insist that it fits their ideology and struggle to make it pass the tests of truth. When it fails, many grasp the fourth assumption, claiming the text does not say what it says, but has another meaning hidden beneath the surface.

Modern fundamentalists follow the Reformers and retain the first three assumptions when they read Scripture, while modern biblical scholars do not. I will return to this contrast in chapter 6.

The issue at this point is to find an interpretation of Genesis 2 and 3 that meets the literary correspondence test of truth, stays close to the text, and avoids ideology. Such a sound interpretation can function as a test case for other interpretations encountered later.

To find such an interpretation, I have turned to a famous contemporary literary critic, Harold Bloom, who is a practiced reader of English literary works, yet knowledgeable about the Hebrew narrative, for he has written a book on it (Bloom 1990). On central theological points, Bloom's interpretation follows modern scholars without becoming snarled in the arcane coils of Hebrew scholarship. It stays close to the text, and it is fresh, rich, and interesting. My using his interpretation does not imply that I think he presents the true analysis of the narrative. I do not. I do not think there is a single, true exegesis. The text is too complex for that. But some interpretations correspond more closely to the text than others and avoid obvious ideological entanglements. Bloom's fits these criteria. It will serve as a test case later in the book for the evaluation of a diversity of interpretations.

Before presenting Bloom's interpretation, a review of the biblical narrative of Genesis 2 and 3 may be helpful.

The narrative opens in a lifeless place. God creates a man, Adam, from clay, then creates a garden, Eden, for the man to inhabit and cultivate. God gives Adam the fruit of all the trees of the garden for food except one, the fruit of the tree of the knowledge of good and evil, declaring that if the man eats fruit from that tree, he will die that day.

God then sets out to create a partner for Adam. God creates all the animals and shows them to Adam, but Adam finds no fit partner among them. So God puts Adam to sleep and creates a woman from his rib, and the man finds her to be a satisfactory partner. The man and woman are naked but not ashamed.

A serpent approaches. It asks the woman about God's ban on eating from some of the trees in the garden. The woman tells the serpent of the prohibited tree and God's promise of death if they should eat its fruit. The serpent contradicts God, saying that eating from it will not bring death, but knowledge that will make the pair like gods. Finding the tree lovely and the promise of wisdom enticing, the woman eats the forbidden fruit and gives some to the man who also eats. As a result, they see that they are naked and cover themselves with aprons of leaves.

God enters the garden, and the couple hides. God calls Adam, asking where he is, and the man replies that he is afraid because of his nakedness. When God asks how the man knows he is naked, the man says that the woman gave him some of the forbidden fruit. The woman in turn says that the serpent tricked her, and she ate the fruit, too.

God then curses all concerned, the serpent with moving on its belly and enmity to human beings, the woman with increased birth pain and subordination to the man, and the man with hard agricultural labor in ground now also cursed. God also curses Adam with death, a return to the dust from which God created him. Adam names his wife Eve, and God clothes them with animal skins. Then, thinking the couple may become even more like gods by achieving immortality through eating the fruit of the tree of life that also grows in the garden, God drives them out of Eden and places cherubim and a flaming sword to guard it.

This story is familiar to most Christians, but Bloom's interpretation of it will come as something of a surprise.

Harold Bloom

Bloom (1990, 175–87) begins his interpretation with God's shaping of the first human being. He compares God's methodology in Genesis with that of other creator-gods in the ancient world. Whereas most creators use a potter's wheel to shape human beings, God does not. Like a child making a mud pie, God creates the first man without benefit of technology. In comparison with other ancient deities, God seems inept. Bloom continues the theme of God's ineptitude by noting that God does not readily find a fit partner for Adam. God tries and tries and tries, creating a myriad of animals, none a suitable partner for Adam. Then God tries another way, putting Adam to sleep and having him give birth, as it were, to woman. God seems to have learned from previous attempts, for she has been engineered from Adam's rib, not patty-caked from mud. God may again be inept in placing the tree of the knowledge of good and evil in the garden as a prohibition that becomes a temptation.

Bloom comments on the misogyny lying behind so many interpretations of Eve. He notes that the creation of Eve is the only narrative of the creation of a woman in all the ancient literature we possess. In Genesis, it receives six times the space allotted to the creation of Adam. As noted, Eve is not patty-caked from clay but carefully constructed from Adam's rib. God creates her as a partner to help Adam, not as a subordinate. Bloom says that in reaching for the forbidden fruit, she is the active, imaginative partner, Adam a passive imitator.

Bloom does not see the serpent as evil. Rather, it is a smooth character (usually translated as "crafty"), a pun in the Hebrew on Adam and Eve's being smooth (usually translated "naked"). Bloom notes that the serpent is not a liar. Being an animal, the serpent lives only for the day. When it says that Adam and Eve will not die, it correctly foretells that they will not die that day, as God had promised they would. Nor is the serpent presented as malevolent. The biblical text never states its intentions.

Bloom thinks Adam and Eve behave childishly throughout the narrative. They are childish in succumbing to the serpent, in hiding from God, in saying that they are hiding because they are naked, and in blaming others for their own behavior. In the end, God punishes them horribly for behaving like children. Bloom considers their punishment far too harsh for their misconduct. Not only are they subject to God's explicit curses of labor in childbirth and toil in farming, but God also casts them out of the home created for them. They suffer an incomprehensible catastrophe, a domestic tragedy of estrangement from God who has been both father and mother to them.

Yet these punishments do not change Adam and Eve's nature. It is never degraded or corrupted. Bloom does not find the catastrophe that Christian theologians call *the fall* in the text. On the contrary, he notes that the text explicitly says Adam and Eve become more like gods after they eat the fruit of the tree of knowledge (Gen. 3:22). He is also aware that the text says God casts them out of Eden not because they have disobeyed, but because God fears they will eat the fruit of the tree of life and gain immortality (Gen. 3:22-24), making them even more like gods.

Bloom approaches the narrative with no discernable ideology, and his reading corresponds closely to the text. It also corresponds closely with a wide consensus among scholars of the Hebrew Scriptures. Scholars versed in the text do not find a fall in Genesis 3 (Barr 1993; Westermann 1984, 276–78), and they have concluded that, if a fall occurs anywhere in Genesis, it occurs slowly as the years lived by the patriarchs declines from nearly one thousand years with Methuselah to only 120 years for Moses. The great catastrophe in Genesis is Noah's flood, but it does not change human nature. Human nature is just as wicked after the flood (Gen. 8:20) as before (Gen. 6:5). Indeed, scholars agree that the idea that a fall occurs in Genesis 3 is found nowhere in the Hebrew Scriptures. Nor is it prominent in the New Testament. Jesus does not mention it; nor do the authors of Hebrews, Peter, James, or the Johannine tradition. Indeed, in Scripture in its entirety, the event of Genesis 3 is mentioned only in Romans 5, 1 Corinthians 15, and 1 Timothy. The idea that a fall occurs in Genesis 3 dates to the late first century (Westermann 1984, 276).

So according to textual evidence and scholarly consensus, Bloom has presented a sound interpretation, although his is not the only sound one possible. Because his interpretation is sound enough, comparing other interpretations with it will test them for the literary truth of correspondence. I turn now to an exegesis that also corresponds closely to the text but begins with an ideology. This interpretation shows how readings may stay close to the text yet result in widely different interpretations. The exegete is an anonymous gnostic Christian.

A Gnostic Christian

Gnostic Christians come to the text of Genesis 2 and 3 with a highly developed theology. They believe in a supreme, good God. They think salvation comes through knowledge. (*Gnosis* means *knowledge* in Greek. The Gnostic interpretation is in Pagels 1989, 69.) They believe the material world is evil and that a separate, evil god created it. The Gnostics bring their theology to the text, making their interpretation ideological. Gnostics naturally view the tree of knowledge as good. They think eating its fruit leads toward salvation. They also naturally construe the God of Genesis 2 and 3 as evil. Not only is God the creator of the material world, God tries to keep Adam and Eve from eating the fruit of the tree of knowledge. After Adam and Eve eat the fruit, God is angry, envious, and fearful. God envies Adam and Eve their new knowledge, envies them for being more like gods. Fearing they will become even more godlike by eating the fruit of the tree of life and achieving immortality, God banishes them from the garden.

The Gnostics see God not only as envious, but malicious. God's curses do not constitute just punishment for Adam and Eve's deed, but are excessively harsh. In contrast, they see the serpent, the bringer of knowledge, as honest and good. It tells Eve truly that the tree will bring the couple knowledge of good and evil, not death that day as God had said.

Two points are important here. First, beliefs matter. From the Gnostic point of view, it is easy to see God as envious and unjust and the serpent as honest and good. Second, the Gnostic reading may be ideologically motivated, but it corresponds very closely to the text. God does not want Adam and Eve to attain knowledge, forbidding them the fruit of the tree of knowledge. God does not want them to become immortal; that is why God banishes them from the garden in which the tree of life grows. The reason for their banishment is that they would become more godlike, for they have already attained one of the gods' attributes, knowledge of good and evil. God's motive could be envy.

God's punishments seem harsh, indeed, a point Bloom emphasizes. Adam and Eve have behaved like disobedient children, a role they continue to play as they hide from God in the garden and blame others for their misdeeds. God treats them as hardened sinners, hounding them from home, augmenting their anguish, and dictating their death.

The serpent brings enlightenment. It is also honest. From its point of view, it tells the truth about death. Furthermore, as the serpent said they would and as God himself acknowledges, Adam and Eve attain knowledge when they eat the forbidden fruit.

The Gnostic interpretation of the serpent brings out an important aspect of the narrative. In the narrative, the serpent is an animal, not a supernatural being. Of course it speaks—but then, this is Eden. Perhaps all the animals can talk, for Eve shows no surprise at the serpent's eloquence. God's anger and curse are aimed at a simple animal, changing its method of locomotion and setting it at enmity with human beings, an enmity shared by all the large beasts of prey.

This is no demon, certainly not the prince of demons (von Rad 1961, 85; Anderson 1987, 155).

Moreover, the author of the narrative could not have thought of the serpent as a demon and definitely not as Satan, their prince. To interpret the serpent as a demon or Satan is anachronistic. Even the most extreme scholars place the writing of Genesis 2 and 3 no later than the Babylonian exile. It was probably written almost five hundred years earlier; if Moses wrote it, then hundreds of years before that. Belief in demons entered Judaism more than three hundred years later than the exile, only two hundred years before the birth of Jesus. Neither demonology nor the concept of Satan was part of Jewish culture at the time the Genesis narrative was written.

Furthermore, the narrative never states, as later Christian authors will, that God created Adam and Eve immortal. In fact, the narrative suggests they were originally mortal. By placing the tree of life in the garden and not prohibiting the consumption of its fruit, God seems to have intended for Adam and Eve to become immortal later by eating its fruit. Perhaps they would have needed to continue to eat it to maintain their immortality. After Adam and Eve eat the fruit of knowledge, God appears to have a change of mind. God forbids them the fruit of immortality, thereby keeping the promise that if Adam eats from the tree of knowledge, he will die.

Like the Gnostics, orthodox Christians bring an ideology to the text. Orthodox Christians are certain that God is good, that the serpent is demonic, and that eating the fruit of the tree of knowledge brings ignorance. (This is undoubtedly a strange assumption, wildly at odds with the text—a notable mark of an ideologically motivated reading.) The most influential interpreter of the fall in western Christianity was the Bishop of Hippo in northern Africa whom the church later canonized, Saint Augustine (354–430).

Augustine

Augustine derives much of his interpretation of Genesis 2 and 3 from his peculiar reading of Paul's Epistle to the Romans. Modern scholars think Augustine made two serious errors in his interpretation. In Romans 7:14-24, Paul uses metaphors of captivity and enslavement to express his frustration with his own inner conflict, saying that he has been captured and enslaved in spiritual warfare, reminding his biblically knowledgeable readers of the Hebrews' slavery and captivity in Egypt and Babylon:

> For we know that the law is spiritual; but I am of the flesh, sold into slavery under sin. I do not understand my own actions. For I do not do what I want, but I do the very thing I hate. . . . I can will what is right, but I cannot do it. For I do not do the good I want, but the evil I do not want is what I do. . . For I delight in the law of God in my inmost self, but I see in my members another law at war with the law of my mind, making me captive to the law of sin that dwells in my members. . . . Who will rescue me?

Although the youthful Augustine had read this passage as Paul's quandary before his conversion, the mature Augustine reads it as applicable afterward. He concludes that, despite Jesus' atonement and our baptism, Christians are still slaves to sin. We have no free will. The early Christian theologians, John Chrysostom and Origen, held the opposite view, as do modern scholars (Pagels 1989, 106). Scholars now think Augustine's earlier reading is the better one, that Paul's question, "Who will rescue me?" with its immediate thanksgiving to Christ (Rom. 7:25), was answered by Jesus' death and resurrection. Paul has been rescued already. The catastrophe of captivity and enslavement is over; Jesus has saved Paul from slavery to sin. Paul is free.

Western theologians who read Paul as Augustine does are under Augustine's influence. The Eastern Orthodox Church, whose New Testament includes all of Paul's letters but whose antecedents are not Augustinian, credits us with free choice, as I note in chapter 4.

The other passage Augustine misread is Romans 5:12. Augustine used a Latin translation rather than the Greek original, and the Latin translation says in English, "sin came into the world through one man . . . *in whom* all men sinned," whereas the original Greek reads "*because* all men sinned" (emphasis added; see Pelikan 1971, 299, and Urban 1986, 134–37). The Latin mistranslation of *because* as *in whom* leads Augustine to think all people are somehow contained in Adam and carry the guilt for Adam's sin. The belief that we are guilty for Adam's sin causes Augustine to think infants who die unbaptized are damned.

Augustine's misreadings of Paul lead him to misinterpret Genesis 2 and 3. This is not the only influence that leads him to misread this particular text. Genesis 1 says we are created in God's image and so is inconsistent with Genesis 2, which has us created from mud. Paul, whom Augustine often follows, is not a careful reader of the narrative, and he depends on the Greek translation of his day rather than on the original Hebrew. Augustine expects Scripture to be coherent, so he sometimes strains to make it so, as did his predecessors and successors. The point here is not that many things influenced Augustine's misreading of Genesis 2 and 3. The point is, he misread it.

Augustine thinks that the disobedience of Adam and Eve leads to a much greater disaster than Genesis 2 and 3 actually describes, far greater than Bloom's domestic tragedy of estrangement. For Augustine, there is a terrible fall from sublime heights to wretched depths, a horrendous catastrophe in which Adam and Eve and all their progeny become totally corrupted and utterly alienated from God, each other, and themselves. In order to find such a fall in Genesis 3, Augustine departs from the text. He inflates the original nature of the first couple, exaggerates the character of their sin, and amplifies their punishment. Because of his embellishments, his interpretation of the narrative fails the test of correspondence, for his account of events differs significantly from the account in Genesis 2 and 3.

Augustine depicts Adam and Eve as very noble originally. He goes beyond and often against Genesis 2 and 3 to give them free will, full health, full knowledge, the chance for immortality by eating of the tree of life, the ability not to sin, an inclination to choose the good, and the ability to persist in this blessed state (Kelly 1960, 362). From this portrait, they appear safe from all corruption, immune to all temptation. Yet, they are far from incorruptible, for according to Augustine, Adam and Eve become corrupt even before they are tempted and well before they commit their devouring deed. Augustine depicts the act itself as almost an afterthought: "It was in secret that the first human beings began to be evil; and the result was that they slipped into open disobedience. For they would not have arrived at the evil act if an evil will had not preceded it" (Augustine [413–426] 1984, 571). According to Augustine, they had turned away from God before the deed was done.

This interpretation fails the test of correspondence. The account in Genesis says little or nothing about the original character of Adam or Eve. As Bloom notes, Adam is patty-caked from clay, hardly an indication of his perfection. Eve is more carefully engineered. However, the only comment that might indicate the character of either is that they "were both naked, and were not ashamed" (Gen. 2:25b). This probably indicates innocence. Innocence is what we would expect from people who are newly created and lack experience. When the serpent approaches them, they act as if they are innocent and naïve, even forgetful like youngsters in a candy store, impetuously following the latest suggestion, impulsively fulfilling their immediate desires. As Bloom notes, in the narrative they seem to be disobedient children rather than corrupt sinners.

Furthermore, God's condemnation of the serpent clearly indicates that the sin of the pair lies in their deed itself, not in their prior corruption. This is also Paul's position in Romans 5:18a where Adam's deed itself is the origin of sin. After that deed, God in Genesis 3 judges the disobedient pair. If human nature changes, it changes as a consequence of the deed. Its change does not precede and cause the deed, as Augustine asserts ([413–426] 1984, 547).

Not only does Augustine inflate the original nature of the first couple and misplace and exaggerate the character of their sin, he also embellishes their punishment. His embellishments appear to negate the goodness of God. Even without embellishments, the punishments raise questions about God's benevolence. Bloom considers the pronounced punishments "incommensurate . . . [with] the childish offenses that provoked them" (1990, 184). The Gnostics, too, consider God's punishments too harsh, and they impugn God's goodness partly because of God's cruelty. Augustine's more punitive God appears to be more vicious than either Bloom or the Gnostics think. His portrait of God is not consistent with the orthodox Christian doctrine of God's omnibenevolence.

Augustine's embellished punishments involve radical changes in Adam and Eve's nature, changes also conveyed to their progeny forever. Borrowing Paul's metaphor, Augustine finds the fallen pair wholly enslaved to sin. No longer can they choose to do good. No longer can they decide to obey God. Their progeny suffer the same degradation. For Augustine, all of us have become the helpless slaves of sin.

Augustine's assessment of the change in human nature does not correspond to what is said in the text of Genesis and sometimes directly contradicts the text. First, the list of punishments in Genesis 3 does not include a change in human nature. As Bloom emphasizes, and almost all scholars of the Hebrew Scriptures agree, there is no fall in the narrative. Furthermore, some of Adam and Eve's progeny are able to be good and obey God. For example, Genesis refers to Noah as "a righteous man, blameless in his generation" (Gen. 6:9). Genesis 6 maintains that he obeys God exactly in the construction of the ark and the rescue of the animals—"Noah did this; he did all that God commanded him" (Gen. 6:22). Augustine's interpretation of the text fails the test of correspondence.

It also fails the test of coherence. Augustine depicts Adam and Eve as perfect when originally created. Their attributes of perfection include the ability not to sin. Yet they sin. Moreover, Augustine claims that they become corrupt before they are tempted. As his biographer comments, even Augustine thinks of Adam and Eve's deed as "a sin beyond reason" (Brown 1967, 393).

Their sin is unreasonable. It is unreasonable for the perfectly endowed Adam to be smitten by pride when his will is inclined toward the good and his capacity is such that he can persist in this state. It is beyond reason for Adam and Eve with their perfect knowledge to desire more, thereby succumbing easily to the blandishments of the serpent. Augustine's emphasis on Adam and Eve's perfection and the ease of their obedience to this one simple and memorable command when surrounded by so much delicious and delightful fruit makes their sin inexplicably irrational. Genesis does not make Adam and Eve's behavior unreasonable, only childish. Augustine makes it incoherent.

Augustine's interpretation of Genesis 2 and 3 is also canalized. It follows closely Burkert's analysis of the canalization of catastrophe and atonement, although Augustine reverses Burkert's order. Augustine is certain that Jesus' awful crucifixion and painful death provide a wonderful atonement for which he is incredibly grateful, as he says throughout his *Confessions* ([397] 1961). Being both awful and wonderful, the atonement seems to require a comparably awful and wondrous catastrophe, which Augustine supplies by misinterpreting Genesis 2 and 3. Burkert draws attention to this tendency to balance catastrophe and atonement. Moreover, he notes that if the transgression is thought to be against a deity, then the deity's response is always perceived as justified. Augustine tries to justify God's terrible punishments by making the transgression horrible. Burkert comments that if the suffering is universal, all human suffering is perceived as divine punishment. Augustine sees all our sufferings as punishments. In this, he is mistaken, as I argue in chapters 8 and 9.

Augustine's interpretation of Genesis 2 and 3 fails both positive tests of truth. It is also canalized. His interpretation is ideologically motivated, and it is false.

Unfortunately for the history of Christianity, western Christianity adopts Augustine's misinterpretation of Genesis 2 and 3. It also retains Augustine's name for the doctrine derived from his exegesis, the doctrine of *original sin*. The original or first sin is Adam and Eve's eating of the forbidden fruit, a sin they clearly commit in Genesis 3. However, Augustine's doctrine of original sin also includes the idea that a fall occurs in Genesis 3 that changes human nature so that everyone is subsequently a depraved slave of sin. Thus, the doctrine of original sin provides a model of human nature. In its Augustinian version, that model shows us to be corrupted and depraved slaves unable to do anything but sin.

Not only does Augustine's model of human nature fail the tests of truth related to the text of Genesis 2 and 3, it is a radical departure from the model of human nature held by the early church and preserved in the Eastern Orthodox Church to this day. Before Augustine, the church emphasized Christians' moral freedom and moral responsibilities (Pelikan 1971, 281–84). The church thought Adam and Eve sinned because they abused their freedom, and we sin because we misuse ours. The church's emphasis on freedom opposed pagan fatalism, a fatalism so pervasive that the Roman emperor Tiberius stopped sacrificing to the gods because he thought they could not change fate (Pelikan 1971, 281).

Augustine appears to embrace pagan fatalism, reversing the early Christian message of liberation (Pagels 1989, 99–120). He thinks Adam and Eve were originally free, but that they desired even more freedom. They desired moral autonomy, and this was their sin (Pagels 1989, 99). Augustine's serpent tempts Adam and Eve with liberty (Pagels 1989, 120), but when Adam and Eve eat the forbidden fruit, liberty is what they lose. After the fall, Adam and Eve are no longer free. They are constrained to sin necessarily.

If Augustine's position here seems confused, it is. The confusion occurs because Augustine does not define freedom as the ability to choose between good and evil. Instead, he defines freedom as obedience, making the freest, most perfect creatures those who obey God out of necessity (Kelly 1960, 362). According to Augustine, Adam and Eve originally lacked one perfection. They could choose evil. As long as they obeyed God, they were free. When they disobeyed God, they chose evil and became its slaves. Augustine's version of freedom influenced the entire western church. After Augustine, the church defines freedom as loving service to God and depicts lack of freedom as bondage to evil.

Ominously for rational theology in the western church, Augustine's position is self-contradictory. It asserts that necessary obedience to God is freedom, whereas necessary obedience to evil is bondage. Necessary obedience cannot be both freedom and bondage. The definition of freedom Augustine bequeaths the western church fails the test of coherence. Nonetheless, the church adopted it. The church thereby lost the simple and coherent definition that preceded Augustine and that is once again influencing theology and moral philosophy: the definition of freedom as the ability to make choices between goods or choices between good and evil, choices that make a difference to our lives. Under this ancient definition, we are far freer than Augustine supposes.

Augustine was never a systematic thinker. His writings are largely responses to crises. However, it appears that what happened in Augustine's thought is similar to what occurs later and more clearly in the systematic Calvin. Augustine appears to approach Genesis 2 and 3 with convictions about God borrowed from Scripture and philosophy. The convictions are that God is omniscient, omnipotent, and omnibenevolent. If God has these attributes, then logically the creation must be perfect, and the creation includes Adam and Eve. Thus, Augustine arrives at his very noble couple, ignoring the patty-caked clay figure of Genesis 2.

As the Roman Empire crumbled around him, Augustine became increasingly aware of the negative side of the human situation, filled with suffering and death. Furthermore, he examined his own experience of sin in his *Confessions* ([397] 1961) and found himself enslaved. Given the perfection of Adam and Eve in the beginning and a chaotic and sinful world later, something terrible must have occurred. When he turns to Genesis 3, Augustine finds an appalling fall. Research in human psychology indicates that people who want to believe something find ways to dismiss data that contradict their belief and to distort details in evidence that is more tractable so they can plausibly continue to sustain their conviction (Baumeister 1997, 307). The discovery of the Interpreter bolsters these results, demonstrating how readily we devise false explanations we find credible. Augustine ignores the details and embellishes the narrative, inventing the evidence he seeks, creating and then preserving his belief in a primordial catastrophe. His interpretation is ideologically motivated.

I conclude this chapter by emphasizing four points. First, because Christians are like other people, their response to having an atonement is typical of the canalized response Burkert discovers in people throughout the world. As soon as Christians construe Jesus' crucifixion as an atonement, they search for a catastrophe to explain it. They find a catastrophe in the narrative of Genesis 2 and 3, the narrative of Adam and Eve's sin and God's punishments. Second, imposing an ideology on a text deeply influences the interpretation of that text. Gnostic Christians presuppose an evil creator and a saving knowledge, then find these in Genesis 2 and 3. Those Christians we today term *orthodox* presuppose a good creator and a catastrophe. These they find in the same text. Third, there is no fall in Genesis 2 and 3. Sin has another source. The lack of a catastrophe at our origin means Jesus' crucifixion carries a different message than we have thought. Fourth, Augustine's concept of free will is self-contradictory and therefore false. People are far freer than Augustine thinks. Western Christianity needs a new, better concept of freedom, one based on choice.

The concept of free will is not the only Augustinian concept in western Christianity needing correction. Also requiring revision are the doctrines of original sin.

Chapter 4

Original Sin

This chapter is a continuation of the last. It applies the coherence and correspondence tests of truth from chapter 2 to three doctrines of original sin, all purportedly derived from Genesis 3. It also asks whether the doctrines are canalized and, if so, how completely. The three doctrines of original sin are from Christianity's three principal branches: Protestantism, Roman Catholicism, and Eastern Orthodoxy. In order to describe the doctrines simply, I present them from the point of view of a single, central theologian from each branch of the church. The theologians are John Calvin (1509–1564) for Protestantism, Saint Thomas Aquinas (c. 1225–1274) for Catholicism, and Saint Athanasius (c. 296–373) for Orthodoxy.

It may be well to mention again that the doctrines of original sin have two separable parts. One part makes a historical claim about Adam and Eve. All the branches agree that Adam and Eve disobeyed God's direct command and ate proscribed fruit. The other part of the doctrine of original sin makes a psychological claim. It provides a model of human nature. The three branches have different models of human nature. This chapter focuses on the three models. It uses the phrases "doctrine(s) of original sin" and "model(s) of human nature" interchangeably and begins with Protestantism.

Protestantism has two main founders, John Calvin and his older contemporary, Martin Luther. Luther, an Augustinian monk, and Calvin, a lay theologian, were both deeply influenced by Augustine. Because Luther's doctrine of original sin mirrors Calvin's and Calvin is the more systematic theologian, in this book Calvin represents Protestantism.

Calvin and Protestantism

To read Calvin's *Institutes of the Christian Religion* ([1559] 1995), from which all references here to Calvin are taken, is repeatedly to be told that Augustine is right, his predecessors and successors wrong. Calvin follows Augustine closely. He, too, says that Adam and Eve were noble and free before the fall. At the fall, they lost their freedom and their nobility. They lost the image of God that was in them, "the entire excellence of human nature" (I:165). Their good nature was replaced by "blindness, impotence, vanity, impurity, and unrighteousness" (I:214). Fallen humanity is not merely bereft of God's image, but "prolific in all kinds of evil" (I:218). People are now entirely slaves to sin, for our nature is biased in such a way that we choose to sin; we cannot do otherwise. With Adam and Eve's fall, the entire creation became corrupted, for it had been created for human use (I:214). Thorns and thistles sprang up and choked out fruitful plants.

Calvin bases his interpretation of Genesis 3 on the convictions that God is powerful and just. He reasons that such a God must have created human nature and all creation to be good. If people claim this is not so, they impugn God's justice (I:160). However, we suffer and die. There must be some explanation for what we perceive as evils. Calvin assumes that pain and death are punishments, severe ones. Because God is just, the sin that evoked such severe punishments must have been prodigious (I:212). The fall must have been catastrophic. It affected everything and everyone. After the fall, we are the subjects of original sin, "a hereditary corruption and depravity of our nature, extending to all parts of the soul" (I:217). Everyone carries this corruption, even infants who, if they have not yet produced the fruits of sin, have at least the seed of it within them (I:217).

Calvin offers a cure for this terrible catastrophe. The catastrophe is so complete that human nature and human will cannot be transformed. They must be replaced. We are not wounded or diseased, needing cure, but utterly corrupted. We are not to be pitied and redeemed but recreated, for God hates us as we are (I:220). We need a new nature (I:219) and a new will (I:255); otherwise, we are alienated from God, even though Christ suffered and died (I:463).

Calvin's views fail the test of coherence in at least three different ways. First, they are not coherent with orthodox Christology. According to the councils of Nicaea and Chalcedon, Jesus Christ is divine and human. He has two natures and two wills, one divine, the other human. He acquires his human nature and human will at the incarnation and carries them through death into heaven and glory. His human nature and human will are not replaced by some other nature and will: they remain human. If his human nature and his human will do not need to be replaced, then neither do ours, because we are equal to him in our humanity. Atonement may transform human nature. It does not replace it.

Second, Calvin's interpretation of the narrative is not consistent with the orthodox doctrine that God is omniscient and omnibenevolent. A good and just God would not knowingly create creatures and place within their ready reach the means of their utter corruption while foreseeing that they will grasp the fruit and eat. Such a deity comes across as being either ignorantly inept (Bloom) or sinisterly sadistic (Gnosticism). Calvin's incoherence here has its roots in the text. The text does not portray God as perfect, but as unduly punitive. Calvin wants to claim that God is perfect. At the same time, he wants to interpret Adam and Eve's sin as catastrophic. A perfect creator who creates a perfect creation that suffers a catastrophic fall cannot be made coherent, even by Calvin.

When confronted with the charge that his God is unjust, Calvin can only reply that God's justice and human justice are not alike (II:225–30). But such a reply fails another test of coherence with Christian theology, because Christianity maintains that we are to imitate God in Christ. Are we then to tempt our brothers and sisters in Christ to their own downfall, as Calvin's God seems to do to Adam and Eve?

Third, Calvin himself believes the orthodox doctrine that God is omniscient and omnibenevolent. Calvin thinks God intended the fall of Adam and Eve, foresaw it, and ordained it. He believes Adam and Eve corrupted themselves (II:233). They sinned freely. From this, he extrapolates the thesis that God saves some people while damning others arbitrarily, merely because God wills to do so (II:202–11). Taken together, these ideas are a jumble. There is no way to make them even appear coherent.

Calvin's work fails the test of literary correspondence as well. Because Calvin claims that the only authority for truth is Scripture, the test of correspondence here asks whether Calvin's interpretation of Genesis 2 and 3 corresponds with what the chapters actually say. It does not. Rather than reading Genesis closely, Calvin follows Augustine. Therefore, his interpretation suffers the same exaggerations and deficiencies as Augustine's. In Genesis 2 and 3, Adam and Eve are not as noble as Augustine and Calvin portray them. As Bloom reminds us, God patty-cakes Adam from clay, hardly a recipe for nobility. Bloom also argues that Adam and Eve behave like mischievous children, not noble adults. Their actual sin seems rather small. They disobey God carelessly and rashly rather than malevolently. After God discovers their transgression, God does not change their nature as Calvin thinks. Rather, God alters their situation by increasing their pain in labor, setting them at enmity with serpents, and casting them from their home so they are sure to die.

It is true that eating the fruit changes them. It opens their eyes, giving them insight into their situation. Scholars differ about the meaning of this awakening. Do they now know sex? Lust? Shame? Good and evil? Everything? The narrative seems to many to be a coming-of-age story in which children discover what adults already know—sexual desire, the discipline of life together in marriage, childbirth pains for the woman, hard labor for the man, and death at the end of it all. Adam and Eve's corruption is hardly the point of the narrative.

Reading Calvin, I have been struck with his reasoning. It often seems sound. It is reasonable that if God created everything good and yet we experience the evils of pain and death, a catastrophic change occurred between God's original creation and our experience of the world. It is reasonable that if pain and death are punishments for sin, the sin must have been terrible. However, the very coherence of his thinking here drives and distorts his interpretation of Genesis 2 and 3 so that his interpretation does not correspond to the text. This is heavily ironic, for Calvin spends the first part of the *Institutes* hailing the truth of Scripture and acclaiming the corruption of human reason. Here is one of his summary comments:

> For if we reflect how prone the human mind is to lapse into forgetfulness of God, how readily inclined to every kind of error, how bent every now and then on devising new and fictitious religions, it will be easy to understand how necessary it was to make such a depository of doctrine [the Bible] as would secure it from

either perishing by the neglect, vanishing away amid the errors, or being corrupted by the presumptuous audacity of men. (I:66)

Ironically, despite his conviction that Scripture provides a bulwark against human error, in the end Calvin depends more on his private reason than on a careful exposition of Genesis 2 and 3.

Calvin is caught in a dilemma of his own making. He is not a critical reader of Scripture, and he refuses to allegorize. He wants to embrace the plain sense of Scripture, but Scripture is not so plain. Genesis 1 portrays God as omnipotent and benevolent, the author of a good creation. Genesis 2 and 3 portray God as inept and ignorant, even vicious. Trying to reconcile these two different portraits often drives Calvin into confusion. Furthermore, he trusts Augustine's misinterpretation of Genesis 2 and 3, which he follows closely, adding even harsher punishments to God's decrees.

Augustine's misreading of the narrative and his doctrine of original sin invade the western church and, through Calvin and Luther, capture Protestantism. Augustine's success, which is also Luther's and Calvin's, suggests that his model of human nature appeals to something deep within us. Elaine Pagels (1989, 145–49) thinks Augustine's model of human nature and its origin appeals because, paradoxically, it gives people a sense of power. Augustine and Calvin give Adam and Eve tremendous power. According to them, the first couple's actions drastically alter nature and humanity. Moreover, according to Pagels, Augustine suggests that our suffering occurs because of our moral lives, lives over which we have control as we do not over our physical and emotional pain and suffering. Furthermore, she thinks Augustine convinces us of what we already most deeply feel, "that pain is unnatural, death an enemy" (Pagels 1989, 147).

Pagels's answer to the appeal of the Augustine/Calvin interpretation of Genesis 2 and 3 and their doctrine of original sin is useful, but weak. Augustine and Calvin have tapped into deeper roots in our humanity than Pagels exposes. They have evoked two correlated canalizations. The first is the catastrophe-atonement canalization analyzed by Burkert. The second is the canalization of evil.

The Canalization of Evil

In *Evil: Inside Human Cruelty and Violence,* Roy F. Baumeister (1997) analyzes evil from the perspective of modern psychology. He does not try to justify the existence of evil (a matter I address in chapter 10) but to explain how human moral evil, especially cruelty and violence, comes into the world. He discovers that we treat evil in an unrealistic, canalized manner. He calls his discovery of our canalization of evil the *myth of pure evil*. He demythologizes our canalization by showing that actual evil is far different from our canalized version.

Baumeister concludes that actual human cruelty and violence are products of personality and circumstance. Frequently, the victims of violence participate in their victimization, for violence is often the result of an escalation of violence between victim and perpetrator. This explains why most murders are committed by someone who knows the victim. Since evil is a product of escalation, it grows gradually. Baumeister notes that cruelty and violence may be the result of egocentricity and/or the desire for material gain or it may be the result of our idealism, the cause of some of our worst atrocities. Rarely do violence and cruelty stem from sadism.

As Baumeister shows, this is not how people commonly view evil. When we speak of evil, report it in news stories, or write about it in movie scripts and novels, we enhance and distort it, painting the victim, the perpetrator, and the events in black and white. Baumeister (1977, 72–75) says our canalized version of evil has eight characteristics. The Augustine/Calvin model of our fallen human nature has the same eight. Here I compare them, beginning each time with the Augustine/Calvin model.

First, Augustine and Calvin claim that all human beings are totally egocentric and that Adam and Eve fall through egocentric pride and disloyalty. They both maintain that we are blinded by our egocentricity and cannot see our pridefulness. The canalized version of evil says evil people are egocentric, they have too much self-esteem, and because of these qualities, they are arrogantly blinded to themselves and their situation.

Second, Augustine and Calvin insist that harmony reigned before the fall. The fall destroyed our harmony and concord. The canalized version of evil claims that the normal world is peaceful and predictable and that evil disrupts this peaceful order, bringing chaos.

Third, Augustine and Calvin assert that evil has been with humanity from shortly after the creation of the first human beings to the present. Evil is old and intractable. The canalized version of evil says that evil is ancient, constant, and relentless.

Fourth, Augustine and Calvin both extol the innocence of Adam and Eve, making them far nobler than the Genesis narrative indicates. They also turn the serpent into a demon full of malice. The canalized version of evil says victims are pure and innocent, beset by malicious beings.

Fifth, Augustine offers no motive for Adam and Eve's pre-fall corruption. It is inexplicable and unreasonable. The canalized version of evil emphasizes incomprehensibility of motive. In it, the evildoer simply inflicts gratuitous harm on innocent victims. If there is any motive at all, it is pleasure.

Sixth, Calvin especially emphasizes the voluntary nature of evil. Human nature is biased so that people are pleased to do evil. We are slaves who wish to be enslaved by sin, and so we are. Our intentions are bad. In the canalized version of evil, evil people intentionally harm the innocent.

Seventh, both Calvin and Augustine say that people are totally depraved. Not only are we driven by emotions, our reason is helpless to assert control; indeed, our reason in general is impotent. The canalized version of evil maintains that evil people find it difficult or impossible to control their emotions.

Eighth, for Calvin and Augustine, Satan is the adversary of God and humanity. At the fall, we become adversaries, too, estranged from God, ejected from paradise, at enmity with one another, isolated from nature. We have become evil aliens. In the canalized version of evil, the evil person is an alien outsider.

Because Baumeister's study is from modern psychology with no interest in the fall or in theology in general, the perfect fit between his analysis of our canalized version of evil and the Augustine/Calvin model of human nature is astounding. Baumeister's analysis shows the canalized version of evil is unrealistic and does not correspond to the way the world is. In doing so, it shows the unrealistic character of Protestantism's doctrine of original sin as a model of human nature. Augustine and Calvin's model has mesmerized us because it is canalized. Its being canalized should alert us to its falsehood. As I argue in chapters 7, 8, and 9, human nature is complex. In it, egocentricity commingles with charity and injustice with love. Our best attributes undergird our worst sins. Calvin's model is too dark and too simplistic. The only author I know who uses it, stays close to the biblical text, and also does justice to the complexity of human nature, is the English poet, John Milton (1608–1674). Books 9 and

10 of his *Paradise Lost* ([1667] 1966) retell the events in Genesis 2 and 3 as a fall of epic proportions.

I have now finished exploring the Protestant doctrine of original sin. It fails both tests of truth. It is incoherent in several respects. It fails to correspond with the biblical narrative and strays far from Bloom's interpretation of it. Moreover, the doctrine is doubly canalized. It balances Christianity's magnificent atonement by a disastrous fall, thus conforming to Burkert's analysis of our canalization of catastrophe and atonement, and it follows point for point Baumeister's evidence for our canalization of evil. We need a doctrine of original sin that can better pass the tests of truth. Such a model developed under the pen of the central theologian of Catholicism, Saint Thomas Aquinas.

Aquinas and Catholicism

Unlike Protestantism, Catholicism does not look solely to the Bible for truth. It also looks to councils of the church, to tradition, and to the hierarchy, especially the Pope, who became infallible in 1870 if speaking ex cathedra on faith and morals. Therefore, whether Aquinas's views on original sin pass the test of correspondence to Scripture is not as important for Catholics as it is for Protestants. Because the hierarchy and tradition have made Aquinas the premier theologian of the Catholic Church, and I have chosen him because he is the foremost Catholic theologian, for me to ask whether Aquinas's views correspond to the standards of councils, traditions, and the Pope would produce a circular argument. Therefore, I examine Aquinas's relationship to Scripture. My primary resource for Aquinas's views is his *Summa Theologicae* ([1271] 1964, vol. 26).

Aquinas begins with the familiar position that before the fall, harmony reigned. He arranges the harmonious human psyche into a tripartite hierarchy in which reason and will submit to God, the nonrational parts of a person to reason, and a person's body to the soul. As long as this harmonious subordination continues, people retain God's sanctifying grace, the indwelling Spirit.

The fall wrecks this harmony. At the fall, God withdraws sanctifying grace from humanity (McBrien 1994, 188). This withdrawal destroys what Aquinas calls *original justice*, a person's right relationship with God (36–43, question 82, art. 3 and 4; Urban 1986, 150). It also destroys each person's own harmony, making the soul subject to the senses and reason to desire, and it annihilates peace among people.

According to Aquinas, all is not lost at the fall, although much is enfeebled. The essential nature of what it is to be human is not lost or even diminished, for "the essential nature of a specific being . . . cannot be destroyed nor even diminished by sin" (Vandervelde 1981, 31). However, God can withdraw divine gifts from creatures, and if they are withdrawn, the creatures suffer loss. Aquinas considers original justice a gift from God, something to be transmitted from generation to generation as a part of human nature (O'Brien 1964, 130–31); if it is destroyed, human nature darkens, becoming confused and disordered. Human reason also dims. Aquinas thinks that humanity retains its rational nature after the fall, but reason does not dominate our nonrational parts as it once did. Because humanity's inclination to virtue resides in its reason, the natural inclination to virtue remains, but it is tainted by sin.

Aquinas maintains that original sin is a deficiency, not a positive force for evil. This view Calvin explicitly rejects ([1559] 1995, I:218). For Calvin, the loss is replaced by active sin, an active will to do evil. Aquinas's weaker view leads him to say that people have some ability to help themselves. The fall did not destroy freedom of will. People can still choose to love God and one another with God's help. Aquinas sees the relationship between God and humanity as one of cooperation. Nonetheless, Aquinas follows Augustine in defining freedom as freedom to do good, whereas lack of freedom results in sinning. Although he emphasizes natural human choice, he does not see moral freedom as the ability to choose freely between good and evil.

Much of Aquinas's discussion fails the test of correspondence to Scripture. First, his model of human nature contains concepts that are not in the text. Genesis 2 and 3 do not mention human faculties or their relationship to one another. These ideas entered Christianity through pagan Greek philosophers, especially Plato and Aristotle. Genesis does not mention sanctifying grace or original justice.

Second, Aquinas makes the fall larger than it is in Scripture, exaggerating the distance between Adam and Eve's nature at their creation and after their sin. His portrait of Adam and Eve as a fully adult pair abets his tendency to exaggerate. Genesis 2 and 3 portrays Adam and Eve as Bloom indicates, immature and naïve before their sin and equally childish after it.

Third, the change that occurs in Genesis 3 is not a degradation of human nature as Aquinas maintains, but a growth in knowledge. Adam and Eve acquire knowledge of good and evil. The first couple does lose some things, for example, pleasure in labor and the friendship of serpents. Although Scripture mentions these losses explicitly, they seem unimportant to Aquinas. In fact, in the *Summa Theologicae* and elsewhere in his discussions of original sin (collected texts in Gilby 1955, 118–43), Aquinas evinces little interest in the Genesis text. He is far more concerned with other authorities, especially Aristotle and Augustine.

Despite his lack of interest in the narrative, his model does sometimes correspond to parts of Genesis 2 and 3. The biblical Adam and Eve can be construed to be in harmony with God before their disobedience and they seem deprived of that harmony thereafter. Although God does not explicitly withdraw from them after they sin, their banishment from the garden where deity walks does set them at a distance.

Whether Aquinas's position as a whole completely passes the test of coherence is hard to say. His detailed exposition is replete with technicalities, the technicalities make it extremely complex, and its complexity sometimes makes it seem paradoxical. In spite of this, its fundamental outline is clearly coherent. That outline is accepted by the modern Catholic Church in its *Catechism* of 1994 (95–103). Here the fall is a historical deed occurring at the beginning of human history. The first sin is disobedience, and it affects human nature, which loses its original harmony. Original sin itself is a state in which people are deprived of original justice, a state in which their nature is wounded but not totally corrupted. Original sin is not active, but privative. There is nothing incoherent here.

The complexity and technicality of Aquinas's doctrine mean that in its entirety it cannot be canalized, for it is too clearly a product of reason and erudition. Moreover, Aquinas's fallen human beings are not black and white stereotypes, but multihued individuals. They are complex, confused, and conflicted. Their spiritual lives are filled with struggle as they long for virtue but sin instead. Cooperating with God is a messy affair, filled with doubt and joy. His fallen human beings do not necessarily love evil or take pleasure in it. They are not totally alienated from God, and they are not purely egocentric, but are capable of loving God and one another. Nonetheless, some of Aquinas's essential points follow the two canalizations discussed above. His view of a catastrophic fall fits the canalization of catastrophe and atonement analyzed by Burkert. His doctrine of original sin has some of Baumeister's eight characteristics of the canalization of evil: Adam and Eve are innocent victims, evil is old and intractable, and order and stability give way to disorder and disharmony.

Aquinas's doctrine of original sin fares better than Calvin's. It is only partly canalized. Being coherent, it also passes one of the tests of truth. It partly satisfies another, for it corresponds somewhat to Scripture, although its details and larger abstract concepts are not in Genesis 2 and 3. However, it contradicts a central feature of Bloom's exegesis and the text of Genesis 3 itself when it claims that Adam and Eve's nature changes. In addition, Aquinas misses entirely Adam and Eve's childishness. In the end, his is a darker view of Genesis 3 than either the text or Bloom's interpretation permits. A brighter doctrine of original sin flows from Athanasius and the Orthodox Church.

Athanasius and Orthodoxy

The Orthodox Church is not well known to Christians in the West, so a brief introduction may be helpful. For fuller treatment, see Timothy Ware (1993) from whom the information here is taken.

Very early in Christian history, the church began to develop two separate traditions, one Latin, the other Greek. The center of the Latin tradition was Rome (West), of the Greek tradition, Constantinople (East). The Greek-speaking church expanded into eastern Europe and Russia beginning in the ninth century. In the eleventh century, the Greek and Latin churches split formally over theology and ecclesiology.

As with the later Protestant split, the ecclesiastical issue was the power of the Pope. The Orthodox Church refused to accept the Pope as supreme head of the church. It expected the bishops to meet together in councils to make decisions. The year 1054 saw this matter come into open conflict. Since then, authority in the Orthodox Church has rested on Scripture, tradition, the first seven ecumenical councils, the Nicene Creed, church theologians (especially those of the fourth century), and certain doctrinal statements made by subsequent leaders in the Orthodox Church. Because the church decided which books are to be treated as Scripture and the church interprets

Scripture, the Orthodox Church thinks Scripture ultimately gets its authority from the church, not the other way around, as in Protestantism. The Orthodox Church has the same New Testament as the western churches. However, whereas the West uses the Hebrew Scriptures for its Old Testament, the Orthodox church uses the Septuagint.

The Septuagint, also known as the LXX, is a translation of the Old Testament Hebrew Scriptures into Greek, completed about 132 years before the birth of Christ, supposedly by seventy-two translators (all information on the Septuagint is from Cross 1957, 1240–41). All Christians used the Septuagint from Paul's time until at least the end of the fourth century, and they considered it divinely inspired. It contains all the books in the current Hebrew Bible, which are the same as those in the Protestant Old Testament, as well as those books in the Roman Catholic Bible known to Protestants as the Apocrypha. The Greek text differs considerably from the Hebrew text in some instances, both in content and meaning. For example, the Septuagint leaves out some passages of the Hebrew books of Job, Jeremiah, and 1 Samuel and changes the order in Jeremiah and Ezekiel. In Genesis 3:16 where the Hebrew clearly suggests sexual desire ("yet your desire shall be for your husband"), the Greek evades this connotation by making the clause read (in English) "'your return will be to your husband,' i.e. you will keep coming back to him" (Wevers 1993, 45).

This information is relevant to the current discussion. If authority is spread so broadly in the Orthodox Church, who will best represent it? If the church's interpretation of Genesis 2 and 3 is authoritative, then why not trust that authority rather than examining the text ourselves? If the text is different from that used in the West, then how can we fairly compare the Orthodox interpretation of it with those of the western branches of Christianity? Fortunately, all these questions have answers.

To proceed in reverse order, the text of the Septuagint is available and so are commentaries on it. John William Wevers (1993, 20–50) compares the Hebrew and Greek texts of Genesis 2 and 3. There are few differences, only two relevant to this discussion. In the Septuagint the serpent of Genesis 3:1 is merely wise, with no connotations of craftiness, and connotations of sexual desire are not part of God's curse of Eve. This means that those who use the Septuagint are less likely to make the serpent a demon and to judge lust a component of original sin than those working from the Hebrew and its Latin and English translations.

Although the Orthodox Church considers its interpretation of Scripture authoritative, it recognizes many interpreters, not one. This brings us to the question of whose interpretation to choose. I have chosen a classic theologian in the Orthodox tradition, Saint Athanasius, Bishop of Alexandria, Egypt. I have several reasons. First, he is probably the most familiar of the Greek-speaking theologians to those brought up in the western tradition. For centuries in the West, both Protestants and Catholics used a creed that carries his name and some of his ideas, although he did not write it. Second, he is a fourth-century theologian, and these theologians are favorites of the Orthodox Church. Third, he wrote an extensive commentary on Genesis 2 and 3. Fourth, the work is available in English. I refer to Athanasius's *De Incarnatione* ([c. 318] 1977, 26–31).

According to Athanasius, God's natural grace suffuses creation from the first, and God never withdraws it. God creates Adam and Eve and all the other animals in their natural state, mortal and subject to decay. At the same time, God blesses Adam and Eve with additional, special grace so they participate in God's word and image. In this state, they possess immortality and supernatural knowledge, but only while they continuously contemplate God. Freshly created, they are naïve children, having "the beauty of innocence with which they were created" (1977, 30, n. 5). Because they are innocent, the serpent easily deceives them. When they disobey God and fall, God withdraws special grace, and Adam and Eve descend to their natural state of ignorance and mortality. They become ignorant because they lose the knowledge of God as soon as they begin to contemplate material things (the tree of knowledge—Athanasius tends to allegorize the narrative). They lose the image of God but they retain their free will, for it is a natural attribute. Their progeny suffer the consequences of the fall but do not bear the guilt of the primordial pair.

Athanasius's model allows fallen humanity to turn to the contemplation of God and receive God's special grace in this life. By God's special grace, we can (and do) cooperate with God toward our own salvation. This is not a doctrine of merit but of free grace, since God's grace, whether natural or special, is always free (Ware 1993, 222). Athanasius's model provides for the salvation of unbaptized infants and even for Jeremiah and John the Baptist to have led sinless lives (Kelly 1960, 347–48). It also allows for our deification. As

Athanasius says, "[Christ], indeed, assumed humanity that we might become God" (1977, 93, n. 54). His view is far more optimistic than Augustine's or Calvin's or even Aquinas's. The Orthodox Church today retains his optimism.

Athanasius's account passes the test of coherence. God creates all animals subject to the natural laws of decay and death, but gives people special graces as long as we obediently contemplate the divinity. When we cease to be obedient, God withdraws special grace, leaving us in our natural state. This works especially well in Athanasius because Adam and Eve's special graces are dependent on their continuous contemplation of God; when they turn to lesser matters, they would logically lose God's special grace by their own action. It is logical as well that their progeny would exist in their natural state but not retain God's special grace, for we, too, contemplate the material world rather than God. This is particularly likely since we live outside the Garden of Eden. Being just, God does not hold Adam and Eve's progeny guilty for their parents' deed.

Athanasius's model corresponds quite closely to Genesis 2 and 3. In Genesis 3, Adam and Eve sin very soon after they are created. They appear to be neophytes who have not learned about deception. That they succumb so easily to the serpent's blandishments adds to the sense of them as innocent and unsuspecting children. The model agrees here with Bloom's interpretation. Adam and Eve's banishment from the garden where God walks is easily construed as God's withdrawal from them. All our authors agree on this point. Because their banishment also separates Adam and Eve from the tree of life, it maintains their natural state of mortality, fulfilling God's promise in Genesis 2 of death if they eat the forbidden fruit. Here Athanasius carefully and deliberately follows the text. Neither Genesis 2 or 3 mentions free will, so Athanasius's retention of it corresponds to the narrative as well as with Bloom's interpretation. By free will, Athanasius and the Orthodox Church mean the freedom to choose between good and evil (Ware 1993, 223–24).

Athanasius's model seems to fail to correspond with the Genesis narrative when he claims that the pair lose knowledge at the fall. The Genesis account has them gain it, as God notes (Gen. 3:22). Yet even here, Athanasius tries to stay close to the text. He argues that Adam and Eve both gain and lose knowledge. They gain knowledge of good and evil while losing their knowledge of God. Given the tragic rift that Bloom finds between the pair and God, a rift that would seem to lead to their loss of knowledge of God, Athanasius's analysis of the narrative seems to follow the text.

The Athanasian model is fairly naturalistic, a good sign that it has not been canalized. He naturalizes mortality, having all earthly creatures created mortal. He naturalizes pain. All earthly creatures feel it. Neither natural pain nor death is a punishment for sin. Rather, God punishes Adam and Eve by withdrawing supernatural gifts, leaving us in our natural state. Adam and Eve's catastrophe is small, almost ordinary. It does not fit the canalization of evil. Adam and Eve are not cast in black and white, but in varied colors. They are innocent and childlike, yet egocentric. They lose divine grace but do not become totally corrupt. Athanasius is the only one of our theologians to leave us with humanity much as modern science sees it, a part of the natural world, with death as our natural end.

In this chapter, I have applied two tests of truth to three doctrines of original sin, the doctrines developed by the major branches of Christianity. I have asked whether the doctrines are coherent and correspond with Scripture. Protestantism's doctrine fails both tests and is also doubly canalized; therefore, it is highly likely to be false. Catholicism's doctrine fares better, but it still fails parts of the test for correspondence and is somewhat canalized. Orthodoxy's doctrine passes the tests and is not canalized. This means its model of human nature, as so far tested, is the most likely to be true.

However, the inquiry thus far has ignored the test of consilience and disregarded the central concern of the test of correspondence, namely whether the text of Genesis corresponds with the way the world is. It has also neglected to ask whether Genesis 2 and 3 cohere with other sections of Genesis. The following chapter addresses these questions. The result leads to the demise of Adam and Eve.

Chapter 5

The Demise of Adam and Eve

A cataclysm in Western thought occurred between about 1830 and 1930. In 1830, most scientific models of the world had as their foundation the narratives of Genesis 1–9, beginning with God's creative word and ending with the subsidence of Noah's flood. A century later, no scientific models incorporated these narratives or even referred to them in passing. Many authors have told the story of this cataclysm in myriad ways. This chapter depicts it as the result of three processes: first, the rise of a critical approach to the Bible based on evidence internal to the text; second, the development of knowledge of the global distribution of living organisms and fossils; and third, the consilience of scientific theories whose beginning may be dated to Charles Darwin's circumnavigation of the globe on the *Beagle* in 1831–1836 and whose ending no one knows.

This cataclysm has had many results, one being the demise of Adam and Eve. By the *demise of Adam and Eve,* I mean primarily the slow death of a model of the universe that had survived for more than a thousand years. But *demise* implies more than death. It also means relinquishment of high office and transfer of authority. In Christianity, Judaism, and Islam, Adam and Eve had held high office as the progenitors of all humanity. They had held authority, the authority of Scripture. Adam and Eve do not merely die. A coup supplants them. Their high office and authority pass to critical thought in general and to science in particular. The current culture wars resound with aftershocks of this cataclysm.

This chapter tells the story of the cataclysm by applying the three tests of truth to various models of the world, then inquiring about the consequences. The first section of the chapter compares the model of creation in the narrative of Genesis 2 and 3 with the model presented in Genesis 1 and asks whether the models are coherent. This comparison applies the coherence test of truth and involves evidence internal to the biblical text. The second section asks whether the model in Genesis 1–9 corresponds to common observations concerning the distribution of plants, animals, and fossils across the globe. This inquiry employs the correspondence test of truth. The third section examines scientific models in general and Darwin's model in particular to ask whether they meet a third test of truth, Whewell's consilience of inductions. The final section argues that the main threat to Christianity is not science in general or the theory of evolution in particular, but careful reading of Scripture, which by itself brings about the demise of Adam and Eve. The next chapter applies nuanced scriptural scholarship to the text. Here, I read the text simply, first applying the test of internal coherence.

Coherence and Genesis 1–3

The narrative I refer to in this chapter as Genesis 1 stretches on to Genesis 2:3 where God rests after having finished the creation. Thus, in this chapter Genesis 1 is shorthand for Genesis 1—2:3 as previously Genesis 2 and 3 has been shorthand for Genesis 2:4b—3. (Scholars are uncertain whether Genesis 2:4a belongs to the first narrative or to the second.) Genesis 1 narrates God's creation of the cosmos and living beings. It has a repetitive, poetic, liturgical style, with six words or acts or days of creation prefaced by "and God said," and each terminated by "and God saw that it was good." Genesis 2 and 3 do not have this style and focus on the human drama, but they cover some of the same material as Genesis 1. Therefore the two narratives loosely cohere with each other. In both, there is a God. In both, God creates plants, animals, and human beings. In both, water plays a significant role. But here their coherence ceases, for many of the details do not mesh, not even those about water.

Genesis 1 mentions water in two different places, verses 6-10 and 20-22. In 6-10 God creates a dome to separate the waters, the dome being the sky, presumably solid so the waters above it cannot leak through. The waters above the sky are not mentioned again in Genesis 1, but they return in Genesis 7:11 as the "windows of the heavens" open and water from above the sky floods the Earth. These are supernatural waters, the waters of chaos. The waters below the sky God gathers together into seas, separating them from the dry land. At work, God is a powerful creator and ruler whose word separates, controls, and orders.

In the later verses, God commands the waters to bring forth sea monsters and swarms of other living creatures. Although these waters are the seas we see, they retain a supernatural, creative element as they literally produce living creatures. Again, God's word separates, creates, and organizes.

The only waters in Genesis 2 and 3 are in 2:5-14. They are more naturalistic than those in Genesis 1, and God's relation to them is more anthropomorphic. Here flows a river with four branches, two of which are known today, the Tigris and Euphrates. Rain is mentioned. God stands on the bank and with intimate hands creates a man, with divine breath gives him life. The rivers water the garden God creates. Rather than being the creator who commands and orders at a distance, God stands within creation and tenderly mothers the new creature into being.

These two narratives treat water differently. In one, it is supernatural, symbolic, chaotic yet life giving, in the other, natural. They also treat the process of creation and the creator differently. In one, God is distant, powerful, and commanding. God's very word brings the universe into being. In the other, God is intimate and motherly, kneading creation with tender hands, giving it divine breath for life. These two pictures are so different that scholars believe people with very different interests wrote the two narratives centuries apart (Friedman 1987; Westermann 1984, 74–278). Further evidence for this view is that each of the narratives calls God by different names.

Moreover, Genesis 1 and 2 give the biological creation in a different order. Genesis 1 has God first create vegetation, then sea dwellers, birds, land creatures, and human beings. In Genesis 2, God first creates a man, then a garden of vegetation, animals, birds, and a woman. Although a serpent appears in Genesis 3, Genesis 2 does not mention the creation of reptiles or fish.

Furthermore, the two narratives treat the creation of humanity differently. In Genesis 1:26-29, God creates male and female together in the image of deity, gives them dominion over the Earth and its creatures, and gives them every plant and every tree for food. In Genesis 2, God creates the man first, using earthly clay and divine breath, then seeks a partner for him. After many unsuccessful attempts, God puts the man to sleep and creates a woman from the man's rib. For food, God gives them the fruit of all the trees of the garden except one, the tree of the knowledge of good and evil. Some intentions seem similar here. In Genesis 1, God gives the people dominion over the Earth and its other inhabitants; in Genesis 2, the man names the animals, implying dominion. In Genesis 1, God creates the man and woman in the image of deity; in Genesis 2, God gives the man divine breath to make him a living being. Each narrative seems to imply that humanity contains something of the divine. Yet, the narratives handle God's gifts of dominion and divinity very differently. In all these matters, Genesis 2 fails the test of coherence with Genesis 1. The details contradict each other.

More importantly for our purposes, Genesis 1 does not narrate the main event of Genesis 2 and 3, Adam and Eve's disobedient eating of the fruit of the tree of knowledge, yet it covers enough of the same material to contradict the prohibition of the forbidden fruit in Genesis 2. In Genesis 1, God tells the pair they can eat freely of all the plants and all the fruits of the trees. Genesis 1 knows no prohibited tree. It never mentions a tree of knowledge. In Genesis 1, humanity had no forbidden fruit to tempt, no ominous command from God to disobey. The first pair's alleged act of disobedience in Genesis 3 could not occur in the world described in Genesis 1. If Genesis 1 presents an accurate model of the way the world is, then Adam and Eve's disobedience never occurred. Adam and Eve may have been historical figures, but they neither committed nor transmitted original sin.

However, Genesis 1 may not accurately represent the way the world is, or was. Perhaps a better way to find out about the world would be to observe it. *Biogeography,* the study of the distribution of living and fossilized organisms on Earth, uses direct observation. Perhaps it can shed light on the biblical accounts of creation in Genesis 1–9, telling us whether these accounts of the creation of plants and animals taken as a whole correspond to the way the world is in relevant respects and sufficient degrees.

Correspondence and Genesis 1–9

Genesis 1–9 offers three accounts that touch on the distribution of plants and animals on Earth. Genesis 1 gives a very general description, noting only that on the third day God gathered the waters into one place, separated them from dry land, and created vegetation; on the fifth day made fish and birds; and on the sixth, created the other animals, including human beings. Genesis 1 does not tell much about what to expect when exploring Earth's flora, fauna, and fossils.

Genesis 2 is more specific. Here God creates a garden from which a river flows, dividing into four branches, Pishon, Gihon, Tigris, and Euphrates. Although the first two rivers are unknown today, the last two flow from the mountains of eastern Turkey, join, and drain into the Persian Gulf. God creates humanity and all the living creatures in this area. From here, they spread out to populate the Earth.

However, Genesis 6–8 tells of horrific rain God sends to flood the Earth, destroying almost everything not aboard Noah's ark. As the flood subsides, Noah's ark comes to rest somewhere in the mountains of Ararat (Gen. 8:4). These mountains extend from present southeastern Turkey into northwest Iran. After the land dries, Noah, his family, and a male and female of each species leave the ark, again multiply, and migrate until they populate the Earth. Never again does God so utterly destroy Earth's creatures.

The two narratives giving a specific geographical location from which all the animals on Earth migrate mention locations so similar they may be considered the same. According to Genesis, people and animals migrated from southeastern Turkey into all the places we find them today.

From what we now know of biogeography, this model from Genesis is not similar enough in relevant respects and sufficient degrees to the way the world is to pass the test of correspondence. Consider koala bears. These animals now live nowhere but Australia (except those shipped to zoos and the like). In Australia, they enjoy a warm, dry habitat of wooded grasslands. The savannas of Africa provide similar habitat, lie closer to Turkey, and are accessible from Turkey by land. Yet, no koala bears migrated to Africa. Instead, according to Genesis, they started from Turkey, headed east across several rugged mountain ranges and the entire land mass of Asia, found their way into tropical Malaysia, crossed the water to Indonesia, and then swam across enormous distances for so small a terrestrial mammal, landed in Australia, then migrated south into the Australian wooded grasslands. Meanwhile, all the koala bears not migrating to Australia died out. Small, defenseless marsupials whose major activity is sleep and whose diet is eucalyptus leaves could not have migrated this long and difficult way. Had they been hardy enough to have done so, they would not have died out in every place but Australia. Moreover, had there been such a dying, fossils would remain, but not one has been discovered.

Or consider Townsend moles. These animals live along the west coast of North America from southern British Columbia to northern California and nowhere else. Adults weigh about five ounces. The moles tunnel underground in moist areas where the soil is loose and eat insects and roots. If they migrated from Turkey, either they crossed the Asian landmass, swam the frigid waters of the Bering Strait, and braved the snows and permafrost of Alaska or swam across the Atlantic Ocean and crossed North America. Either journey would have meant crossing thousands of miles of land and water uninhabitable to them. How would they have done this? Moreover, it seems likely that some, finding good habitat nearby, would have settled down in places like Syria. Yet, we find them nowhere but on the west coast of North America.

Study of biogeography produces hundreds of thousands of cases like these, cases of animals and plants living nowhere near Turkey despite possible habitats for them in the area: animals and plants not notable for their mobility, their defenses against predators, or the variety of their diets. We would have to invent wild tales of impossible travels and deaths in order to think that they migrated from Turkey to where they now live, then died out in Turkey and along all the routes of their migration, yet left no fossils.

By the end of the eighteenth century, knowledge of biogeography was sufficiently extensive that many people had rejected the Eden/Noah's ark version of the geographic origins of plants and animals. They replaced it with two quasi-biblical models that were in competition with each other when Darwin set out on the *Beagle* in 1831. According to both, God created pairs of each species and placed each pair in an appropriate environment. The simpler model held that each species had only one center of creation. Animals and plants found across the globe migrated from their single point of origin. However, all too often the biogeography of a species made nearly impossible its migration from a single point of origin. The competing theory held that God had made multiple pairs of some species and placed each pair in different locations. This explained how species came to be where they were known to be, but it multiplied miracles, something most scientists wish to avoid.

When Darwin began his voyage, he accepted the simpler model because he thought its competitor lacked evidence. He reasoned that, if there were multiple centers of creation for each species, then members of the same species would be in many parts of the globe whether they were capable of long migrations or not. As Darwin argues at length in *On the Origin of Species* ([1859] 1964, 346–410), many animals and plants are capable of such migrations, but terrestrial mammals are not. Therefore, they constitute the test case: "But if the same species can be produced at two separate points, why do we not find a single mammal common to Europe and Australia or South America? The conditions of life are nearly the same" (352–53) so that a species put there could easily have survived. Indeed, plants and animals native to Europe often thrive when transplanted to Australia and the Americas.

Darwin thought the evidence pointed to single centers of creation. He expected to find each species radiating out from its central creation point into habitats similar to the original. However, when Darwin reached South America, this is not what he found. On the continent, he found similar species in diverse habitats. On the islands nearby, he saw diverse species in similar habitats. Moreover, the island species resembled the continental ones. These biogeographical arrangements confounded Darwin's expectations. In addition, he discovered that fossils in South America, as in Europe and Australia, resembled the living animals in the area where the fossils lay. Resemblance to living species was especially close in fossils found near the surface of the earth. As he searched deeper into the earth and therefore backward in time, the fossils were increasingly different from living species. Darwin was puzzled. He was also a cautious man. When he returned to England, he took the evidence to the greatest experts of his time and awaited their assessments.

In England, the expert on fossils was Richard Owen (the cases are in Bowlby 1990, 220–22). It was he, not Darwin, who demonstrated that the fossils Darwin had recovered in South America were not the same species as the living ones, although they resembled the living species. Darwin's friend, Charles Lyell, had already demonstrated that the same applied to the marsupials of Australia, and everyone concerned knew about European fossils. There is a pattern. Each continent has its own types of species. The fossils on each continent are different species from the living ones and yet resemble them. Each continent seems to have animals designed specifically for it that have changed over time. This evidence convinced Darwin that species could change. They are neither eternal as Plato and Aristotle claim, nor immutable, as the Bible seems to suggest.

John Gould was the expert on birds. He showed that the mockingbirds Darwin had brought back from the Galapagos Islands off the west coast of South America were three distinct species. Because Darwin had noted which island each bird had inhabited, Gould's analysis showed each island contained its own distinct species, all closely related to species on the continent. This is not what would be expected had God created each species separately. There would have been no reason for God to create different species for similar habitats. This evidence convinced Darwin that living species are related to each other by descent. If they are related by descent, this explains other, previously puzzling facts, namely, that species can be classified according to how closely they resemble each other, and that the trend over time is for species to proliferate and diversify. The evidence also suggests that geographical barriers such as mountains, rivers, and oceans that separate and isolate populations promote speciation.

As biogeographical evidence accumulated, the strictly biblical model of the special creation of species and their migration from Turkey to the habitats they now occupy rang increasingly hollow. As more information became known, the model seemed to resemble the world in fewer and fewer respects, and the explanations offered by those who wished to keep the model became thinner and more fantastic. As that model failed, another developed and eventually replaced it. The new model is Darwin's theory of evolution by natural selection. Other than the evidence already examined, one of the strongest arguments in its favor is Whewell's test of truth discussed in chapter 2: the consilience of scientific models.

Consilience in Science

In the middle of the nineteenth century, science posed many puzzles. One reason the scientific community accepted evolution after Darwin published the *Origin* was that Darwin's theory of evolution solved many of them. Before Darwin, no one understood why the best classification of organisms was by resemblance or why the most natural classification seemed to be a hierarchy of groups subordinate to groups. And although those people who classified organisms knew that some resemblances were good for classification whereas others were not, they did not know why. Darwin provided reasons. Most resemblances among species occur because the species descended from a common ancestor. However, some resemblances develop among unrelated species because they inhabit similar environments. Whales are not fish but mammals, yet they are fish-shaped because they have adapted to their aquatic habitat. They resemble fish because of adaptation, not because they inherited their fish-like shape from fish.

No one relying on the theory that God created each species separately could explain why biologists had such difficulty telling the difference between varieties within a species and separate species. Darwin offered an explanation. Varieties are incipient species, and evolution leaves the demarcation lines between species unclear. No one understood why embryos of disparate species were so similar, but the adults so dissimilar. Darwin had a solution. Natural selection operates most forcefully when animals are old enough to have to find food, shelter, and mates. Therefore, adults become extensively modified over time as those best able to find food, shelter, and mates survive to reproduce. Lacking such environmental pressures, embryos change but little. Biologists had long noted the presence in many species of organs or bones that seemed undeveloped and useless, like the human appendix and the snake's pelvis and hind limbs. Some, such as teeth in whales or chickens, only appeared in embryos. Why would these useless, rudimentary characteristics appear in these animals? Darwin had an answer. Although no longer useful, they were useful in the organism's ancestors and have been retained through inheritance.

Under creationist theories, the geographical distribution of organisms across the globe seemed increasingly inexplicable. Darwin had a solution. He explained biogeography by the evolution of one species into another. If God had created each species, it was difficult to explain their imperfections. Darwin explained them. Organisms modified by natural selection need not be perfect, only sufficiently adapted to their environments to survive to reproduce. Moreover, species are not engineered from a plan. They evolve from one another, and new species must be built upon the material and organization supplied by ancestral species, leading sometimes to awkward compromises.

Questions arose about why the fossil record contains gaps. Darwin provided an answer. Most organisms are never fossilized, for they are eaten and/or decompose instead of being buried and mineralized. Typically, only big bones are fairly impervious to these processes. Even if organisms do become fossils, erosion may erase the record. Where fossils exist, people must find them. Where no river has dug a gorge, fossils may lie buried and undiscovered. Although Darwin does not mention it, the digging of canals and deep coal pits in the nineteenth century unearthed many fossils that otherwise would never have been found.

All these explanations in the *Origin* constitute consiliences, the uniting under one theory of diverse areas of scientific knowledge—paleography, biogeography, anatomy, embryology, and classification. In this regard, Darwin's book is brilliant, comparable to Newton's *Principia Mathematica* (1687). (Darwin's was a best-seller; all 1,250 copies of the first printing sold out on the day they became available [Bowler 1989, 187]). Nowhere in this multiplicity of consiliences is there need to refer to Genesis's narratives of origins. Indeed, the last sentence of the *Origin* implicitly rejects Genesis 1 and 2 and ignores the Genesis flood:

> There is grandeur in this view of life, with its several powers, having been originally breathed into a few forms or into one; and that, whilst this planet has gone cycling on according to the fixed law of gravity, from so simple a beginning endless forms most beautiful and most wonderful have been, and are being, evolved. (490)

God's breath may have created organisms, but God created only a few forms, or one. The many species we see around us evolved from that original creation. God did not create them directly.

Darwin's consilience was only the first of many in and around biology, too many to discuss in detail here. I review the most recent biological consilience at length in chapter 8. In the rest of this section, I devote most coverage to the first post-Darwinian consilience, for it completes Darwin's original theory. Known as *neo-Darwinism* or the *New Synthesis*, it connects the theory of evolution with the science of genetics. It required the work of many scientists and developed in three major phases and a series of minor ones from 1900 to 1950.

The New Synthesis begins with the new century. In 1900, three biologists working independently discovered genes and laid down the basic rules of inheritance. These are Hugo de Vries, Karl Correns, and Erich von Tschermak. In reviewing previous publications, all three came across a paper Gregor Mendel had published in a small Austrian journal in 1866, anticipating their discoveries by thirty-four years. Hence, their discoveries carry the name of that obscure botanical monk.

Mendelian genetics maintains that genes govern each characteristic of an organism, and each organism carries two genes for each characteristic, one donated by each parent. Different characteristics are inherited independently of each other. Biologists have since discovered that the Mendelian "laws" are only partly true, but their original simplicity aided the scientists who worked with them.

Indeed, the belief that different characteristics are inherited independently proved important for the next major phase in the consilience between genetics and evolutionary theory, the development of population genetics. When people think of inheritance, we usually think of characteristics being passed from parents to offspring, that is, we think of individuals contributing and inheriting certain characteristics. Yet, a more fruitful way to conceive of inheritance is to think statistically in terms of populations. Learning to think statistically about populations of organisms involved a consilience between abstract mathematical statistics and the concrete problem of heredity in natural populations. Three men deserve credit for this synthesis, R. A. Fisher, J. B. S. Haldane, and Sewall Wright. Fisher's book, *The Genetical Theory of Natural Selection* (1930), laid the foundation for a series of books that constitutes the final major phase of the New Synthesis. These works united the new model of population genetics with biological models already in existence.

The first book in the synthesis was Theodosius Dobzhansky's *Genetics and the Origin of Species* (1937). The title itself indicates a deliberate effort to effect a consilience between the new genetics and Darwin's work. Dobzhansky argued that the main mechanisms underlying evolution and the diversity of living organisms are the gene changes and mutations already familiar to biologists working with laboratory populations. In their turn, gene changes and mutations are molded by natural selection, migration, and the geographical isolation of a population that may result in speciation.

Next came Julian Huxley's consiliation, *Evolution: The Modern Synthesis* (1942), the book that provided the name for the phenomenon that was occurring. Ernst Mayr published *Systematics and the*

Origin of Species (1942) the same year. *Systematics* is another word for classification. Mayr developed evolutionary criteria for biological classification and also dug into two interesting Darwinian conundrums. First, each species is composed of individuals that vary with respect to each other. Not only is this known from direct observation, it is also a necessary part of evolutionary theory, for without variation, species could not evolve over time. Yet, systematists must recognize individual organisms as members of the same species or members of different ones, so species must be, in some sense, stable, unified, and recognizable. Second, population geneticists had showed that natural selection tends to stabilize species, yet species evolve. What are the evolutionary mechanisms for speciation? Like Dobzhansky, Mayr emphasizes the reproductive isolation of small populations, the very evidence for species transformation Darwin had seen in the Galapagos.

George Gaylord Simpson made paleontology a part of the synthesis in his *Tempo and Mode in Evolution* (1944). His main thesis is that the mechanisms already familiar to geneticists could account for the data fossils provide. He dealt with the temporal nature of the fossil data by arguing that the mutation rates known from work in the laboratories of the 1930s and 1940s match the rates of change found in the fossil record. Again, he emphasizes small populations and reproductive isolation as the mechanisms underlying the most common type of speciation. To explain the gaps in the fossil record, he evokes Darwin's arguments about the rarity of fossilization and discovery, then adds to these the typical small size of speciating populations. Few transitional organisms ever exist to be fossilized. When large numbers of the new species appear and fossilization is statistically more likely, the transitional organisms are gone.

G. Ledyard Stebbins's *Variation and Evolution in Plants* (1950) brought botany into the consilience. It is the last great work of the Synthesis.

In all, the New Synthesis reconfigures Darwin's original consilience to fit the facts of biology emerging in the middle of the twentieth century. It makes genetics central and brings evolution under the aegis of statistics to explain in some detail how evolution occurs. By 1950, the theory of evolution was playing a central role in most areas of biology. Much had changed since Darwin's voyage on the *Beagle*. Then, scientists turned to the Bible to understand many aspects of biology. Now in their works of consilience, scientists never refer to Scripture. No longer do they feel the need to cite the narratives of origin and flood found in Genesis. These narratives no longer seem relevant to understanding the world. The new models replace Genesis because the new models explain accumulating evidence and better demonstrate the unity of organic nature.

Soon, new discoveries produced new consiliences. So unified has science become since Darwin's day that it is impossible to offer an adequate overview of the consilience that has taken place. This consilience among different scientific fields—physics, chemistry, geology, biology, astronomy—tests the truth of the models involved and strengthens our assurance that all the models correspond fairly closely to the way the world is. Here four central consiliences must represent the whole and reveal something of its magnitude.

In 1953, Francis Crick and James Watson discovered that DNA, the chemical key to heredity, exists in the form of a double helix. Almost immediately, biologists could understand the process of chromosomal duplication and many aspects of heredity at the chemical level. This discovery expanded the biological consilience by bringing chemistry into discussions about genes, explaining how they work and how genetic diversity develops without mutations by the recombination of genes in sexually reproducing organisms. Knowledge of DNA also helps in the classification of organisms and in the dating and classification of fossils

Ten years later, geologists showed that the continents move. Alfred Wegener first proposed the idea of continental drift in 1912, suggesting that the granite of the continents floats on the basalt beneath them. The first evidence for this idea had come with the mapping of the east coast of the Americas and the west coast of Africa. They seem to fit together like a jigsaw puzzle. Furthermore, the rock strata appear to have once been continuous, and the species on each coast are so similar that they seem to have once been living in contiguous geographical areas or, as Darwinians relate, species so similar seem to have once been one species. Nonetheless, before 1963 scientists rejected the idea of continental drift because there was no known mechanism to move continents.

The granite of the continents is not a single piece but is fractured into separate plates. Geologists discovered that these plates do not drift. Instead, they are being pushed apart by the welling up of hot magma between them. The sea floor is spreading. The concomitant crashing together of plates opposite the areas of spreading builds mountains. This theory of continental motion and mountain building is called *plate tectonics*.

Plate tectonics helps biologists account for the present locations of organisms on Earth and better comprehend the history of life. Plate tectonics has further substantiated the theory of evolution. It has provided an important consilience between geology and biology.

Interestingly, the stories of the discovery of evolution and of plate tectonics provide parallel examples of how scientific theories come to be accepted. In both cases, early theories had been proposed that seemed to explain the evidence in hand. Darwin's grandfather, among others, had written a book on evolution; Wegener proposed continental drift. Yet, scientists rejected both ideas because no one could adequately explain how such things could occur. No one knew of a mechanism to change species into other species or to move continents. Once viable mechanisms were proposed, scientists accepted each theory with amazing rapidity.

This caution in accepting theories that do not adequately explain the data is typical of science. It is also warranted. We know why because we know about the Interpreter, so ready to invent plausible but false explanations rather than leave phenomena unexplained. We also know much about how the human mind tends to distort evidence to support desired conclusions and about its penchant for developing and believing without adequate evidence explanations that fit canalizations. We now know why the careful testing of theories in all disciplines is necessary if we want to ascertain the truth.

There have been other important discoveries in the increasing scientific consilience. By the 1920s, scientists had discovered the expansion of the universe. Two major theories about the origin of the universe developed around this discovery. In 1948, Hermonn Bondi and Thomas Gold proposed that the universe had always existed and had always been much the same. This *steady state universe* predicts the continuous creation of matter to balance the universe's expansion.

The competing theory says that the universe began in a sudden, terrific explosion and has been expanding ever since. Fred Hoyle somewhat snidely named it the *Big Bang*. George Gamow predicted that radiation from the Big Bang should have continuously lost energy and would now exist as uniform background radiation of about five degrees above absolute zero. In 1965, Arno Penzias and Robert Wilson announced the detection of microwave background radiation about three degrees above absolute zero spread uniformly across the sky. Their discovery supported the Big Bang and refuted the steady state theory, which did not predict any background radiation.

Since then, astrophysicists have discovered much about the universe and have seen further into it, a view that involves looking backward in time because the speed of light is finite, so light takes time to travel to us. The farther away the objects we see, the further back in time they exist. Astrophysicists discovered that the chemical elements making life possible on Earth are created in stellar fires and explosions. We may accurately, if somewhat romantically, describe ourselves as *stardust*. Stardust makes possible our DNA and all that follows from it. This has been a consilience between astronomy, chemistry, and biology of remarkable beauty, perhaps implying intelligent design. I return to the subject of design in chapter 10.

With every intention of suggesting a consilience with the New Synthesis of the 1930s and 1940s, Edward O. Wilson in 1975 called his monumental compendium on sociobiology, *Sociobiology: The New Synthesis*. As the consilience of evolutionary theory with genetics built the New Synthesis, the consilience of the New Synthesis with ethology (the scientific study of animal behavior) and sociology (the scientific study of human social behavior) constructed *sociobiology*.

Sociobiology is the scientific study of animal social behavior from a genetic and evolutionary perspective. Its study of human behavior emphasizes our continuity with other animals. In its study of the social behavior of other animals, sociobiology has been enormously successful, becoming a huge subdiscipline of biology with its own journals and institutions in just thirty years. Its studies of human behavior have been more controversial and are more immature, but they have already provided considerable insight into human conduct and have produced nascent theories of human nature, which I discuss in chapters 7, 8, and 9. Because sociobiology receives detailed treatment later, I will say no more about it here.

The consiliences that have been occurring in science perform at least three functions. First, they support with evidence the assumption that the universe is one, orderly, and law-abiding. Second, they provide mutual support for the models that fit into the consilience. If the theory of evolution lay outside such a consilience, it would be suspect no matter how much about species it explained. The fact that it is a core theory in the scientific consilience lends strong support to the value of its model of the way the world is. Third, the scientific consilience is now complete enough to tell a creation story of its own.

This creation story begins with astrophysics—the Big Bang, and the construction of galaxies, stars, and planets, which I explore more fully in chapter 10. The story then becomes Darwinian, as life emerges in Earth's primordial seas, a life made possible by the stellar synthesis of the heavy elements like carbon, and deeply influenced by the fracturing of the original, continental plate and the subsequent isolation of species on separate, dynamic continents and islands, matters discussed in detail in chapter 7.

Chemically, all life seems to be related. From chemistry, anatomy, and physiology informed by knowledge of evolution, we can locate ourselves on the bush (not tree) of life. We are animals, mammals, primates, *Homo sapiens*, wise beings, more closely related chemically to chimpanzees than foxes are to dogs. This part of the new creation story allows us to study the behavior of other animals as a mirror for our own, to combine the theories of evolution, genetics, and animal behavior in order to understand something of ourselves.

Adam and Eve are not in this story. No scientist argues against their historical existence. None has to. The Genesis creation narratives are not consilient with the rest of what we know. They are irrelevant to the newer, bigger, consilient, scientific saga. The new saga's explanatory power marks the demise of Adam and Eve.

The Demise of Adam and Eve

This book argues that science and Christianity can be reconciled. I began by noting that science supports Christianity because science investigates the material universe and its order, a universe and an order that Christianity claims God created. Logically, Christianity should say science examines God's creation and, in doing so, teaches us about God's plans and values. Logically, Christianity should see science as a support, demonstrating that the universe is the orderly, magnificent creation of an unimaginably powerful and purposeful God.

The largest philosophical error keeping Christians and atheists alike from adopting the view that science supports Christianity is the assumption that science proves the truth of *philosophical materialism*. Philosophical materialism is the view that nothing exists but matter. Science either assumes philosophical materialism is true or limits its domain of inquiry to the material world. If it assumes the truth of philosophical materialism, it cannot prove its own assumption. If it limits its domain of inquiry to the material, it cannot prove or disprove the existence of the immaterial. Science cannot prove the truth of philosophical materialism.

Furthermore, Einstein's equations and the development of the atomic bomb demonstrate the interchangeability of matter and energy, so science itself demonstrates that classical matter is not all that exists. And quantum mechanics calls into question the very concept of matter, an idea I elaborate in chapter 10. Thus science tends to undermine philosophical materialism.

Evolution seems the most dangerous science to many Christians, usually for one of two reasons, both false. First, they think it seems to remove God from the universe. But unless God is an object like other objects, standing anthropomorphically beside the Tigris and Euphrates, God cannot be removed from it by science. In his *Systematic Theology* (1951–1963), Paul Tillich argues convincingly that God is not an object among other objects, but rather the ground of all being. God is not only "out there" creating, but "in here" creating. It is poor theology to overemphasize God's transcendence, or out-there-ness, at the expense of God's immanence, or in-here-ness. Classical Christianity has always tried to balance God's transcendence and immanence, to emphasize that God is both separate from and beyond creation and also working within it.

Second, some Christians think evolution undermines the infallibility of Scripture. However, evidence from Scripture itself shows passages to be self-contradictory and therefore necessarily fallible since two self-contradictory accounts cannot both be true. Familiar are the contradictions between Genesis 2 and 3 and Genesis 1, between Luke's and Matthew's infancy narratives, and between the picture of Jesus presented in John's Gospel and in the Synoptics, but there are myriad others (for more, see Friedman 1987).

Moreover, the theory of evolution is not the only scientific theory to contradict Scripture and was not the first. Nicolas Copernicus (1473–1543) first contradicted the Bible with the theory that the sun is at creation's center, not Earth. Biogeography contradicted Scripture before Darwin wrote the *Origin*.

Although the fallibility of Scripture is clearly an important problem for many Christians, where the theory of evolution is concerned, its fallibility is not the central issue. The central issue is the demise of Adam and Eve, the destruction of the doctrine of original sin. Superficially, the challenge seems to come from science. If Adam and Eve are not historical figures, they did not, as historical fact, disobey God. There was no act of original sin, no fall, no corruption of human nature. Pope Pius XII ([1950] 1956, 287), whose church accepted modern biblical criticism as a valid approach to Scripture in 1943, explains:

> There are other conjectures, about polygenism [multiple centers of human creation] (as it is called), which leave the faithful no such freedom of choice [to research and debate]. Christians cannot lend their support to a theory which involves the existence, after Adam's time, of some earthly race of men, truly so called, who were not descended ultimately from him, or else supposes that Adam was the name given to some group of our primordial ancestors. It does not appear how such views can be reconciled with the doctrine of original sin, as this is guaranteed to us by Scripture. . . . Original sin is the result of a sin committed, in actual historical fact, by an individual man named Adam, and it is a quality native to all of us, only because it has been handed down by descent from him.

The issue is not the inerrancy of Scripture but the destruction of the doctrine of original sin with the demise of Adam and Eve.

The Catholic *Catechism* (1994, 98) emphasizes the Pope's point. In a boldfaced subheading, it declares, "Original Sin—an essential truth of the faith," then it continues,

> Although to some extent the People of God in the Old Testament had tried to understand the pathos of the human condition in the light of the history of the fall narrated in Genesis [this is false; the Old Testament personages antedate the concept that there was a fall in Genesis], *they could not grasp this story's ultimate meaning, which is revealed only in the light of the death and Resurrection of Jesus Christ. We must know Christ as the source of grace in order to know Adam as the source of sin.* . . . We cannot tamper with the revelation of original sin without undermining the mystery of Christ. (Emphasis added)

Pope Pius and the *Catechism* confirm my own argument. My argument has been that Christians were convinced Jesus' terrible crucifixion made atonement, and they sought a horrific historic catastrophe to explain the cross. Eventually this led them to Genesis 2 and 3. The *Catechism* says that without knowledge of Jesus' death and resurrection, we cannot correctly interpret Genesis 2 and 3. Here, the *Catechism* confesses that we must import Christian theology into the narrative to find there the catastrophic origin of sin and the corruption of human nature. That is, to find the fall in Genesis 2 and 3, we must read the text with our ideology in hand.

Chapters 3 and 4 demonstrate the truth of the *Catechism's* confession. They show that the doctrine of original sin is not in Genesis 2 and 3. The doctrine(s) stem from Christian theological beliefs and misreadings, especially the egregious misinterpretations of Augustine and Calvin. Moreover, as this chapter argues, the events narrated in Genesis 2 and 3 never happened.

Thus far, the examination of Scripture has been limited to the early chapters of Genesis. However, the question of the truth of Scripture is a broader question, one that has exercised readers since the first books of the Bible were written. The next chapter explores the vexing and historically varying issue of the relationship between Scripture and truth.

Chapter 6

Scripture and Truth

Ancient interpreters of Scripture, Gnostics, Athanasius, Augustine, Aquinas, and Calvin all lived before the revolution in biblical scholarship that began in the eighteenth century. Yet, all of them were aware that coherence and correspondence characterize truth. All also had faith that Scripture conveys the literal words of a good and truthful God. Their interpretative problem was to read Scripture so it was coherent.

Before the Reformation, interpreting Scripture was a fascinating task because the interpreters thought Scripture contained cryptic messages, that the surface meaning often concealed deeper significance. They found much esoteric significance in allegorical expositions. The Reformation banned esoteric, cryptic, and allegorical readings of the text, making the task of interpreting Scripture less exciting and more difficult.

Modern fundamentalists and evangelicals who consider Scripture inerrant follow the Reformation tradition, although they must now read with conscious literalism. John Gerstner (1982) gives a modern argument for the evangelical perspective. R. C. Sproul (1996) reproduces the statement on biblical inerrancy by the Council on Biblical Inerrancy, the relevant part of which is abstracted in the paragraph below.

The council says God inspired the whole Scripture and all its parts, "down to the very words of the original" (1996, 23; emphasis removed). Because God inspired the writing, the origin of Scripture is divine, not reducible to human insight or altered human consciousness. Yet, although God caused the writers to use the words they employed, God never overrode the authors' personalities, but used their personalities and their distinctive literary styles. It is true that only the original autographs were inspired, but transmission has been sure, and our manuscripts reproduce the originals accurately. Science may not be used to reject what Scripture says. Tests of truth [such as those discussed in chapter 2] may not be used to evaluate Scripture. Apparent errors and inconsistencies will eventually be resolved (from Sproul 1996, 23–46).

Here ancient faith in Scripture addresses modern concerns. By the middle of the twentieth century, biblical scholarship contained elaborate discussions about the personalities and styles of the authors of Scripture. Problems of transmission had long been apparent. Science had consolidated a new creation story. Historical and scientific errors and Scripture's internal inconsistencies had made scholars question its truthfulness and, therefore, its inspiration.

The difference between modern biblical scholars and ancient and evangelical interpreters is not that the latter reject the tests of truth. They do not, but they do not consider them criteria for evaluating Scripture. Scripture is not to be evaluated; it is to be believed. Because ancient and evangelical interpreters come to Scripture knowing it is true, it must, by definition, be coherent and correspond to the way the world is. Thus, one of the interpreter's jobs is to demonstrate the truth of Scripture by showing that it is coherent and that science and history correspond to it.

By contrast, modern biblical scholars are not committed to the coherence of the text. They think the Hebrew Scriptures and the New Testament contain irreconcilable inconsistencies. One task of the modern biblical scholar is to explain how the inconsistencies originated.

When modern biblical scholarship began, the problem of coherence was particularly acute for the Hebrew Scriptures. Faith said they contained God's very words, but scholars had three versions: the accepted Hebrew text, the Septuagint, and a version of the Torah used by the Samaritans, discovered in 1616. The versions differed. Moreover, each contained internal inconsistencies. In contrast, correspondence hardly posed a problem, for little evidence to contradict Scripture was available. As late as the middle of the eighteenth century, apart from the development of a solar-centered astronomy, neither science nor history posed insuperable problems. Thus, the question of coherence drove the scholarship.

When modern scholarship began to examine the Gospels, the most acute problem soon became correspondence. Which words and acts attributed to Jesus in the Gospels correspond to those of the historical Jesus?

Although I have assumed in previous chapters that Scripture may be read intelligently without knowledge of modern biblical scholarship, knowing the best biblical scholarship facilitates accurate comprehension. On the other hand, reliance on poor biblical scholarship can lead to errors. Both the scholarship and the biblical text need critical examination.

I begin my comments on the Hebrew Scriptures with widely accepted scholarship, then discuss more contemporary work. The discussion is limited to the *Torah*, the first five books of the Hebrew Scriptures, also known as the *Pentateuch* or the *Five Books of Moses,* because ancient tradition named Moses as their author. The first three chapters of Genesis are of particular interest in this book, so they receive the most attention here. As noted, the initial scholarly problem was coherence.

Coherence and the Torah

For centuries, Jews and Christians believed Moses wrote the Torah, and God directly inspired his writing so the Torah was literally the words of God. As long as Jews and Christians thought this, they tried to reconcile the seeming inconsistencies. When interpreters ceased their efforts at reconciliation and let the incoherencies stand, they had to acknowledge that there were irreconcilable contradictions in the Torah. They recognized doublets and triplets of narratives, several names for God, different characterizations of God, and diverse literary styles. The inconsistencies were not chaotic. A particular name for God was coupled with a particular characterization of God and with a particular literary style. A different name for God would be attached to another characterization of God and another literary style. Together, such consistent similarities and differences led biblical scholars to develop the *documentary hypothesis* of the origin of the Torah. The documentary hypothesis holds that the Five Books of Moses are not a single document, but have been compiled from a number of documents and from orally transmitted recollections. The Torah contains two distinct traditions: one the tradition of Israel, the northern kingdom of the Jews, and the other the tradition of Judah, the southern kingdom of the Jews.

Scholars ascertained that two documents now integrated into the Torah sprang from each of these traditions. Scholars call the documents of the northern tradition *D* and *E*. D stands for much of the book of Deuteronomy. E stands for *Elohim,* the name for God in a separate document. Scholars name the southern documents *J* and *P*. Throughout J, God is called *Yahweh* (which begins with *J* in German, long the language of biblical scholarship). The P document is characterized by priestly concerns like law and ritual. The creation narrative in Genesis 1 is a P document; the narrative of Genesis 2 and 3 comes from J. J, E, P, and D are documents, not individuals, although scholars occasionally use one of the letters to stand for the final editor or *redactor* (another word for editor) of the respective documents.

The documentary hypothesis has withstood more than a century of criticism and outlasted numerous alternative hypotheses. Richard Elliott Friedman summarizes the current situation:

> There is hardly a biblical scholar in the world . . . who would claim that the Five Books of Moses were written by Moses—or by any one person. Scholars argue about the number of different authors who wrote any given biblical book. They argue about when the various documents were written and about whether a particular verse belongs to this or that document. They express varying degrees of satisfaction or dissatisfaction with the usefulness of the hypothesis for literary or historical purposes. But the hypothesis itself continues to be the starting point of research, no serious student of the Bible can fail to study it, and no other explanation of the evidence has come close to challenging it. (1987, 28)

The hypothesis originated in the eighteenth century. It still stands, virtually alone.

However, scholars have developed competing hypotheses. One of the most recent is that of Isaac M. Kikawada and Arthur Quinn (1985) who argue that Genesis 1–11 is a unified document by ancient standards, and that we are wrong to apply modern standards to it. However, their case fails on two substantial grounds as well as on minor ones (McCarter 1994). First, their criteria for unity are too broad; their criteria apply to almost any narrative, no matter how composed. Second, scholars have both biblical and extrabiblical evidence that sacred literature in biblical times was composed by combining and editing documents. For example, the composer of 1 and 2 Chronicles borrowed extensive material from Samuel and Kings. The Samaritan version of the Torah expands Exodus with material from Deuteronomy. The Dead Sea Scrolls use similar techniques. Thus, we have firsthand evidence outside Genesis that ancient editors composed sacred texts by compilation (McCarter 1994, 31). There is every reason to suppose that ancient redactors composed Genesis 1–11 by a similar process.

P is especially easy to separate from the other documents and is unusually coherent (Blenkinsopp 1994, 15). Genesis 1 is entirely from P. Its style is consistently poetic and liturgical and its theme homogeneous. Yet, Genesis 1 shows signs of being composite. Creation occurs in six days, but there are eight works of creation; creation happens by word, but also by action (Westermann 1984, 82).

J is even more composite than P. Genesis 2 and 3 are J documents. Yet, Claus Westermann, one of the greatest contemporary scholars of Torah, thinks Genesis 2 originated in a separate tradition from Genesis 3 (Westermann 1984, 192). They have different themes. Genesis 2 moves from incompleteness to completeness; Genesis 3 is about law-breaking and punishment (Westermann 1984, 191–93). Furthermore, it is possible to subdivide Genesis 3. The punishments are from different traditions. Expulsion alone was the original punishment (Westermann 1984, 195; 256–57). The tree of life comes from a different tradition than the tree of knowledge; the guardian and the flaming sword blocking the way to Eden are also from separate traditions (Westermann 1984, 272–75). If Westermann is correct that J combines these traditions without sufficiently melding them, he has exposed one foundation for the diversity of interpretations of Genesis 2 and 3. The narrative is inconsistent, leading interpreters in numerous directions.

Finally, Westermann judges that there is no fall in Genesis 3. As noted in chapter 3, his judgment reflects a broad consensus among Torah scholars. The tradition of a fall in Genesis 3 dates only from the first century C.E. The original narrative never intended to be historical. It is not about history, not about heredity, and not about the abstract notion of sin (Westermann 1984, 276–78). Rather, it is about the condition of human beings when the J document was edited, but also concerns our condition at all times insofar as Genesis 3 reflects our biological constitution (Westermann 1984, 20–21, 262). Neither

Genesis 1 nor Genesis 2 and 3 answers the questions theologians have put to them. Rather, the three initial books of Genesis emphasize mystery and ambiguity—the mysteriousness of creation and the mystery and ambiguity of evil (Westermann 1984, 174, 256).

For now, Westermann represents the culmination of scholarly work on the documentary hypothesis as applied to Genesis. Other scholars have tired of trying to separate traditions and trace their origin. *Canonists* want to cease the search for sources and return to the canonical Torah, the final version handed down to us. They consider the canonical text the appropriate source for theological reflection (Blenkinsopp 1994, 14).

Structuralists want to study the literary structure of the text. Robert Alter's (1981) emphasis on thematic and verbal resonances in the text has been influential. An example of his technique and influence occurs in Friedman (1995), who picks up Alter's tracing of the plea "recognize this" in the stories of the deception of Jacob by Judah and Judah by Tamar and explores resonance after resonance, uncovering a common theme of deception and revenge that extends from Rebekah's and Jacob's deception of Isaac through Joseph's sojourn in Egypt.

One of the simplest verbal techniques for creating a resonance is the pun. Jacob falls in love with Rachel and works for her seven years, only to find that her father, Laban, has deceived him and substituted his eldest daughter, Leah, on Jacob's wedding night. In turn, Jacob deceives Laban in the matter of some ewes and rams. In Hebrew, *Rachel* means *ewe* and *Leah* resembles the word for *ram*. "Laban, who deceived Jacob by substituting Leah for Rachel, is repaid by losing his ewes and rams (his Rachels and Leahs). Here again, the payback subtly refers back to the original offense" (Friedman 1995, 230–31).

As a structuralist, Friedman speculates that the theme of deception and revenge may stretch across the entire Genesis narrative, from the serpent's deception of Eve and God's punishment of the offenders through the last chapter of Genesis. Here Joseph finally breaks the cycle when he forgives his brothers and promises to help them rather than seeking revenge (Gen. 50:15-21). If the theme does extend back to Genesis 2 and 3, the J document (into which these narratives fall) seems to criticize God for punishing Adam and Eve rather than forgiving them—another intriguing interpretation of Genesis 3!

Feminist scholars want to expose the ideology they think under-lies the text. The ideology is *patriarchy,* rule by men (literally, by fathers), men all-too-willing to degrade women. Feminist scholars consider Genesis 2 and 3 a patriarchal text. A few extreme feminists insist that we should not consider patriarchal texts canonical or inspired or even valuable precisely because they are patriarchal and, therefore, convey an unethical message. However, the majority think women can reclaim patriarchal texts for themselves. They read Eve as the protagonist of Genesis 3. The most outstanding of these interpreters are Phyllis Trible (1973, 1978, 1984) and Elisabeth Schüssler Fiorenza (1984, 1993, 1998). Mainstream biblical scholar-ship has profited from the feminist scholars' insights, although a few male scholars ignore the feminists' work and continue to pro-duce patriarchal interpretations of the Genesis narrative (Milne 1995, 265).

How a disparity between feminist and more traditional inter-pretations of Genesis 2 and 3 can arise is painfully obvious. In Gen-esis 3:1-6, Adam does not talk to the serpent, Eve talks to it. She explains God's prohibition. Eve is the theologian, not Adam. She is active and independent. Adam is silent and passive, the recipient of the fruit Eve gives to him, which he consumes without reaction or argument.

Trible sees Eve as heroic. Eve takes the initiative, questions God's command, and acts. Adam is compliant, a mere follower.

But Jerome T. Walsh (1977), using the same interpretative tech-nique as Trible while ignoring feminist analyses, reaches the oppo-site conclusion. He finds God establishing a hierarchy. God is supreme, Adam the highest created being, Eve subordinate to him, and the animals subordinate to human beings. The serpent and Eve disrupt God's hierarchy. They assert themselves unduly. They ques-tion God, the supreme authority, and bypass Adam altogether. For his part, Adam does not take the responsibility demanded by his place in the hierarchy. Eve's usurpation is not heroic; it is sinful. Adam's subordination does not show the superiority of women; it displays Adam's sinful weakness. (I have depended here on Milne 1995, 264–66 for the contrast between Trible and Walsh.)

The differences between the interpretations seem to depend on whether the interpreters admire intelligent and assertive women.

Thus far, this book has examined almost a dozen analyses of Genesis 2 and 3. Even the best biblical scholars disagree with one another. Their disagreement has led me to introduce yet another interpretation, my own. I follow no particular school of biblical exegesis. I merely try to make my interpretation correspond closely with the text without peering through ideological spectacles. Although I wrote my interpretation before reading Westermann's, my interpretation comes amazingly close to his. However, it discloses what Westermann fails to make explicit. Genesis 2 and 3 convey a new kind of truth: symbolic truth.

Symbolic Truth in Genesis 2 and 3

The narrative of Genesis 2 and 3 is symbolic. The names tell us this. In the narrative, *Adam* is not the name of a person. It is the Hebrew word for *man*, derived from the Hebrew word *adamah*, the term for *clay*, *soil*, or *earth*. As Bloom notes, a good translation of *Adam* would be *earthling*. Since Adam is male, I will call him *Earthman*. In the narrative, God creates Earthman from earth. When God curses Earthman, God says Earthman will eat the produce of the earth in painful labor, then turn into earth at death. Earthman's life, labor, and death are in the earth. So were the life, labor, and death of almost every man in preindustrial agricultural society. Human life was ruled by the necessity of tilling the earth in order to survive. Earthman's life symbolizes a life of agricultural labor, a harsh and repetitious life that sometimes must have felt cursed.

Eve is not the name of a person, either. It is Hebrew for *lifebearer*, or, as the New Revised Standard Version translates the explanation in the text, *childbearer of all living*. I will call her *Childbearer*. God creates Childbearer from Earthman's rib. Just as Earthman is tied to the earth from which he came, Childbearer is tied to Earthman from whom she came. When God curses her, the curse involves sexual desire for her husband, subordination to him, and great pain in childbearing. The curse binds her to Earthman in painful labor, just as God's curse of Earthman ties him to the earth in painful labor. As Earthman's life centers on the earth and the propagation of crops, Childbearer's life centers on her husband and the propagation of children. Childbearer's life symbolizes the life of almost every woman before the advent of effective birth control, a painful and repetitious life that sometimes must have felt cursed.

The Genesis narrative portrays life as men and women in the agricultural world of the Hebrew Scriptures experienced it. Men labor in the fields, producing food to sustain life. Women labor in childbearing, producing children to sustain the generations. Men and women must live this way because we are mortal, symbolized in the narrative by Adam and Eve's banishment from access to the tree of life. Were we immortal, we would not need to till the earth to sustain our lives, nor would we need to bear children to maintain the generations.

Here is a new kind of truth: symbolic truth. For almost anyone in preindustrial, agricultural societies like that of the Hebrews at the time, Adam and Eve under God's curse were a revealing symbol of the lives people led. However, Adam and Eve are not an adequate symbol of other lives at other times—of hunters and gatherers, industrial peoples, state and corporate bureaucrats, or information collectors and consumers. This is another reason liberals are wrong to think of the narrative as a myth capturing truths about human nature or the human situation. The myth is too narrow. It describes the lives of peasants.

It is also too broad. As a characterization of biological roles, it reaches beyond humanity to encompass the entire organic world. It portrays the fundamental tasks of all organisms—to garner resources and reproduce, generation after generation, or die and become extinct. The narrative captures a powerful truth in symbols. At this level of generalization, it corresponds remarkably well to the Darwinian view of nature.

After presenting the Darwinian view of nature and human nature in chapters 7 and 8, I will return to the inadequacies of the liberal analysis of Genesis 2 and 3. In chapter 11, I use modern scholarship to explore the Gospels, so it is important here to examine the impact that the tests of truth have had on them. The greatest impact has come from the correspondence test of truth.

Correspondence and the Gospels

Biblical scholarship on the Gospels follows a pattern similar to scholarship on the Hebrew Scriptures. For many centuries, Christians had faith that the Gospels present an accurate portrait of Jesus and his times. Matthew, Mark, Luke, and John were understood to be the authors of the Gospels. Christians thought Matthew and John knew Jesus, while Mark and Luke were in the generation portrayed in Acts. Although there are four Gospels, Christians believed they conveyed a single message. They also believed that God inspired the Gospel authors in much the manner affirmed by ancient interpreters and modern evangelicals.

On the other hand, even casual readers could see that the first three Gospels are similar to one another and sometimes alike, word for word. Scholars named them the *Synoptic Gospels* because they "see together." In them, Jesus' sayings are short, pithy, and memorable. He rarely talks about himself and often speaks of the kingdom of God. Casual readers could also observe that the Gospel of John is different from the Synoptic Gospels. Its order is unusual, unique events occur in it, and Jesus speaks in long discourses, mostly about himself.

When scholars sought the tradition that best corresponds with the historical Jesus, they asked themselves whether the Synoptics or John portrays Jesus more accurately. They arrived at a broad consensus scholars still maintain today. The presentation in the Synoptic Gospels corresponds better to the historical Jesus. John's tradition captures the reaction of one segment of the early church to the risen Jesus, who is often called the *Christ of faith*. The Gospel according to John was the last one written. An anonymous Jewish convert composed it around 90 C.E. Its author did not know Jesus.

This decision left open the question of the origins of the similarities and differences among the Synoptic Gospels, a question termed the *synoptic problem*. Why were some passages alike, word for word, some too similar for their similarity to be accidental, yet some material unique to a particular Gospel? Only Luke, for example, has the story of the Prodigal Son (Luke 15:11-32), the Pharisee and the tax collector (Luke 18:10-14), and Zacchaeus up the sycamore tree (Luke 19:1-10). Only Luke relates that Jesus and John the Baptist are relatives (Luke 1:36).

On the synoptic problem, too, scholars have reached a broad consensus. The first Gospel to be written is the Gospel according to Mark, composed around 70 C.E. by an anonymous Gentile convert, probably living in Rome. The Gospels according to Matthew and Luke are later, also anonymous, and depend on the Gospel attributed to Mark. (Hereafter, as is customary, I refer simply to Mark, Matthew, Luke, and John, without implying they are the authors.)

Material common to Mark and Luke or Mark and Matthew or Mark, Matthew, and Luke originally derived from Mark. In other words, Mark's Gospel is an essential source, known and used by Matthew and Luke. Material common to Luke and Matthew not found in Mark is from a source now lost to us, a source scholars dub Q from *Quelle*, the German word for source. Together, these ideas about sources constitute the *two-source hypothesis*, the sources being Mark and Q. The two-source hypothesis ignores material peculiar to Matthew or Luke. Scholars refer to these materials as *M* and *L*, respectively. The inclusion of M and L gives scholars the *four-source hypothesis*, the sources being Mark, Q, M, and L.

These hypotheses address the existing canon. However, approximately sixteen other Gospels survive from the first three centuries. Some clearly narrate legends, but others apparently contain historical information. The Jesus Seminar, with more than two hundred Jesus scholars, includes the Gospel of Thomas when it assesses the historicity of the sayings of Jesus. This suggests that scholars today depend on the tests of truth to discover the historical Jesus rather than on the criterion of canonicity to tell them what is true.

As with the Hebrew Scripture sources, J, D, E, and P, the Gospel sources Mark, Q, M, and L have additional sources beneath them. Scholars have attempted to recover these other sources. One of these sources is Jesus, and the search for the historical Jesus attempts to distinguish what Jesus said and did from what others attribute to him. Oral traditions carried news of Jesus' deeds and words to the generation after him. Oral memory would have retained short, pithy, memorable sayings rather than lengthy discourses, which is one reason scholars consider the Synoptic Gospels more historically reliable than the Gospel of John.

To compose his Gospel, Mark uses oral traditions and perhaps written documents based on them, but he also borrows from the culture around him. Much of his passion narrative is built from rituals surrounding the procession and deification of the Roman emperor (Schmidt 1997), thereby enriching the passion narratives theologically, if also distorting them historically. Mark also appropriates details from the Septuagint. To Mark, doing so would have made good sense, for he is convinced that Jesus is the Jewish Messiah who fulfills Scripture. Mark's sources lack what he considers significant details. Because he believes Jesus fulfills Scripture, Mark logically believes that he can recover the lost details from Scripture. Mark reads Greek, so he turns to the Septuagint for the details. Jesus' entry into Jerusalem on a donkey is directly from Zechariah 9:9 and the thirty pieces of silver given Judas for betraying Jesus from Zechariah 11:12-13. Much of the scene on the Mount of Olives is from 2 Samuel 15–17 where David (Jesus) flees from his enemies across the Kidron valley and up the Mount of Olives, weeping as he goes, but prepared to accept God's will. David (Jesus) is betrayed by a kiss.

Anyone drawing a portrait of Jesus that corresponds to what the historical Jesus said and did must consider this information. The four-source hypothesis is important because it allows scholars to distinguish sources from Gospels. Matthew, Mark, and Luke may all relate the story of blind Bartimaeus (Mark 10:46-52; Matt. 20:29-34; Luke 18:35-43), but the narrative has only one source (Mark). One criterion of historicity is that a saying or event is more likely to be historical if it comes from two or more sources. The same saying or event found in different contexts and occurring in different forms is also likely to be historical. These constitute versions of the consilience test of truth. Most of the other criteria of historicity involve the test of correspondence.

Without using the terms employed here—coherence, correspondence, and consilience—John P. Meier (1991, 167–95) includes a thorough discussion of the criteria of historicity, as do the books on the Gospels from the Jesus Seminar (Funk, Hoover, and the Jesus Seminar 1993, 16–34; Funk and the Jesus Seminar 1998, 1–36). Here are some of the criteria that apply the correspondence test of truth to the search for the historical Jesus.

Short, pithy, and memorable Gospel sayings are likely to come straight from an oral tradition that remembers Jesus' words without much alteration, although it has translated them from Aramaic into Greek, so caution is always necessary.

Events and sayings that embarrass the early Jesus movement are likely to be historical; otherwise, they would not be in the Gospels. For example, John's baptism of Jesus is an embarrassment because it makes John appear superior to Jesus, whereas Jesus' followers think Jesus superior. Yet, all the Gospels tell of Jesus' baptism, so it must have been too widely known not to have been recorded. In reaction, all the Gospels struggle to show that John is inferior to Jesus. Luke (3:21-22) and John (1:29-34) record Jesus' baptism while avoiding explicit mention of John as the person who baptizes him.

We know the Jewish authorities reject Jesus and the Romans execute him. Jesus angers and frightens people. Any portrait that shows him only caring for others and conforming to Jewish expectations is false. In contrast, sayings and deeds of Jesus that contravene social expectations, especially ones that insult and anger, are likely to be historical. Moreover, they must have been an embarrassment to the early church, which sought accommodation with both Jews and Romans and tried to present itself as innocuous and Jesus as victimized.

Predictions attributed to Jesus in the Gospels require careful scrutiny. Some scholars want to say that the early church created all Jesus' predictions, but this is probably too sweeping. Close to his death (say, at the Last Supper), Jesus may have expected the end, for he knew human psychology and could be sure that his behavior aroused anger and fear in the authorities. He might have anticipated his crucifixion shortly before it occurred.

One of the most interesting examples of a prediction in the Gospels is the saying of Jesus that the Temple will be destroyed so that "Not one stone will be left here upon another; all will be thrown down" (Mark 13:2; Matt. 24:2; Luke 21:6). This is a controversial passage, about which there is no scholarly consensus. The Jesus Seminar divided evenly over whether the saying goes back to Jesus (Funk, Hoover, and the Jesus Seminar 1993, 108–9). The saying has only one source, Mark, but the prediction occurs in other contexts, for example at Jesus' trial (Mark 14:48; Matt. 26:60), so it is fairly well attested by the sources. The Romans destroyed the Temple in 70 C.E., and the Gospels were composed after its destruction, so the authors knew that the wooden parts of the Temple burned while many of the stones remained in place. Mark, Matthew, and Luke have knowingly recorded a prediction whose details are false. To me, it sounds as if this prediction was so well-known as coming from Jesus that all three authors felt compelled to record it, even though they knew its details were false.

Some sayings and deeds clearly should not be attributed to Jesus. Those acquired from the Septuagint or from the surrounding Gentile culture should not. Nor should those that require knowledge Jesus could not have obtained, for example, knowledge of events occurring only after his death. Common sayings from folklore or from first-century Jewish wisdom are more perplexing. These sorts of sayings were typically attributed to people considered sages, whether they said them or not, because sages were thought to repeat known wisdom. Jesus may have spoken words of common wisdom, but scholars cannot distinguish his words from those merely attributed to him, so many scholars have made a blanket decision not to attribute wisdom sayings to Jesus.

Once scholars have developed a central core of sayings and deeds that fit these criteria and, therefore, almost surely portray the historical Jesus, they can use the portrait this material gives of Jesus as a model against which to test other materials attributed to him. If the new materials are consistent with the model, they are likely to be historical, too. Thus, historical Jesus scholars also employ the consilience test of truth as they develop a reliable portrait of Jesus.

The Jesus Seminar, with more than two hundred voters, thinks Jesus said and did approximately 17 percent of what the Gospels attribute to him (Funk and the Jesus Seminar 1998, 1). If we consider that Jesus was an obscure figure in a minor province of the Roman Empire, this 17 percent represents a comparatively massive amount of knowledge. We know much less about far more prominent figures from the era. Most of our knowledge of Jesus comes from the Synoptic Gospels' portrait of Jesus in Galilee. If we eliminate John's Gospel and the passion narratives and examine only the Galilee material in the Synoptic Gospels, the 17 percent figure jumps to a historical accuracy of almost 50 percent. This is a very impressive number for ancient documents whose authors did not have our view of what constitutes historical writing. So, although 17 percent seems low at first glance, on reflection it is high, representing an amazing knowledge of Jesus' deeds and words. From this material, the Jesus Seminar develops the following portrait of Jesus.

He is an itinerant.
He is an exorcist, accused of being possessed by demons.
He is a social deviant followed by deviants, whom he accepts.
He breaks Sabbath and purity laws (largely why he is a social deviant).
He rejects conventional family ties.
His home village rejects him. (Funk and the Jesus Seminar 1998, 32–34)

It is a portrait many other scholars accept. Some are feminists.

Feminist scholars have found a home among Jesus scholars, and they have made valuable contributions to Jesus scholarship. Feminists have found Jesus congenial. He rejects the ideology of patriarchy. He welcomes women into his circle. Women claim leading roles in the early church. Feminist scholars have helped their colleagues discover the role of women in the Jesus movement and better understand Jesus' acceptance of the socially marginalized. Feminists have helped others appreciate how socially liberating women of the first century found the Jesus movement. In scholarship on the historical Jesus, feminists scholars' contributions have been welcomed, appreciated, and integrated into the mainstream.

Scholars' willingness to apply the tests of truth to Scripture, and Scripture's frequent failure of the tests, raise the question of the authority of Scripture.

The Authority of Scripture

Ancient interpreters and today's inerrantist evangelicals clearly grasp the fundamental issue for the authority of Scripture. To be authoritative, Scripture must be true. A false authority is not an authority, but a deceit. The ancients and evangelicals consider Scripture to be God's words, and because God is truthful and omniscient, Scripture must be coherent and correspond to the way the world is. The ancients and evangelicals never use these criteria to test Scripture for truth because they already have faith in its truthfulness. Instead, they use them as interpretative devices. They interpret Scripture so it is coherent and use Scripture to evaluate science and history. If Scripture is true, science and the modern historical reconstruction of biblical times are false.

Moderns who do not take an evangelical stance have answered the question of the authority of Scripture in two distinct ways. Rather arbitrarily, and merely to emphasize the distinction, I will attribute the two separately to theologians and scholars. Ancient theologians answered the question of the authority of Scripture by proclaiming that God inspired it and therefore it must be true. Over time, as theologians used the tests of truth to evaluate the quality of the inspiration, the criterion of inspiration weakened and faltered, and theologians tried other criteria. Some rested scriptural authority on the truth of events like the Exodus, even if God did not inspire the biblical account of it, and even if the account distorts history. However, this approach makes history authoritative, not Scripture. Others located authority in personal religious experience, making experience authoritative instead of Scripture. Robert Gnuse (1985) reviews and critiques all these attempts. His conclusion is that none of the efforts to ground authority in Scripture succeeds (1985, 124). If there is an authority, it must be found elsewhere.

Modern scholars take a different approach. Their scholarship itself provides two answers to the question of the authority of Scripture. The first answer involves the search for sources of Scripture to explain Scripture's inconsistencies, using the coherence test of truth. The search for sources explains many inconsistencies, but it undermines the authority of the Torah. Three results have been particularly significant.

First, the Torah cannot be God's words, if God's words are true. Although God may have inspired Scripture in some sense, human beings with various agendas composed it, and the coherence and correspondence tests of truth have falsified some or much of what they have said.

Second, although the sources disagree with each other, no scholar has developed successful criteria for ascertaining which are the impostures and which is the authoritative source, if there is one. Moreover, J, E, D, and P each performs a unique function in the Torah. None can be eliminated without seriously impairing Scripture.

Third, the search for sources leads into an endless historical twilight. After J, E, D, and P have been separated, inconsistencies remain. These documents, too, are composite. Ideally, for Scripture to be authoritative, scholars would search for sources until they arrive at the one true source, like discovering the source of the Nile, or finding God. But there is no God at the end of the search, if there is an end—merely another fragmentary source, lying among the ruins of the authority of the Torah.

Applying the correspondence test results in even greater disappointment for those seeking authority in Scripture. No scholar can ascertain whether the words of Scripture correspond to God's words, for we have no proven transcript of God's words with which to compare it. Moreover, if God's words correspond to the way the world is, much of Scripture cannot be God's words, for much in it conflicts with scientific and historical studies that pass the tests of coherence, correspondence, and consilience. If those words for which we have tests are not God's (because they fail the tests of truth and God is true), it is unlikely that the words of Scripture for which no tests are available are God's words, either.

Scholars concerned about the authority of Scripture try to answer these conundrums explicitly. They interpret Scripture so it is amenable to science by speaking of figurative language and myth. They reinterpret the historical sections of Scripture as theological statements. They construe as moral those parts of Scripture modern sensibilities find immoral; for example, feminist scholars search yesterday's patriarchal narratives for aspects that affirm women.

In all such interpretations, authority comes from sources other than Scripture—from science and history as they pass the tests of truth, and from modern moral sensibilities. But to interpret Scripture so it corresponds to other authorities is to grant authority to other sources and, ultimately, to the tests of truth, not Scripture. To interpret Scripture so it corresponds to other authorities is also to interpret Scripture ideologically.

Scholars also read Scripture as literature, ascertaining, say, J's message hidden in the structure of the Torah, as Friedman (1995) does for the deception stories. Unfortunately for the authority of Scripture, even an interpretation that stays close to the text and accurately reveals J's message leaves open the question of whether J's message comes from God. Searching for sources behind J that perhaps will carry us closer to God only condemns us to the endless historical twilight.

So, the effort to maintain the authority of the Hebrew Scriptures while submitting them to tests of truth has failed. This failure carries us back in a vicious circle to the ancients and evangelicals. In order to believe the Hebrew Scriptures authoritative, interpreters must believe them true and then interpret them so they meet the tests of truth. But then the final authorities are the tests of truth. In the beginning as in the end, the tests of truth are authoritative, not the Hebrew Scriptures.

The same circle envelops the New Testament. Yet the New Testament's authority is more salvageable than that of the Hebrew Scriptures because the New Testament fares better under the tests of truth.

Incoherence in the New Testament does not pose the same kind of problem it creates for the Hebrew Scriptures because the New Testament deliberately offers different accounts of Jesus' life in four separate Gospels. Moreover, Luke speaks of his version as one among many and explicitly says it is based on investigation, without mentioning inspiration (Luke 1:1-4), which appears to legitimate a search for sources. Luke (Acts 5:1-11, 15:1-35, 18:24—19:7) and Paul (1 Cor. 1:10-31, 3:1-23; Gal. 1:6-9, 2:11-14) show early Christian leaders disagreeing and assemblies that include novices and dissenters. In admitting its own inconsistencies and the struggles of the early church, the New Testament invites the reader to inquire into the text and seek resolution. It seems to say that, although some of the reports may be biased or mistaken, and although many people struggle to understand the Gospel message rightly, the message itself is coherent and historically accurate.

Nor do the sources vanish into endless historical twilight. They stop at Jesus. He is the source, not only for the Gospels, but also for Paul's personal revelations. Having him as the source leads scholars to search for a coherent portrait of Jesus in the New Testament that corresponds to the Jesus of history.

The question of authority in the New Testament begins with the question of why we should consider Jesus an authority and ends with the question of why we should consider a particular portrait of Jesus authoritative. Focusing on Jesus removes the burden of authority from the canon of Scripture, which is helpful because Scripture itself does not say that the canon we have is authoritative (Barr 1983, 23).

There are at least two different reasons we might consider Jesus an authority. First, we might believe him to be the Messiah, the *Logos,* the Son of God, the elevated, divine person of passages of Scripture (especially of John, Paul, and the Letter to the Hebrews), the creeds, and the Pope, either because we consider Scripture or the church or the Pope authoritative or because we have personally experienced the resurrected Jesus.

Second, we might consider Jesus a great Jewish prophet, as Islam does, or a sage or moral leader worth following, without casting him into the Jewish or Greek roles of Messiah or *Logos.* He might be an authoritative religious and moral figure for whatever reasons we usually deem people authoritative religious and moral figures.

Central criteria for considering a particular portrait of Jesus authoritative are given above. In brief, the portrait must pass the familiar tests of truth.

The New Testament's authority, then, has its source in Jesus, whom we may consider an authority for a number of reasons. Beyond Jesus, its authority comes from the authenticity of its portrait of Jesus, which scholars must uncover by applying the correspondence, coherence, and consilience tests of truth to historical, cultural, and sociological materials located primarily in the canonical Gospels, but also situated in a wide range of other sources, from the Gospel of

Thomas to the sociology of religion. This new century is particularly fortunate in inheriting a fairly broad scholarly consensus on the historical Jesus. I summarize that consensus in chapter 11.

Having interpreted Genesis 1 and 2, studied the Christian doctrines of original sin, witnessed the demise of Adam and Eve, and explored the truth of Scripture, it is time to turn to science to see whether science and Christianity may be unified by doing without Adam and Eve. Uniting them will require replacing the model of human nature provided by the doctrines of original sin with that supplied by sociobiology. To understand sociobiology's model of human nature it is necessary to know the theory of evolution.

PART TWO
THE UNIFICATION
OF SCIENCE AND CHRISTIANITY

Chapter 7

The Theory of Evolution

The theory of evolution by natural selection is one of the oldest unfalsified theories in science. It has demonstrated explanatory and predictive power and has proved hermeneutically rich in nearly every field of biology. Showing impressive resilience, it has incorporated almost a century-and-a-half of new scientific discoveries and withstood rigorous philosophical queries.

This chapter tests the truth of the theory using the criteria discussed in chapter 2: coherence, correspondence, and consilience. It also asks whether the theory is canalized. Discussion in Chapter 2 of the correspondence test of truth emphasized that theories are about models, that models simplify the world, and that models must resemble the world in relevant respects and sufficient degrees. The theory of evolution is no exception. Furthermore, like most scientific theories today, the theory of evolution is a statistical theory. Its predictions hold for groups, not necessarily for individuals. These points apply equally to the theory's extension to sociobiology presented in chapter 8. Theories of human nature are also necessarily about simplified models subject to the limits of statistical application. This means that evolutionary theories of human nature and theological theories of human nature begin with fundamental parameters in common, for both simplify the complexities of human motivation and behavior, and neither successfully predicts individual human behavior.

The best explanation of the theory of evolution is still Charles Darwin's ([1859] 1964). For a brief, clear, modern presentation, see James Rachels (1991, 6–61). A thorough discussion that also addresses common misunderstandings is Daniel Dennett (1995).

My explanation here begins with the coherence of the theory of evolution by natural selection.

Coherence and Natural Selection

One of the most appealing aspects of the classical theory of evolution is its accessibility. Grasping it does not demand obscure mathematics or observations made with esoteric technology. Understanding it requires only common observation and simple logic. Moreover, three observations suffice. First, offspring differ from each other. For example, a litter of puppies whose parents are black and white will have some puppies that are mostly black, others mostly white, others variously spotted. The puppies will differ in other ways. Some will be bigger, some will be more resistant to diseases, some will mature faster, some will be more aggressive, and so on. We are all familiar with such variations.

Second, many characteristics are inherited. If the parents are black and white, we expect their offspring to have these colors, too. If the parents are large dogs with long hair and pointy noses, so will their offspring be. Two collies will not produce a dachshund. Everyone knows this.

Third, more offspring are born than survive to reproduce. In domestic plants and animals, people often control survival and reproduction by *culling* and *selective breeding*. We cull the unwanted and breed those we consider most desirable. In the wild, culling agents include diseases, parasites, predators, starvation, and the inability to mate. The most resistant organisms survive and reproduce. This, also, is well-known.

Simple logic shows that populations of organisms with these three familiar characteristics will change over time. To change over time is to *evolve*. Here is the logic. Imagine a first generation. Natural forces cull some of its members before they reproduce. Because the members differ from each other, the culling eliminates some characteristics from the first generation. The surviving members reproduce. Because their offspring inherit their characteristics, the second generation resembles the survivors. The cycle recurs in the second generation. Natural forces cull members of the second generation before they reproduce. Because the members differ from each other, the culling eliminates some characteristics. The survivors reproduce. The third generation resembles the survivors in the second generation. As this cycle recurs, later generations come to differ more and more from the first generation.

Darwin begins *On the Origin of Species* with a discussion of the evolution of domestic populations. He bred pigeons, and he spoke and corresponded widely with other animal breeders. He notes that breeders considered animals "quite plastic." They say they can change their flocks and herds almost at will by culling and selective breeding ([1859] 1964, 31). Darwin calls the practice of culling and selective breeding *artificial selection.*

Darwin draws an analogy between artificial selection and *natural selection.* Natural selection is what nature does. Like a breeder, it culls and selectively breeds. Natural selection and artificial selection are very much alike except that natural selection has no end in view, no goals, no rational design. Organisms selected to breed, those that survive to reproduce, are merely those best adapted to their local environments at the time.

The rediscovery of the gene in 1900 and the New Synthesis of the 1930s and 1940s changed the definition of natural selection and emphasized its lack of goals. Natural selection is now defined as a change in gene frequencies, and the types and rates of changes are formulated mathematically, making biology more like the physical sciences than it was in Darwin's day.

In sexually reproducing organisms, genes change in every generation. They change without mutation because sexual reproduction mixes the genes of male and female, a mixing known as *recombination.* In this way, variation increases in a species over time, all other things being equal. Even so, when molecular techniques became available, biologists were surprised to discover how much genetic variation exists within species. Of course, some of the variation is due to mutation.

Mutation and recombination both occur randomly, that is, without respect to the benefit of the organism and without any overall plan or rational design. One result of the random nature of mutation and recombination is nonviable organisms. For example, women who are impregnated often have natural abortions very early in their pregnancies, so early that they are unaware of the abortions. As many as half of all human pregnancies may terminate in this way. This is one form of natural selection. Although mutation and recombination occur randomly, selection acts to eliminate harmful genetic combinations and mutations while maintaining the ones that help the organism survive to reproduce. Helpful variations increase as time passes.

Because nature has no goal or plan and because genetic alterations occur randomly, critics of Darwin's theory often say that natural selection is random and that random events cannot produce highly organized beings. This is a misunderstanding. Consider artificial selection again. The breeder supplies neither variations nor heritability. Nature supplies these to the first generation randomly, without goal and without respect for the good of the organism. The breeder selects characteristics like speed and breeds the fastest, culling the rest. In artificial selection, selection is not random. Only the fastest are selected.

Neither is natural selection random. Certain aspects of each organism's environment occur regularly, like wolves tracking a herd of deer. The wolves cull the slowest. The fastest deer escape hungry jaws and survive to reproduce. Over time, the whole herd becomes faster. Becoming faster requires specific anatomical and physiological changes. The future herd may have lighter bodies, longer legs, and greater lung capacity. The wolves do not plan it this way; indeed, they would prefer slower deer. Nevertheless, their hunting patterns select for survival the lightest and deepest breathing deer with the longest legs, and these deer pass their characteristics on to the next generation. Selection of this sort is *directional,* not random.

This discussion should clarify another aspect of Darwin's theory, one sometimes missed by experts. Evolution occurs in *populations.* Populations evolve, not individuals. The individual is born, survives, and reproduces. The individual is the unit of selection, but not the unit of evolution. Herds, flocks, gaggles, schools—these constitute the units of evolution. This is one reason evolution is hard to recognize. Another is that we have difficulty knowing what changes to look for, a matter I discuss below. A third is that the evolution of one species into another in most organisms large enough to see usually takes thousands or millions of years. Individual human beings typically cannot witness the entire event.

The logic of Darwin's theory has four important implications for understanding our place in nature. First, Darwin explains the apparent design of organisms without reference to a designer, without reference to God or to God's miracles. The diversity of species on Earth has come about by natural causes. In the nineteenth century, this was shocking news.

It was perhaps especially shocking in England where almost everyone who was literate had read William Paley's *Natural Theology* ([1802] 1970), an argument for the existence of God based on design in nature. Paley's biological argument is as simple as it is convincing. He asserts that there are only two ways organisms can come to be. Either they come to be by random forces or by intelligent design. He then compares organisms to watches (the kind with springs and gears). He notes that watches are intricate and complex and all the parts work together so that the whole operates as a unit. We would never think watches came to be by random forces. That would be impossible! Indeed, we know they have an intelligent designer, a human engineer. Organisms are also intricate and complex and all the parts work together so that the whole operates as a unit. They, too, could never have come to be by random forces. There is only one other option, Paley declares. They must have an intelligent designer: God.

When Darwin offered a third option for how organisms come to be, he wrecked Paley's argument. Darwin's third option is a kind of designer, but a natural one without intelligence, consciousness, or plan. That designer is natural selection. No longer do organisms require an intelligent, supernatural designer to explain their existence.

Second, Darwin changed the western concept of what needs explanation in nature. Western thought had been formed by the biblical book of Genesis, which assumes that creatures were originally at peace and that the origin of conflict needs explanation, so it explains the origin of conflict. Augustine, Aquinas, and Calvin follow Genesis. In contrast, Darwin shows that conflict is inherent in nature. Organisms compete with one another for resources and to reproduce. After Darwin, the existence of cooperation requires explanation. Chapter 8 explains it.

Third, reproduction has its own selection mechanism, *sexual selection*. In sexual selection, potential sexual partners select each other for various attributes. Sexual selection and natural selection can select conflicting characteristics. The female may select the male with the brightest feathers; his bright feathers may attract predators. As with much in evolution, compromises occur. Evolution is a tinkerer, not an engineer (Jacob 1977).

Fourth, because we are part of nature, and resources and reproduction are nature's recurring and sustaining themes, we can predict with certainty that the themes we find most attractive are resources and reproduction—money and sex. These two topics account for two-thirds of our conversations and fill our fiction (Dunbar 1996, 5). They occupy center stage in soap operas and sitcoms. Resources and reproduction interest us as nothing else does. Now we know why. These are the themes of life itself.

Thus far, I have demonstrated the coherence of Darwin's theory of evolution by natural selection and highlighted some of its implications. In the search for truth, however, coherence does not stand alone. We would feel more certain that species evolve from one another if we could watch them speciate. In the following section, I look at speciation among living organisms and fossils. These examples offer two tests to determine whether the theory of evolution, although a very simple theory, corresponds with the way the world is in relevant respects and sufficient degrees to make accurate predictions.

Correspondence and Speciation

To watch a population evolve into a new species, *species* requires definition. In 1942 Ernst Mayr proposed the most widely used definition: "Species are groups of actually or potentially interbreeding natural populations which are reproductively isolated from other such groups" (Mayr 1982, 273). *Population* refers to all the organisms constituting an identifiable unit. Several similar species together form a *genus*. *Potentially* interbreeding populations are geographically separated, but if they were integrated, they would interbreed. Because biologists want to analyze nature, populations must be natural ones. Biologists working in zoos and laboratories can manipulate separate species to produce viable offspring in artificial environments, but biologists still consider them distinct species.

Reproductively isolated means that organisms do not interbreed in the wild even if they inhabit the same locale. Many mechanisms produce reproductive isolation. Flowering times may differ. Reproductive organs or mating behaviors may be incompatible. Even if two organisms do successfully have sex, they may be sterile or their offspring may be sterile. Such organisms are members of separate species.

When Darwin looked at the flora and fauna of the Galapagos Islands, he saw speciation. (Chapter 5 gives the historical details.) More exactly, he observed various phenomena and inferred that some island species had descended from other island species and that all the island species had ultimately descended from ancestors on the mainland. When he wrote the *Origin*, he commented on what he had seen and the conclusions he had drawn (Darwin [1859] 1964, 388–406).

He saw many *endemic species,* species found nowhere else. He saw that the island species resembled those on the mainland, that they were all similar to American species and different from those in Africa. He found neither terrestrial mammals nor frogs, toads, or newts. Was this God's doing?

Being omnipotent, God could have populated the islands with terrestrial mammals and frogs, toads, and newts. God could have put African types on the islands rather than American ones. Many would have thrived in the habitat. Yet, the only organisms on the islands were American types capable of crossing hundreds of miles of salt water. There were bats: mammals to be sure, but mammals that can fly. There were many species of birds, but mostly marine species. There were many plants whose seeds are easily transported by birds. Animals like frogs, toads, and newts, whose eggs and larva immediately die in salt water, were absent. Also missing were terrestrial mammals, none powerful swimmers. He reasoned that the original inhabitants of the islands migrated from the mainland, reproduced variations of themselves, and speciated on the islands.

Modern genetics helps explain why new species so often appear on islands. On the mainland, a species may have millions of members. All their genes will number in the trillions. Collectively, their genes constitute a *gene pool.* No subset of the species carries the entire gene pool.

If a small subset of a species lands on an island, it carries only a small subset of the species' genes. It also represents only an anatomical and physiological subset of the mainland species. On average, its members may have longer necks, shorter toes, duller coloration, less efficient hearts, and greater disease resistance. As these organisms interbreed, they pass on only a subset of the species' genes and, with them, a subset of the species' characteristics.

Furthermore, the organisms have entered a new habitat. Probably fewer predators and fewer food sources live on the island because only a few other continental species would have arrived and thrived there. Thus, both the genetic makeup of the new island population and the selection pressures on it differ from those of the mainland species. Logically, changes will occur in succeeding generations of a population with changes in genetic makeup and selection pressures. Sometimes these changes will result in the evolution of new species.

Mayr predicted this consequence in 1954. Almost thirty years later, he noted that Hampton Carson's work on speciation had substantiated his prediction (Mayr 1982, 602–3). Carson (1982) and others (summarized in Powell 1997) studied speciation in the fruit fly *Drosophila* on the Hawaiian Islands.

In evolutionary biology, islands are not only landmasses surrounded by water, but metaphors for any areas providing geographic isolation. In this metaphoric sense, islands can form anywhere and be composed of anything. For example, a river may rise permanently and isolate a few members of a species from those on the other side. A mountain may form and isolate species members on either side. All the early-blooming members of a species of flowering plant may die because of climate cooling, isolating the remainder. A tree-dwelling species may exploit a new food source and begin residing on a new species of tree. From the point of view of the isolated population, all these events resemble migration to an island. They all function to isolate a small population from the rest of its species. Isolation promotes speciation.

The Hawaiian Islands are actual islands. They ride northwest on the Pacific tectonic plate. As the plate moves, it passes over a hot spot in Earth's mantle. This hot spot produces volcanoes, and the Hawaiian Islands consist of a series of volcanoes that arose over the hot spot, then moved northwest with the Pacific plate and cooled.

As each new island formed and cooled, a subset of one species or another of *Drosophila* moved to it and speciated. Moreover, because of the volcanic nature of the islands and their movement to the northwest, every island provided metaphoric islands within itself. New volcanoes created new landscapes, lava flows divided and remade ecosystems, and new geological features combined with the movement of the islands in latitude and longitude caused variations in wind and rain. All these changes promoted speciation. The Hawaiian *Drosophila* grew to some eight hundred species.

Biologists have named about one hundred of these species *picture-winged flies*. Twenty-seven species of picture-winged flies live on the island of Hawaii. One is *D. silvestrus*. Five ecologically separate populations of *D. silvestrus* live on the island, two in the southwest, three in the northeast. All have bristles on their legs. However, the populations in the northeast have twenty-four to thirty more bristles than the other flies. These extra bristles are an evolutionary novelty.

One or more of the three geographically isolated populations of *D. silvestrus* with extra bristles is probably in the process of speciation. It is geographically isolated, and it differs from the main populations. Moreover, *Drosophila* uses its bristles during mating. The extra bristles may already play a role in sexual selection. Speciation may be just around the corner.

Knowledge of *Drosophila* speciation reminds evolutionary theorists that watching speciation is not like seeing lions turn into tigers. Speciation events are hidden and seemingly insignificant. To see them, biologists must first discover which populations in the wild are separate species—no small task when all being examined are members of the same genus. Second, biologists must find isolated populations within a species—also a difficult task because animals move around, and many plants have seeds and pollen that can be widely scattered. Third, within the isolated populations, biologists need to find relevant differences. Discovering differences that may presage speciation several hundreds or thousands of years from now often proves perplexing.

To study *Drosophila* is to explore a slice of present time, seeing what speciation looks like among natural, living organisms today. *Drosophila* speciation events correspond to predictions from the theory of evolution by natural selection. There are lots of endemic species among geographically isolated populations and subtle differences among closely related species. Many differences, like mate choice, are behavioral. The theory of evolution provides a simple model of the world that corresponds to the world sufficiently to make some very accurate predictions.

When read correctly, the historical record of speciation left by fossils also shows correspondence among theory, model, and world. One of the greatest obstacles to reading the fossil record correctly is a metaphor. People tend to envision the history of life as a chain and to expect newly discovered fossils to provide missing links. However, the chain/link metaphor is misleading. The appropriate metaphor or model of the history of life is a bush. A bush has no central trunk. It is a maze of branches and twigs. A recovered twig may offer little information about the rest of the bush and link to nothing else on it.

Nonetheless, fossil discoveries of the 1980s and 1990s have helped science reconstruct three important evolutionary histories.

They have confirmed that birds evolved from dinosaurs (Ackerman 1998, Shipman 1999). They have given us unexpected evidence that whales evolved in an ancient sea in Pakistan (Thewissen 1998, Zimmer 1998, 117–226) and that terrestrial vertebrates evolved from fish living in Greenland's coastal lagoons (Zimmer 1998, 9–116). The easiest of these histories to recount briefly is the dinosaur transformation.

Two years after Darwin published the *Origin*, Europeans discovered one of the most famous fossils of all time, *Archaeopteryx*. It looked like a dinosaur, but it had feathers. Thomas Henry Huxley, a biologist known as "Darwin's bulldog" for his ferocious defense of Darwinism, suggested that it showed dinosaurs and birds are related. Newly discovered fossils in China have confirmed the relationship. It is that of ancestor and descendant.

One hundred twenty million years ago, near present-day Sihetun in northeastern China, lay a region of lush vegetation and abundant wildlife. A pristine lake provided drinking water for terrestrial animals and a habitat for fish. One day, a volcano in Inner Mongolia belched poisonous gas across the region, killing everything. Then the volcano spewed ash over the dead, burying and preserving them. The results are unusually abundant and well-preserved fossils. Among them is *Sinosauropteryx*, a two-legged, swiftly running carnivore, a theropod dinosaur. For a theropod dinosaur, *Sinosauropteryx* has some interesting features. It is covered with downy filaments that may be protofeathers and has short arms with a hand with only three fingers, like the bones in the wings of a bird. Similar fossil species have a wrist and arms that can move up and down, both features necessary for flight.

Near *Sinosauropteryx* lies *Caudipteryx*, another flightless dinosaur, but with fully developed feathers. In the same area rests *Protarchaeopteryx*, fully feathered and flightless, too, but with features similar to *Archaeopteryx*. Here in one small region of China we find what popular writers call "missing links" in the evolution from dinosaurs to birds.

However, these fossils are not missing links. They do not form an evolutionary chain. The relationship among them is neither chronological nor directly ancestor-descendant. All lived at the same time and were caught in the same volcanic catastrophe. Nonetheless, they illustrate important evolutionary events in significant branches on the evolutionary bush. From them, we can reconstruct enough evolutionary history to be sure that birds evolved from dinosaurs and to model major events marking that evolution.

The other two evolutionary histories—of fish walking ashore and mammals swimming back to sea—are too complex to relate here. I will summarize them by suggesting that they provide seven insights into evolution.

First, *preadaptations* (sometimes called *exaptations*) play a major role in evolution. Preadaptations are features that serve one purpose when they evolve but a different purpose later. Examples of preadaptations from the dinosaur/bird history are the wrist, up-and-down moving arms, and feathers. When they first evolved, they were not used for flight; later they were. When birds got ready to fly, they had the features they needed. This does not mean that they had all the features required for flying efficiently. These evolved later.

Before the 1980s and without adequate evidence, paleontologists had speculated that fish became adapted to land while emerging from fresh water. However, new fossil discoveries reveal that some fish evolved characteristics required for terrestrial living millions of years before they came ashore. While living in salty coastal lagoons, they evolved lungs, legs, and toes. These features were useful in shallow water where walking was as efficient as swimming, and bacteria blooms caused sudden drops in aqueous oxygen. When fish got ready to move to land, they had the necessary equipment. The preadaptations are in the fossils.

Second, organisms making such transitions need not be particularly efficient in their new environments. An early whale fossil found in Pakistan, *Pakicetus*, lived at the eastern end of what was once the Tethys Sea. It swam awkwardly in the shallow water, retaining landlubbers' legs and the head and teeth of a terrestrial carnivore. Ten million years later, at the western end of the Tethys Sea opening onto the Atlantic Ocean, swam *Basilosaurus*, still a carnivore and retaining two tiny back legs, but a whale of a creature, fifty feet long with front fins, a fluked tail, and a spine that could bend backwards, propelling it forward with both downward and upward thrusts of the fluke. Between *Pakicetus* and *Basilosaurus* lay five other fossil species, telling the evolution of an increasingly efficient aquatic hunter and swimmer. (For a discussion of genes in ancestors of whales, see Pennisi 1999.)

Third, evolution sometimes changes many features of an organism at once. *Regulative genes* cause the changes. Regulative genes control other genes. If a regulative gene changes, all the genes it controls, the proteins these genes encode, and the bodies they build will also change.

Fourth, some evolutionary changes, even big ones, occur suddenly. A small change in developmental timing caused the fin of the lobefin fish, ancestor of the fish that went ashore, instantaneously to produce toes instead of fins.

Fifth, some important evolutionary events occur without genetic changes. In birds' legs, the tibia has a crest tying the two leg bones together, helping birds walk with ease. As each baby bird squirms in its egg, pressure that turns tendon to cartilage builds the crest. Pocket gophers have external, furred pouches in their cheeks. Once these pockets were internal. As the gophers evolved longer snouts, the internal pouches migrated forward and turned outward. As soon as the pockets were on the face, facial hair cells made them hairy. Although there seem to be genes for long snouts, pockets, and hair, there are no genes for hairy, external pockets.

Six, evolution runs many experiments. During the Devonian period that began about 400 million years ago, all sorts of vertebrate fish existed—strange sharks, fish with scales like armor, huge relatives of crustaceans, and all kinds of giant lungfish. By the end of the Devonian 46 million years later, many of these forms had become extinct, leaving four major types to survive until today. Evolution's experiments have not ended. In 1991, a sudden freeze in a California lake killed and preserved hundreds of newts. A study of more than nine hundred of their limbs showed that almost one-third were unusual.

Finally, although evolution never repeats itself, it plays familiar themes. Think of the transition from water to land and land to water as an X. (The idea is from Zimmer 1998, 228–29.) The X's cross is where land meets water. Top left to bottom right represents the land-to-water transition; bottom left to top right represents water-to-land. Those animals going into the sea are similar to those arising from it. Both live in shallow water, have long flat heads, snapping jaws, powerful tails, and hunt by ambush. Yet, when examined in detail, they differ so much that from each one's point of view, the other looks like an odd mosaic. Their respective aquatic ancestors and descendants further down the X are also similar. Both have fins, swimming tails, and forelegs, but lack hind legs and hips. Again, the details differ, and each looks to the other like a strange mosaic. The respective terrestrial descendants and ancestors further up the X also have affinities. Both were great travelers and scavengers but poor hunters. Once more, the details differ. Evolution replays familiar themes with variations.

The recent fossil discoveries show strong correspondence with the model of the world the theory of evolution provides. The theory says species will change into other species and that, over millions of years, the changes will be enormous. This is what the fossils show. Almost 400 million years ago, four-legged fish came ashore. Some evolved into mammals. Around 50 million years ago, some of those mammals went back to sea, retaining their distinctive mammalian features but evolving new characteristics making them as adapted to the oceans as the fish around them. More than 120 million years ago, theropod dinosaurs began their evolution into birds. Today the birds number some nine thousand species, from flightless birds as tall as a human being to tiny hummingbirds sipping nectar from flowers, from hunting and scavenging carnivores to snatchers of insects and ravagers of fruit.

In summary, the theory of evolution by natural selection passes the correspondence test of truth in two complementary situations of speciation: speciation in living populations and in fossils.

I now turn to the consilience test of truth. According to this test, a theory is true if it unites various facts or models under one theoretical umbrella. The theory of evolution by natural selection offers a single explanatory umbrella for the origin all species. Here I concentrate on the evolution of our own species. The consilience between our own evolution and that of other species shows us to be an integral part of the natural world. I have taken the information in this section largely from Roger Lewin's *Principles of Human Evolution: A Core Textbook* (1998), because I have deliberately tried to present mainstream paleontological thought. Other works consulted include Richard Leakey (1994), Leakey and Lewin (1992), and Ian Tattersall (1995).

Consilience and Human Evolution

Well before Darwin proposed the theory of evolution by natural selection, biologists had realized that human anatomy resembles that of other mammals, especially primates. In 1758 Carolus Linnaeus, who developed modern biological classification, classified people in the taxonomic order of primates because of our shared anatomical features. Modern chemical analysis shows that humans and chimpanzees are more than 98 percent similar genetically. How did such similarities come about?

Sixty-five million years ago, a mass extinction killed about 70 percent of all existing species. Among those escaping extinction were the ancestors of the primates. The extinction of competitors gave them room to expand and speciate. Primates evolved about 50 million years ago and diversified into almost six thousand species. Today, primates constitute an order of about two hundred species, divided into four suborders: prosimians, new world monkeys, old world monkeys, and hominoids (apes and us).

Hominoids evolved in Africa about 27 million years ago and diversified into some eighty-four species. Today, twenty-four species exist, including our own.

Molecular data show that we and gorillas and chimpanzees, our closest living relatives, stem from a common ancestor. Gorillas first speciated from the ancestral population, and about 5 to 6 million years ago bipedal apes evolved and separated from it as well. The stem species probably most closely resembled modern chimpanzees. Molecular evidence is the only evidence we have for these events because we have not uncovered relevant fossils from the appropriate epoch.

However, the theory of evolution and our knowledge of the evolution of other mammals and primates help us understand some significant points about these events. First, several million years have elapsed since bipedal hominoids separated from quadrupedal ones. The existing quadrupeds, living apes, have had these millions of years to evolve, too. We cannot use information about them uncritically in order to find out about our common ancestor.

Second, anthropologists will never find the missing link between modern apes and us because none exists. Modern apes are not our ancestors, but our cousins. Moreover, evolution does not form a chain with missing links, but a bush whose twigs are not obviously linked together. As a result, although we have thousands of fossils of bipedal apes, we do not know who is ancestral to whom. It is true that, at the behest of the Interpreter, paleontologists have speculated endlessly about ancestors and changed their views as they uncovered each new significant fossil. Nonetheless, we do not know about our ancestors. All we know is which fossils are older and which seem more ape-like or human-like.

Third, as the bushiness of evolutionary histories makes clear, organisms do not form a Great Chain of Being as envisioned by medieval theologians. Medieval theologians speculated that life forms a vast hierarchy whose higher members are more valuable than its lower ones. At the bottom, and least valuable, they placed inanimate objects such as stones. Plants came next, followed by animals. Among the animals, mammals were toward the top, especially the "kingly" lion. (Apes were unknown to medieval Europe.) At the pinnacle of life were men, the most valuable beings on Earth, more valuable than women. It does not take much imagination to figure out who concocted the Great Chain of Being—human males. The meandering, bushy, multidirectional path that evolution follows has proved the concept false.

In the real world, bipedalism evolved among apes millions of years ago, long before any other distinctly human characteristic. Eventually some dozen bipedal species came into existence. Paleontologists have uncovered fossils of most of them.

Paleontologists credit the evolution of bipedalism to climate and ecological change in eastern Africa. Some 5 to 6 million years ago, the climate in east Africa cooled and an originally forested habitat became a mosaic of forest, shrub, and plain, leaving only patchworks of trees in the new ecological space. Apes whose habitat had been thick forest were forced to crisscross grasslands, traveling to scattered clusters of trees in search of food.

Because they were shady, the original forests were relatively cool, and apes were adapted to them. Today, no living forest-dwelling mammal has special features for keeping cool, and this was probably the case with the apes in their original habitat. When they began living in a more open habitat, they lacked cooling mechanisms such as special blood vessel systems in their brains that other savanna-dwelling mammals have. The apes had another asset, however. Like their modern counterparts, they must have been able to sit, stand, and even walk upright. Upright walking is far cooler than quadrupedalism, because less sun strikes the body and breezes move freely above the grasses. Those apes best able to stand and walk upright stayed coolest, survived best, and reproduced. An upright stance has other advantages. Striding is more efficient than apes' four-legged waddle, upright stance gives a better view of predators and food sources and it frees the hands for carrying objects and making gestures. Bipedal apes thrived, multiplied, and diversified in their new habitat.

Paleontologists now think the first bipedal apes were *Ardipithecus ramidus* (fossils from Ethiopia), *Australopithecus anamensis* (fossils from Kenya), and *Australopithecus bahrelghazali* (fossils from Chad). However, Lewin suggests that future paleontologists are likely to follow the classification Tattersall first suggested. Since it seems to me to be the most logical and simple classification of bipedal apes available, I provide it here (from Tattersall 1995), beginning with the oldest of the apes.

Tattersall divides the bipedal apes into three genera, *Australopithecus*, *Paranthropus*, and *Homo*. The *Australopithecus* genus includes the gracile australopithecines and consists of *A. afarensis* and *A. africanus*. I think Tattersall would also include the latest finds, *A. anamensis* and *A. bahrelghazali*, in the genus.

The most famous australopithecine fossil is Lucy, an almost complete *A. afarensis* skeleton dating to 3.5 million years ago, discovered by Donald Johanson in 1975 in Hadar, Ethiopia. Anthropologists have hundreds of fossils of her species as well as famous fossil footprints of three individuals traversing thirty yards of volcanic ash near Laetoli, Tanzania. Lucy and other members of her species had brains of about four hundred cubic centimeters, a little larger than those of chimpanzees. They stood about three feet tall. Their walk was fully bipedal. However, they maintained such arboreal adaptations as curved hands and feet, mobile shoulders, and short legs. Paleontologists generally describe the species as being ape-like above the neck and human-like below it.

The *Paranthropus* genus contains the species anthropologists have called *robust australopithecines*. Tattersall includes four species, *P. robustus*, *P. boisei*, *P. aethiopicus*, and *P. crassidens*. As yet, the *Paranthropus* have no famous, almost complete representatives among the fossils. Rather, they are known through a range of fragmentary fossils indicating creatures with huge molars, flared cheekbones, and a robust build. From their dentition, they appear to have eaten leaves and rough herbage. Some existed contemporaneously with the australopithecines, yet they were probably not in competition as the australopithecines tended to dine primarily on fruit.

Homo is the most recent genus to have evolved. Tattersall places seven species in the genus (in age order): *H. habilis*, *H. rudolfensis*,

H. ergaster, H. erectus, H. heidelbergensis, H. neanderthalensis, and
H. sapiens.

H. habilis had a brain of about seven hundred cubic centimeters
and is the earliest evolved hominoid species known to have used
tools. *H. ergaster* is now thought to have been the first species of
Homo to migrate out of Africa into southern Europe and Asia.
Apparently, somewhere in Europe or Asia a population of *H. ergaster*
speciated, producing *H. erectus,* the only *Homo* species not native to
Africa. *H. erectus* reentered Africa, speciated, and produced *H. sapiens,* who then migrated from Africa and settled throughout the
world. At least, this is the current best scenario.

Anthropologists know a lot about *Homo erectus,* not only because
hundreds of fossils exist from Africa and Asia but also because in 1984
Richard Leakey discovered an almost complete 1.6 million-year-old
skeleton on the west side of Lake Turkana, Kenya. He named the fossil the *Turkana boy.* The Turkana boy was tall. He would have grown
to be an adult almost six feet in height. His brain was 880 cubic centimeters and would have developed to the average for the species, 950
cubic centimeters. Several anatomical features suggest members of his
species did not have a fully developed, spoken language.

Most animal species show *sexual dimorphism,* the male usually
being larger than the female. The large sexual dimorphism characteristic of earlier hominoid species shrank in *H. erectus* to about 25 percent. This change has important behavioral implications. In
mammalian species with large sexual dimorphism, males dominate
females and compete aggressively with each other. Troops tend to be
composed of related females, their offspring, and one dominant male.
Males leave their natal troop and try to take over another troop or
form one of their own. As sexual dimorphism decreases, this pattern
changes. With a differential of some 25 percent, males are less competitive, and troops are composed of several related adult males,
females, and their offspring. Males stay in their natal troop and
females change troops. Male bonding occurs, made easy by the close
relatedness of the males, who are often brothers and half-brothers.
Homo erectus seems to have followed this latter pattern.

H. erectus brought other changes. For the first time, members of
a species seem to have hunted systematically and returned to home
bases where they used fire and made tools methodically. In a judgment supported by details of birth canal size and brain capacity,
paleontologists think *erectus* offspring experienced an extended

period of dependence, which increased the offspring's ability to absorb culture and shaped the adults' parental behavior. In *Homo erectus,* we begin to see much that we recognize as typical of our own species.

Our own species, *Homo sapiens,* evolved in Africa some two hundred thousand years ago. The evidence for this date derives from mitochondrial DNA data, spawning a scenario for our evolution misleadingly entitled the *mitochondrial Eve* hypothesis.

The DNA in our forty-six chromosomes lies in the nucleus of each cell. Mitochondrial DNA occurs outside the nucleus. For recent evolutionary studies, it is ideal. It mutates faster than nuclear DNA, so it can be used to measure recent events. Because it passes only from female to female, it does not undergo recombination, so females inherit it intact. Finally, it is small, containing only 16,569 base pairs in contrast to the 3 billion base pairs of nuclear DNA. Using it, biologists have traced our speciation to a population composed of about ten thousand individuals living two hundred thousand years ago. Naming the hypothesis after Eve, whom most people consider a single individual, has proved misleading. Individuals neither evolve nor speciate. Populations evolve, and speciation occurs within populations.

Homo sapiens's brain capacity is about 1,350 cubic centimeters, comprising about 2 percent of the body's weight but consuming almost 20 percent of the body's energy. Such a brain is an expensive organ to grow and maintain, and its size implies that members of the species, especially females who bear offspring, had ready access to stable, high-energy food and suffered low predation pressure. Evidence from dentition shows that *H. sapiens'* diet consisted of a large portion of meat, a ready source of the energy needed to feed our big brains. Eating meat regularly means systematic hunting, using tools. It may also indicate that males provisioned females and even participated in childcare.

Not much of this is new on the evolutionary scene. As I mentioned, *H. habilis* used tools and *H. erectus* hunted systematically. In *H. erectus* as well, we see the childhood dependence that suggests the ability to acquire culture and to promote male childcare, or at least male provisioning of females. Only symbolic language seems to be *Homo sapiens's* special acquisition.

Because symbolic language left no artifacts until the invention of writing, paleontologists debate whether symbolic language evolved with our species, as some anatomical details indicate, or whether it evolved later than the species itself. Although anatomically modern humans date to two hundred thousand years ago, modern symbolic behavior arrived only recently. Organized burial, symbolic art, complex tools, and the boats that took us across swift, deep seas to Australia date only to about forty thousand years ago. This may have been when we acquired a fully articulated, symbolic language. We may never know when language evolved, for it probably evolved in stages, and it left no fossils.

This section has been about the Darwinian consilience that places us in the natural world among our primate cousins. The evidence for our evolution comes from comparative anatomy, embryology, physiology, and biochemistry, from historical biochemistry (mitochondrial DNA), and from fossils. When paleontologists examine the evidence carefully, they find themselves in some disagreement. It is not perfectly clear when any particular anatomy or behavior evolved. The *Australopithecus* are fully bipedal, yet retain ape-like features in brain, face, shoulder, and leg. *Habilis* used tools; maybe the australopithecines did, too. Nonetheless, systematic, planned tool use comes with *erectus*—or was it *ergaster?* Was it *erectus* that developed a mental template for making tools, or only *sapiens?* When did language develop? Did *erectus* have a protolanguage? Did early *sapiens?*

These very questions tell of the continuity from apes to us. Logically, no one can look at the evidence, then draw a clear line and say, "Here the nonhuman ceased, the human began." We began with the social, diurnal primates; we arrived with art, religion, and language. We evolved for 50 million years. Or has it been almost 400 million as Zimmer (1998, 34) suggests? This is approximately when *Ichthyostega*, our distant four-legged ancestor, first walked onto land. Both dates are part of the Darwinian consilience and mark our place in nature.

The consilience that shows us our place in nature is merely a small part of a larger whole. In chapter 5, I describe many other consiliences Darwin's theory provides, consiliences among classification, biogeography, the fossil record, genetics, plate tectonics, and cosmology and our own DNA. Here, I have focused narrowly on our own evolution. The theory of evolution passes many consilience tests of truth. Considering how vigorously it has been resisted, it is not canalized.

Canalization and Resistance

If something is canalized, we learn it easily, like children acquiring their native language. It seems obvious to us, like agents being the causes of events. When introduced to a canalized idea, we greet it as an old friend. But people have not found the theory of evolution by natural selection either familiar or friendly. Discovering it required global knowledge and patient labor. Even after Darwin explained it logically and with substantial detail, many people rejected it.

Darwin's global travels are well known. He traveled around the world aboard the *Beagle* and became convinced evolution had occurred, but he did not know how. Before he sailed, he had become a fine naturalist. During his voyage, he studied geology as well as plants, animals, and fossils, making important scientific discoveries. After he returned, he immersed himself in other fields of biology and studied philosophy of science. He corresponded around the globe with the best scientists of his day. He himself conducted a wide range of experiments, breeding pigeons, testing seeds for their ability to survive fresh and salt water, and studying barnacles for eight long years, trying to understand their patterns of descent. He kept detailed notes. Finally, he published the *Origin* in 1859, presenting his theory to the public. It had been twenty-eight years since he set foot aboard the *Beagle*.

Many found his book persuasive. Others resisted. Some refused to believe evolution had occurred; others accepted the evolution of all species but our own. Many whom Darwin convinced of the fact of evolution did not accept the theory of natural selection, but they misunderstood evolution as analogous to the development of individual organisms (Bowler 1988). Not until the Mendelian revolution of the early twentieth century did biologists completely understand and accept evolution by natural selection.

Most resistant were the Christian clergy. The Roman Catholic Church did not accept the theory of evolution until 1950, and some individual Catholic clergy continue to rail against it. Many Protestants have never accepted it.

The theory of evolution by natural selection shows no signs of being canalized. It seems unnatural to us, hard to grasp. Yet, the basic theory is simple and accessible. If organisms produce varied offspring, if some characteristics are inherited, if more offspring are born than survive to reproduce, populations will change over time.

These common observations and this simple logic provide the heart of the theory. The rest is substantiating detail.

If we are looking for a local version of the physicists' global theory of everything, the theory of evolution by natural selection is a strong candidate. It is not canalized. It meets all three tests of truth. It is coherent. It corresponds to the way the world is—both the living and the fossil world. Finally, it is consilient, building on theories from physics, chemistry, geology, and cosmology, uniting knowledge from many areas of biology, reaching into our own hominoid past, and helping inform us about our place in nature. As I will argue in chapter 8, the theory of evolution helps us understand human nature, too, once we become familiar with the sociobiological consilience.

Chapter 8

The Sociobiological Consilience

As I describe in chapter 5, modern evolutionary theory represents a consilience between Charles Darwin's original theory of evolution by natural selection and modern genetics, a consilience often called the New Synthesis. In the 1960s, biology underwent another consilience. W. D. Hamilton (1964) combined the New Synthesis with our knowledge of animal behavior to explain animal social behavior from a genetic point of view. After biologists confirmed his predictions and sociobiology had become an established science, Edward O. Wilson announced the new consilience to the public in his *Sociobiology: The New Synthesis* (1975). His title compares this sociobiological consilience with the New Synthesis of the 1940s. Looking back from the new century, the sociobiological consilience appears enormously important. It has triggered the creation of research programs, journals, and scientific societies.

Sociobiology is the genetic study of animal social behavior. Being the study of social behavior, it studies groups. Like its parent theory, it is a statistical theory and applies only to groups, not to individuals. One group it studies is *Homo sapiens*. This chapter explains sociobiology, emphasizing its application to our species. Because sociobiology is a legitimate extension of evolutionary theory, it passes the tests of truth applied to evolutionary theory in the last chapter, so I will not systematically apply them to it in this. However, this chapter supplies evidence of its correspondence and coherence as well as its consilience.

Because sociobiology is a new branch of biology, and because it applies to us, it has been controversial. As is typical of any science, not all the controversies are settled. Some sociobiologists have also been inept with metaphors, sowing considerable confusion in places. Controversies and confusions complicate and cloud the landscape. This chapter tries to simplify and illuminate the sociobiological terrain. I discuss the controversies and confusions only where they impinge on our understanding of human nature.

The classic introduction to sociobiology is Wilson (1975). A briefer, updated work is John Alcock (1989). A lucid explanation of biology and human nature is Timothy Goldsmith (1991). I review his book in Williams (1992). A critical history of the search for human nature using the theory of evolution is Carl Degler (1991). The central concern of sociobiology is the evolution of cooperation, and the principal form of cooperation is altruism.

The Evolution of Altruism

As I explained in the last chapter, classical Darwinian theory is about the evolution of populations by natural selection. In the classical theory, natural selection selects individual organisms, and populations evolve. The New Synthesis discovered that gene frequencies change with populations and that genetic revolutions can occur when new species evolve. In modern evolutionary theory, natural selection is most often defined as a change in gene frequencies. This definition emphasizes the statistical nature of the theory of evolution as well as reminding us that scientific theories are about simplified models of nature.

According to the New Synthesis, organisms compete with each other, and the winner of the competition is the organism passing on the most copies of its genes to succeeding generations. Neither the classical theory nor the New Synthesis adequately accounts for the evolution of cooperation.

Yet, organisms cooperate. Clones, organisms having the same genetic makeup, often form colonies, and some colonies are so cooperative and their parts so specialized that they themselves resemble organisms. Social insects form colonies whose individual organisms also specialize, some being workers, some soldiers, some drones, and some queens. Most birds with helpless young cooperate to raise their mutual offspring. Wolves, foxes, hyenas, chimpanzees, and some hawks hunt cooperatively; foxes and hyenas cooperate to raise communal young; and chimpanzees sometimes share food. We cooperate to rear mutual young, share food, have specialized occupations, and exchange goods and services. One of the central problems of the theory of evolution has been to explain the evolution of all this cooperation.

Sociobiologists have discovered that most forms of cooperation stem from *altruism*. In sociobiology, altruism is a technical term referring to observable behavior affecting reproduction. Altruistic behavior enhances another organism's prospects for reproduction while diminishing the altruist's own reproductive potential. This technical, biological term has a different meaning from the common term, *altruism*. The common term refers to human psychology. People are altruistic if motivated by concern for another's welfare. Much confusion in sociobiology results from combining these two separate and distinct uses of the word. In this section, I use the term altruism exclusively in its technical, biological sense, as a behavior affecting reproduction.

Nature is full of altruistic behavior. Biologists explain the evolution of altruism by the theory of *kin selection*. Kin selection is a form of natural selection in which close kin help one another. The helper may lose reproductive advantages or even die, but because its close relatives possess copies of its genes and the helper has enhanced their reproductive advantages, copies of the helper's genes pass on to succeeding generations.

In a very simplified model, the cooperative organisms mentioned above demonstrate how kin selection works. The most altruistic are the clones. Evolutionary competition requires entities to differ from each other. If they are exactly alike, competition is pointless. Clones are identical, so there is no cause for competition. If one dies without reproducing, copies of all its genes will pass on to succeeding generations anyway, as long as its identical clones live to reproduce. Hence, clonal species like *Nanomia cara* show 100 percent cooperation in their colonies.

Most highly cooperative social insects are in a single insect order, the *Hymenoptera*. The order includes bees, wasps, and ants. The *Hymenoptera* have evolved specialized caste systems at least eleven times (Wilson 1975, 415). Among nonclonal animals, this represents an extraordinary evolutionary feat. None of the other arthropods except the termites has evolved such a system, and in other animals, similar systems have almost never evolved.

The evolution of cooperation in the *Hymenoptera* is not their only peculiar feature. They also are unusual genetically. They are *haplodiploid.* On average, females (the workers) share three-quarters of the copies of their genes with their sisters, half with their own offspring, and a quarter with their brothers (the nonworking drones). Therefore, sisters who help raise sisters pass more copies of their genes to succeeding generations than they would by bearing their own offspring. Predictably, sisters raise sisters. On the other hand, drones would pass on only one-quarter of their genes by helping the colony, but one-half by fertilizing a receptive female. Predictably, they do not work in the colony, but instead, beg food from their sisters, then aggressively compete to fertilize females.

Unlike the *Hymenoptera,* almost all other nonclonal animals are *diploid.* In diploid organisms, offspring receive half of each parent's genes, siblings share half of the copies of each other's genes, on average, and genetic relatedness falls off exponentially as closeness of kinship decreases. Among diploid organisms aside from us, biologists currently know of very few animals with social structures comparable to the *Hymenoptera.* The termites, a few genera of spiders when living in special circumstances (Helmuth 1999), the shrimp *Synalpheus* (Duffy 1996), and the naked mole rat *Heterocephalus glaber* all form hierarchical colonies. Predictably, each colony has one mother and one or a very few fathers. In other words, these colonies of diploid organisms consist of brothers and sisters, each 50 percent related to the other, the maximum relatedness possible in diploid organisms. With these simple, successful mathematical predictions, sociobiology passes significant tests of coherence and correspondence.

Genetic percentages given in chapter 7 may appear to contradict these figures. In chapter 7, I said people and chimpanzees are more than 98 percent genetically similar. Here I have noted that offspring of diploid organisms—including people and chimpanzees—are only 50 percent related to each other. As biologists typically do in these two dissimilar cases, I have treated similarity and relatedness differently. The 98 percent figure represents overall genetic similarity averaged over the two species. The 50 percent figure represents genetic relatedness, in diploid organisms, the amount of maternal or paternal gene contribution to offspring and/or the genetic relatedness of siblings. Overall, the mother and father are very similar genetically, but each contributes only half his or her genes, on average, to each offspring. It is the parental gene contribution and copies shared by close relatives—relatedness—not overall genetic similarity, that predict the amount of altruism.

Genetic relatedness is not the only factor promoting altruism. In various species, anatomy, physiology, behaviors other than altruism, and/or environment play their part. A complete explanation of the evolution of altruism in any particular species would have to take the relevant information applicable to it into account. However, genetic relatedness provides the one fundamental, common explanation for altruistic behavior in species from *Nanomia cara* to *Homo sapiens,* making sociobiology just the sort of consiliating theory that makes good science.

Based on relatedness alone, biologists make accurate predictions about animal social behavior. What will clonal aphids infested with lethal parasitic wasps do? They commit suicide rather than staying in their colony to infect their 100 percent genetically related counterparts (McAllister and Roitberg 1987, 797–99). What is the difference between the colonies of haplodiploid and diploid insects? Haplodiploids, with males related by only one-quarter, produce lazy male drones; diploid termites, whose sisters and brothers are equally related, share the work equally because, reproductively, it pays male as well as female termites to work.

In birds with defenseless young requiring two parents to raise them, males help raise their young. What happens in the harsh climate of the African savannas where even more help is required? Not only do *Merops bullockiodes* parents cooperate to raise their young, older siblings also help, delaying their own reproduction (Fackelmann 1989). Neither unrelated birds nor distantly related birds provide this aid. Sociobiology is full of accurate predictions about animals as diverse as aphids and birds, fish and chimpanzees. It corresponds well to the way the world is.

In theory, altruism can also evolve by *group selection.* Group selection involves the natural selection of groups rather than individuals. Whether group selection occurs in nature is controversial. Its latest and best defenders are Elliott Sober and David Sloan Wilson (1998). The following discussion is based on their work.

Selection theory says that selection can occur at various levels in the organic hierarchy. In classic evolutionary theory, selection directly selects organisms. In gene selection, selection directly selects genes. In group selection, selection directly selects groups.

Selection operates at the lowest level available. If entities at the lower levels vary and reproduce, selection will choose them and ignore anything at a higher level. In thinking about group selection, this is an important point. Consider sexually reproducing organisms like us. Each of us except identical twins is different (we vary), and most of us have children (we reproduce). Our sex cells, the cells of reproduction, are separate from our somatic cells, the cells constructing our bodies. Our somatic cells do not compete, for they are 100 percent related and never pass on to succeeding generations. They die with us. If they competed, our bodies would fall apart. Since they do not compete, selection overlooks them and selects groups of cells containing identical DNA, that is, organisms.

In order for group selection to work, organisms must act like somatic cells. They must almost entirely cease to compete. Ideally, the organisms would be identical and the groups would vary. Then selection would ignore the organisms and select among the varying groups. Clonal organisms are all alike. When they form colonies, selection ignores the separate organisms and selects the colonies. *Hymenoptera* females are genetically three-quarters related, and in colonial species various species-specific mechanisms thwart incipient competition. Selection ignores the organisms and selects the colony. The colonies compete vigorously. They wage war.

In contrast, diploid organisms are maximally 50 percent related. They vary and compete, undermining what Sober and Wilson call their *groupishness,* and their groups disintegrate. Therefore in most diploid organisms, selection selects individual organisms instead of groups.

Biologists interested in group selection have developed several models in which diploid organisms evolve and retain groupishness, but with two exceptions, the models seem to me and to most evolutionary biologists to be mathematical or laboratory artifacts. They do not model the natural world. One of the exceptions involves models using close relatives. This model involves kin selection, if kin selection is a variety of group selection. (As Sober and Wilson note, kin selection can be seen from various perspectives, partly depending on how *group* is defined.) Because biologists originally developed kin selection models to avoid invoking group selection, I will retain their distinction between kin and group selection. In this book, group selection refers to the selection of groups of unrelated or distantly related organisms. Kin selection refers to the selection of close kin.

The other exception involves cultural groups, groups limited as far as we presently know to our own species. Cultures enforce similarity within groups and provide variety among groups (Sober and

Wilson 1998, 132–94), and cultural traits are heritable, that is, we pass them on to succeeding generations. It is possible, even probable, that human cultures have competed and changed as groups, retaining their groupishness. However, natural selection is a change in gene frequencies, and the question remains whether cultural group selection affects genes other than those already affected by kin selection, that is, whether cultural group selection is a form of natural selection. Many, myself included, are doubtful. But whether we evolved by kin selection or group selection, the evolution of altruism in us has left an interesting legacy.

Altruism's Legacy

So far, I have discussed only technical, biological altruism, the behavior of an organism that sacrifices some of its own potential reproduction and benefits another's. No controversy exists among sociobiologists about the evolution of this sort of altruism among close kin.

However, some sociobiologists think altruistic behavior is ultimately selfish because it promotes the survival of copies of the altruist's genes. Many then claim to have uncovered the selfish motives behind human psychological (not technical) altruism. These claims are amazingly common in the sociobiological literature.

Two distinct confusions underlie these claims. I have already mentioned the first, the conflation of the technical, biological term with the psychological one. The technical term refers to observable behavior, the psychological one to unobservable motives, namely, concern for another's welfare. If we describe genes as metaphorically selfish (Dawkins 1976), this means merely that they readily reproduce copies of themselves. It does not mean that the organisms they create are selfish. In fact, as sociobiology has proved, in order to reproduce themselves effectively, genes create organisms that exhibit biologically altruistic behavior. For the same reason, they may also create people with psychologically altruistic motives.

The second confusion is between self and other and regards the locus of the self's attention. The self referred to here need not be a conscious self. Immune systems with their biochemical defenses distinguish between self and other, protect self, and attack other. All living beings must distinguish self from other in order to prolong their own survival.

Any animal that cares for its offspring must distinguish its offspring from itself, for it must behave in certain ways to protect and feed itself and in other ways to protect and feed its offspring. Not only are its behaviors different, so is the direction of its attention. To feed its offspring, it must attend to its offspring's needs, not its own. The tired, hungry bird carries the worm to its chick, postponing the satisfaction of its own hunger. An organism that attends to another's needs rather than to its own is not selfish by definition.

Because the confusion between self and other and related errors about the direction of the self's attention are so embedded in the sociobiological literature—and some of the psychological and theological literature as well—I will hereafter substitute *egocentric* for words like *selfish, egoistic,* and *egotistic. Egocentric* clearly means the centering of attention on the ego, self, or I. For altruism in its psychological meaning of being other-directed and concerned for another's welfare, I will hereafter use *charity*, the English cognate of the Latin *caritas.*

Charity is the King James translation of the Greek word *agape*, a word exclusive to the New Testament, meaning self-denying, other-directed love. It is the charity of 1 Corinthians 13:1: "Though I speak with the tongues of men and of angels, and have not charity, I am become as sounding brass, or a tinkling cymbal" (KJV). It is the love of Jesus' summary of Jewish law as the commandment to love our neighbor (Matt. 22:39; Mark 12:31; Luke 10:27). The relevance of using a word with theological connotations will become clear in chapter 9.

Armed with a new vocabulary, we can ask whether biological altruism can transform into charity. Can behavior directed toward helping another at the sacrifice of the altruist's own reproductive opportunities be motivated by concern for the other's welfare? It would seem that the obvious answer is yes, as long as motives undergird behavior.

However, uncovering motives proves to be a problematic enterprise for science. Science limits itself to working with things people can observe, at least in theory. Motives are theoretically unobservable. Furthermore, Sigmund Freud added a psychological difficulty to the scientific one when he asserted that people's motives are often unconscious. The discovery of the Interpreter has added weight to Freud's claim. Therefore, asking people about their motivation may not uncover their actual motives, even if they answer sincerely. This has posed a real conundrum for psychological research on charity.

The research problem is confounded because almost all psychologists who explore human sociality and charity assume that people are egocentric, then interpret the results of their research to fit their assumption. In psychological research, "rarely is the possibility even entertained that the conflict is between wanting to meet my own needs and wanting to meet others' needs" (Batson 1991, 204). Thus, a working hypothesis metamorphoses into a conclusion that will be proved no matter what the research shows. Here, ideology poses as science.

Sober and Wilson (1998) review both the psychological and philosophical literature on egocentricity and charity, finding it indecisive so that only evolutionary information can resolve the issue of whether human beings have charitable motives. Although I have a different view of the psychological literature because I think Samuel and Pearl Oliner (1988) prove the existence of charity (Williams 1995, 208–16), I also think sociobiology proves its existence. Therefore I am willing to forgo a review of the psychological literature and return to the question asked above: Can behavior directed toward helping others (through the sacrifice of the altruist's own reproductive opportunities) be motivated by the altruist's concern for others' welfare?

By what else? Certainly, it is not motivated by concern for copies of the altruist's genes. First, no one in our evolutionary history knew genes existed, so natural selection could not have selected people concerned about genes. Second, we do not try to increase our genetic representation in succeeding generations. Even to consider doing so seems bizarre. Instead, we enjoy having sex. Third, on the whole, natural selection does not select genes, but organisms, and therefore it produces organisms aware of other organisms, not genes. Fourth, concern for copies of my genes in others would result in concern for their genes, not mine, concern for them, not myself. Clearly, mechanisms for effectively reproducing genes evolved. One of those mechanisms is charity toward kin.

Others who write on human sociobiology reach the same conclusion. Among them are Morton Hunt (1990), Alfie Kohn (1990), and Mary Midgley (1978, 105–42). A humorous and clear critique of the view that metaphorically selfish genes produce psychologically selfish people is Midgley (1983). In the end, the claim needing explanation is the claim that the helper's motives are egocentric. No explanation invoking egocentricity is as parsimonious as the explanation that the altruist's concern for others' welfare motivates the altruist's helpful, sacrificial behavior.

Although sociobiology predicts charity toward kin, it does not predict thoroughgoing charity, nor does it predict that we are naturally benevolent. The caveat that sociobiology relies on a simple model whose predictions can be skewed by confounding factors and whose statistical basis means it does not necessarily apply to the behavior of individuals is important here. Whatever its conclusions, they might not apply to you or me, although they will apply to humanity at large. Furthermore, this caveat should be invoked every time we speak of human nature, whether in the context of sociobiology or not.

Four predictions from sociobiology suggest we are not naturally benevolent. First, since diploid kin are only maximally 50 percent related, sociobiology predicts conflict in our closest relationships, the relationships between parents and offspring, siblings and siblings. Robert Trivers (1974) first made and explored this prediction. On average, offspring are 50 percent related to each parent, but an offspring is 100 percent related to itself. Therefore, offspring will want 50 percent more from each parent than each parent is willing to give. The same mathematics applies to sibling relationships. Each will want more from other siblings than they are willing to give and love them less than they want to be loved.

Second, parents care more for their own children than they do for the children of others. Where parents or other close relatives are in positions of power in the larger community and justice calls for equal treatment for all, nepotism will tend to undermine justice.

Third, if threatened by those who are not family members, kin will unite against them. Hence we have interfamilial feuds and, in larger kin groups, tribal, ethnic, and national wars.

Fourth, group selection is not benevolent. To make their members similar enough to be groupish, groups quell individuality and creativity. They enforce tradition and group mores. Sanctions for infractions can be severe. Social ostracism from a hunting and gathering band typically spells death. Because group selection pits group against group, warfare is likely. Because it emphasizes within-group similarity and out-group difference, dehumanization of out-groups occurs.

Under both group selection and kin selection, racism and genocide are natural. Only within groups is charity likely to flourish.

Mary Maxwell, who is interested in the moral implications of sociobiology for international relations, notes that group selection theory predicts what political theorists find. International moral law is an oxymoron. A single maxim summarizes it: "protect-the-nation" (Maxwell 1990, 124).

So altruism does not result in charity toward all, but charity to close kin, sometimes. A second sociobiological theory about the evolution of cooperation reaches beyond kin. Sociobiologists call it *reciprocal altruism*. Because it does not involve altruism, I will simply call it *reciprocity*.

Reciprocity

Trivers (1971) wrote the definitive article on biological reciprocity. Reciprocity is the exchange of goods and services between organisms not closely related. Reciprocal behavior is egocentric because it enhances each organism's own opportunities to survive and reproduce. Human beings reciprocate for their own benefit. Although reciprocating is advantageous for everyone, an organism can accrue even more advantages for itself if it cheats successfully. This brings tension to reciprocal relationships. Perhaps because of this tension, but more likely because reciprocal behavior requires organisms to remember each other and keep track of past slights and favors, reciprocity is thought to be rare in nature. (For a different view see Margulis and Fester 1991.)

Predictably, the most intelligent species—dolphins, whales, and chimpanzees—appear to engage in many reciprocal exchanges. However, unless observers know the family relationships in a population, they may confuse altruism with reciprocity. Furthermore, if unrelated animals grow up together in artificial environments, they will reciprocate. Their reciprocity may occur because the individuals respond to their nestlings as if they were kin, as nestlings would be in the wild. This behavior, too, would constitute altruism rather than reciprocity (albeit mistaken altruism).

Nonetheless, Trivers argues convincingly that reciprocity is genetic. He cites a now famous example of interspecies reciprocity between cleaner and cleaned fish, a case where relatedness cannot be at issue. The cleaner fish are small and defenseless, a good meal for the big fish they clean. Yet, the big fish do not eat them. Instead, they open their mouths and gills, allowing the little fish to swim in and out, dining on parasites. Both fish gain from their reciprocity. The little fish relish a good meal while the big fish undergo decontamination (Trivers 1971, 40).

Other cases of interspecific reciprocity also occur. Some ants and some plants reciprocate. The plants shelter the ants; the ants provide the plants with nitrogen (Treseder 1995). Many plants exchange their sugars for phosphorus produced by fungi (Schwartz and Hoeksema 1998).

However, we are by far the most extensive reciprocators. Modern economies and modern international trade relationships rest on reciprocity, as do employer-employee relationships and many friendships. Those who live in capitalist countries tend to think of reciprocity as the product of Adam Smith's rationalizing economy and therefore underestimate its naturalness.

Yet, we naturally reciprocate. Marcel Mauss (1967) studied tribal economies. He concludes that gift-giving undergirds them. Tribal members believe gifts possess power, power simultaneously sacred and dangerous. Gifts create strong bonds between donor and recipient. Giving, receiving, and distributing gifts establish and preserve alliances and divisions of labor. Gift giving creates and maintains hierarchies. The giver of gifts is superior, the recipient who does not return gift for gift, subordinate. A man can gain social status and wives by giving more gifts to his rival than his rival can return. Exchange among tribes is lively and continuous, making possible firm and persistent relationships among groups who do not share the ties of close kinship.

Moreover, we naturally think logically when reasoning about reciprocity. *Wason tests* study logical thinking. When first administered, they seemed to show that we think illogically. Curiously, however, almost all the test subjects answered some questions correctly, even if they were unusually complex. These questions employed the same rules of inference as other questions that test subjects answered incorrectly most of the time. Seeing this, psychologists experimented to discover what the questions had in common that the subjects answered correctly. All the questions asked about cheating on social contracts (Ridley 1996, 129).

In the past, I have suggested on grounds of parsimony that we do not have genes for reciprocity, but genes disposing us to do what is rational, and reciprocity is simply rational behavior (Williams 1996b, 278). However, the studies surrounding Wason tests have convinced me I have been mistaken. Moreover, the extent and intensity of our reciprocity and its connection with myth and religion (Burkert 1996, 129–55; Ehrenreich 1997, 7–114; Mauss 1967; Yerkes 1952; Young 1975) tend to remove reciprocity from the realm of the rational. I now think the sociobiologists are correct who claim we have genetic dispositions for reasoning about and engaging in reciprocity.

Like altruism, reciprocity has its dark side, something we have learned from *game theory*. Game theory is a branch of mathematics concerned with conflicts. Tit-for-tat type games best model reciprocal relationships. Simple tit-for-tat games involve two players who must either cooperate or cheat. In reiterated games, the most effective strategy is to cooperate until the other player cheats, then to employ a mixed strategy of cooperation, revenge, and forgiveness. In groups of players, those who cheat eventually drive from the group those who always cooperate, leaving a society composed entirely of cheaters. In order to engage in reciprocity safely, cooperators must be sensitive to cheating and be willing to seek revenge when cheated.

But in the real world, revenge is often unduly brutal, promoting blood feuds. Roy Baumeister (1997, 18–20) argues that the cause is the *magnitude gap*. The magnitude gap is a psychological disjunction between victim and perpetrator. Victims see their victimization as significant; perpetrators view their own acts as insignificant. Victims' sufferings are sustained; perpetrators' pleasures are brief. Victims cannot be victimized without deep emotional involvement; perpetrators disengage emotionally.

Thus, when victims seek what they perceive as equalizing revenge, the former perpetrator views their behavior as excessively vicious. Furthermore, because the roles are now reversed, the new victims judge their sufferings to be far more important and long-lasting than the new perpetrator thinks they are. The result is a spiral of revenge (Baumeister 1997, 160–61).

Reciprocity's dark side appears among social groups as well. In tribal societies when the societies are approximately equal and no third party adjudicates and enforces agreements, peaceful reciprocal relationships are almost impossible to maintain (Keeley 1996, 160–61). As game theory suggests, there are too many factors for the parties to deal with successfully. Even talking peace is difficult because the advantage lies with the party who calls for peace then attacks its disarmed opponents. When equal tribal parties talk peace, they bring warriors and weapons (Keeley 1996, 148).

Moreover, the spoils of victory may be extremely enticing. Consider the pleasure of this Maori warrior as he speaks to the preserved head of an enemy:

> "You wanted to run away, did you? but my meri [war club] overtook you: and after you were cooked, you made food for my mouth. And where is your father? he is cooked:—and where is your brother? he is eaten:—and where is your wife? there she sits, a wife for me:—and where are your children? there they are, with loads on their backs, carrying food, as my slaves." (quoted in Keeley 1996, 100)

And yet, people prefer peace. Many warring tribes accepted colonial pacification easily and with gratitude (Keeley 1996, 145). They just did not know how to maintain peace when reciprocal relationships were the only relationships they had available.

This review of sociobiology has painted a somewhat gloomy picture of human nature. Partly, the gloom stems from examining separately different forms of natural selection and their concomitant dispositions. Although evolution is a tinkerer and has never designed organisms completely from scratch (even in the beginning, it had to use available chemicals and their possible interactions), it does not build Rube Goldberg contraptions. Successful organisms are functioning wholes. We ourselves are organisms whose dispositions work together sufficiently well to have produced a highly successful species. It is worth looking briefly at how biological altruism and reciprocity, charity and egocentricity, work together to produce human sociality.

Human Sociality

In chapter 18 of *Sociobiology* (1975, 379–82), Wilson discusses four pinnacles of social evolution. *Homo sapiens* stands on the fourth pinnacle. We are highly social creatures. Our most energy-consuming social activity, and the most important from an evolutionary perspective, is rearing children. Human children are unique in the animal world in three ways that make human parenting distinctive, too. (For an overview of animal parenting, see Clutton-Brock 1991.)

First, compared with other primates, our children are born about ten months too early because the restricted size of a woman's birth canal makes later parturition lethal. Children's early birth makes them the most dependent mammalian infants. Parents expend great care just to keep them alive.

Second, our children mature slowly, remaining childlike until, with a sudden spurt of growth in adolescence, they become adults. Their extended childhood also demands enormous parental investment.

Third, human children learn more than any other animals. Their parents and others must spend years teaching them.

Moreover, human males care for their children, an activity uncommon in other mammalian species. Some unique features of our species, like women's hidden ovulation and our carnivorous dispositions (unusual in other primates), suggest that we have been successful because men became caregivers, and their first contribution to the family was meat. Terrence Deacon (1997, 401–10) argues that a man did not contribute meat to everyone but only to the woman bearing his children. He thinks this gift lies behind the development of male jealousy, the institutionalization of marriage, and the rise of symbolic language.

Once men began caring for children, parenting became a major commitment for men as well as women. Anyone who has reared children knows how difficult it is. Whatever would make us do it?

A mixed, flexible set of dispositions would help. Concern for the welfare of our children evolves from biological altruism. Parents everywhere care whether their children survive and thrive or not and make many sacrifices for them. Infanticide and neglect largely occur where the possibilities for children's thriving are so limited that, from an evolutionary point of view, it would be foolish to expend the resources required to rear them (Mann 1992).

Most parents also receive pleasure and satisfaction from their children. Pleasure is evolution's carrot, getting us to want to do what we need to do to rear dependent children. People who truly enjoy rearing children will be better parents than those who do not. Their children will thrive and, in their turn, enjoy rearing their own children, because they inherited their parents' genes.

If striven for directly, parental pride and pleasure are egocentric motives. As by-products of caring, they are ambiguous, sometimes judged egocentric, sometimes not. Caring for others is a charitable motive. These motives combine in us so we do the difficult parenting job evolution has given us.

Hardly anyone complains when parents favor their own children over the children of others. If in some world of perfect equity this favoritism seems unfair, it also seems so natural that we are inclined to judge as immoral those parents who neglect their children, and perhaps as pathological those who would cast aside their own children to rear others, especially others not related to them. Favoritism for our own children is necessary if they are to grow to adulthood. Parents who did not favor their own children left no offspring who reproduced. Parents showing favoritism were our ancestors, and we carry copies of their altruistic genes.

Some sociobiologists have called all our favoritism toward our relatives *nepotism*. However, nepotism does not mean favoring one's own dependent children over the dependent children of others. Nepotism is favoritism toward adult relatives by people who hold power or high office in the community. There is an insult to equality here that does not exist where children are dependent and needy, as all young children are. Nepotism substitutes altruism for reciprocity, distributing power, goods, and services inequitably.

Yet, nepotism occurs in every society, in some by design—the design of the powerful. Like caring for one's dependent children, it springs from kin selection, lies close to our reproductive interests, and entices us. Its existence is a lesson in how evolution works. Evolution has neither morals nor designs. A tinkerer by trade, it cares only for survival to reproduce. We judge its products as good or bad, and what we find in this case is that the dispositions required for raising dependent children—good dispositions that get the job done—result in nepotism among adults.

Monogamous societies view nepotism more negatively than do polygamous ones. Monogamous societies have decided to distribute reproductive opportunities equally and extend this equality to other adult relationships. Being groupish, polygamous cultures distribute reproductive opportunities unequally and continue this inequality in nepotism and clannishness. Polygamy and nepotism tend to promote tensions among families and clans.

In our preference for lives of peace and prosperity, one way we mitigate the us-them mentality that kin selection promotes is through manipulating symbols. We have dispositions to cooperate with our siblings, so when we want universal cooperation, we invent fictive kin, proclaiming all people brothers and sisters. We constantly wield this sort of symbolism. To unite college students who are unrelated and come from scattered locations, we establish fraternities and sororities, the English words coming directly from the Latin for *brother* and *sister*. Often, we make certain the Latin root is understood by translating it into English, "This is my sorority sister Tisha," we say. And so we build bonds.

Pierre van den Berghe (1981, 1990) studies ethnic bonds from a sociobiological perspective. One of his conclusions is that tribes and nations build ties among their people by inventing fictive kinship. As he notes, tribes practicing exogamy (marriage outside the tribe) are not composed of close kin because the spouses are from other kinship groups and children carry half the spouse's genes on average. But tribes claim deep kinship ties. So do we, symbolically. To our parents, our spouses are *daughters-* and *sons*-in-law.

Nations make the same sorts of claims, but their claims are even more fictive. Yet, van den Berghe says (1981, 27), to be creditable, the claims must have historical verisimilitude. To claim common kinship in the United States where we know people come from different localities, nations, languages, and races would be useless. The United States is not an ethnic nation but a state, whose people profess loyalty to a constitution rather than to a common ancestor.

We also build larger social bonds through reciprocity. Groups reciprocate. Tribes living as long as forty thousand years ago traded extensively. Trade carried Mediterranean seashells to the Ukraine and northern European amber south (Leakey and Lewin 1992, 324). Among exogamous groups, spousal exchange establishes and maintains alliances, a practice continued among European monarchies well into modern times. However, as European history indicates, neither of these practices keeps the peace. War, sex, and commerce are intertwined so that neighboring groups experience periodic cycles of cooperation and conflict (Keeley 1996, 122).

Sociobiology gives us a model of human nature. Human sociality springs from kin selection and reciprocity. These unite us in charity and fairness, a charity and fairness extended by our symbolic language to build charitable ties to symbolic kin and reciprocal bonds through complex legal contracts and extensive exchange networks. However, our charity and fairness are partly driven by groupishness and egocentricity. In their turn, these produce revenge,

blood feud, dehumanization of others, nepotism, racism, and genocide. Yet, without our egocentricity and nepotism, we would never
survive or successfully rear our children. Our nature is composite
and complex even without the complications and contradictions
arising from culture.

These remarks end a two-chapter exposition of the theory of
evolution, the first testing it for truth and the second developing its
model of human nature. The argument of this book so far culmi-
nates in the next chapter, where I replace the doctrines of original sin
with sociobiology's theory of human nature.

Chapter 9

Original Sin and Sociobiology

The first part of this book applies three philosophical tests of truth to three doctrines of original sin and finds the doctrines either unbiblical or unscientific or both. The second part has argued for the truth of the theory of evolution and showed how sociobiology explains the evolution of cooperation and provides us with a scientific theory of human nature. This chapter puts these parts together. It replaces the theological doctrines of original sin with a scientific understanding of human nature. The results are both surprising and salutary for Christian theology.

Replacement is possible because the three doctrines of original sin held by the three branches of Christianity make two questionable claims, as already discussed. First, they claim the fall is historical, that there was a first human pair who committed the first sin in eating forbidden fruit. Second, they derive from the alleged fall dubious theories of human nature that, with Augustine, become doctrines of original sin. The central concerns of the doctrines may be summarized by posing four questions that have arisen repeatedly in various guises throughout this book. First, are we free? Second, what is the source of sin? Third, can we fulfill Jesus' summary of Jewish law in love to neighbor, or are we helplessly egocentric? Fourth, is our suffering God's punishment for Adam and Eve's sin in us?

The theory of evolution applied to human nature through sociobiology can answer each of these questions, offering scientific replacements for dubious theology. This chapter articulates the answers. I begin with the most fundamental concern, freedom.

Freedom

All three doctrines of original sin offer similar models for the origin of human conflict and bondage. Their narrative models begin with Adam and Eve, a couple who are at peace psychologically, and also at peace with each other and with God. They are also free; that is, they are able to choose between good and evil. After committing the first sin, Adam and Eve change. They fall from their original peaceful state into psychological conflict, conflict with each other, and conflict with God. Moreover, they lose their freedom. Their altered state infects all subsequent human beings and constitutes human nature as we know it.

But as already discussed, these events never happened. They did not happen in the Bible, for there is no fall in Genesis 3. Science has replaced the model with a more substantial and better-substantiated one in which there can have been no first couple and no transmitted sin. Instead, science tells of lineages of bipedal apes evolving from quadrupedal ones, and of some of those lineages evolving into us. The theory of evolution says conflict is part of nature. Conflict is not the result of sin in us, but of diploidy.

As explained in chapter 8, diploid organisms receive 50 percent of their genes from their mother and 50 percent from their father. Siblings are also 50 percent related. Because sociobiology connects the amount of cooperation and conflict among individuals and groups to variation in degrees of relatedness, these figures predict conflict within the nuclear family. As relatedness decreases, conflict increases. The prediction holds amazingly well as weaning struggles, sibling rivalry, and ethnic cleansing demonstrate.

Some people think the accuracy of these predictions implies *genetic determinism.* Genetic determinism is the idea that genes control behavior. If genetic determinism is true, the doctrine of original sin is correct when it says we are in bondage. However, to think sociobiology supports the notion of genetic determinism is both to misunderstand the theory of evolution and to misconstrue how organisms work.

Because the theories of evolution and sociobiology are statistical theories, and statistical theories apply only to groups, the theories neither predict individual behavior nor suggest that genes control it. Moreover, genes by themselves govern nothing. Alone they determine neither physical development nor behavior. Rather, genes and environments work in tandem. This is so even for plants. The classic textbook example is the arrowleaf plant. When it grows on land, its leaves are broad, waxy, and rigid, its root system large. If it grows under water, its leaves are narrow, unwaxed, and flexible, its root system small (Ricklefs 1973, 59). For most plants, environmental illumination acts as a control for genes. Light governs form, height, leafiness, flowering, and fruiting (Moses and Chua 1988). Similar synergy between genes and environments occurs in animals. For example, diet in caterpillars influences their appearance. If they eat flowers, they resemble the flowers they eat; if they eat twigs, they resemble twigs (Greene 1989).

I mention in the last chapter the influence of environment on altruism. Many animals know their siblings because they recognize their nestlings, and they behave altruistically toward them. If non-siblings are nestlings, an animal will behave altruistically toward them as if they were siblings. Environment influences behavior that sociobiology seems to say is completely genetic. This is one reminder that scientific theories are about models, and that the models are far simpler than nature. Sociobiology studies the correlation between genetic relatedness and cooperation and therefore emphasizes genes, but it does not imply genetic determinism.

The opposite of genetic determinism is *environmental determinism*. Environmental determinism is the idea that environments totally determine behavior and that genes play no role. Environmental determinism would place us in bondage as much as would genetic determinism. Fortunately, environments and genes work synergistically. The statistical nature of the theories of evolution and sociobiology and the synergy between environments and genes allow maneuvering room for *freedom*.

Freedom is the ability to make choices between alternatives, choices that affect our lives and those of others. Augustine's definition differs from this, and both Protestantism and Catholicism follow Augustine. I argue in chapter 3 that Augustine's concept of freedom is self-contradictory because he defines both freedom and bondage as necessary obedience, and necessary obedience cannot be both freedom and bondage. I suggest that Christian theology needs a better definition of freedom. Basing freedom on the ability to choose follows common sense, Aristotle ([c. 320 B.C.E.] 1989, 48–58), modern theology (Hefner 1993, 179), and modern science (Goldsmith 1991, 95). It also connects us to nature by allowing other animals some degree of freedom. A brief look at the sorts of choices one species of bird makes will illustrate the freedom that synergy between genes and environments allows. The example is from Goldsmith (1991, 113–14).

Killdeer are birds that nest on the ground. When they have chicks, they defend their nests. If a fox approaches the nest, killdeer will leave it and act as if they have broken wings to entice the fox away from the nest. If the fox fails to notice, the birds will fly on two good wings to another location, then act crippled again. In contrast, when cows approach a nest and the danger is from an inadvertent hoof, the killdeer respond in a completely different manner. They stay near the nest and make themselves conspicuous. As Goldsmith notes, "This process of defending the nest requires the central nervous system of the bird to assess a stream of sensory information and generate a variety of behavioral responses. In short, the killdeer must make a number of decisions" (1991, 113). These decisions affect their lives, those of their chicks, and the lives of foxes and cows.

The birds are free because both genes and environments influence their behavior, allowing room for choice. Sociobiology suggests that birds have genes for altruism and defend their chicks. They also have genes for egocentricity and protect themselves. The pretense that they have broken wings is so typical of the species that it must be strongly influenced by genes. But without particular environments, the genetically influenced behaviors never occur. Broken-wing behavior occurs only in the presence of predators, whereas conspicuous displays happen only in the face of nonpredatory threats. Furthermore, the birds start and stop their behaviors appropriately. Given the situation they perceive, they decide within certain parameters what to do.

The killdeer's choices are real, but they are limited by the birds' limited capacities. If the killdeer had abilities such as complex long-term memories, consciousness, foresight, imagination, reason, symbolic language, and the ability to abstract and self-reflect, they might ponder their plight and decide to nest in trees above the threat of fox and cow. In trees, their young would face other hazards. Flightless, they might tumble from the nest. If the killdeer could foresee such an event, they might feel deeply the conflict between death by fox or death by fall and be torn between options. However, their freedom would not be as restricted as it is now. They would have more choices. They would be more like us.

Our greater capacities make us freer than killdeer. As the example indicates, our greater freedom comes at a cost. The cost is increased conflict. If we had only one option, we would never suffer from indecision or be angry with ourselves and others for making choices later discovered to have painful consequences. If we had only two options, we might choose the better at least half the time. But we have myriad options. Beset with enemies, we can fight or flee, but we can also call others to our aid, invent new weapons, practice deceit, pay tribute, offer our children as slaves, ask for a truce, participate in negotiations involving imaginative outcomes, engage a mediator, and/or build common institutions.

We do not lack freedom. Instead, we have more than we can handle. Often we long to be like the killdeer: if it is a fox, act crippled; if it is a cow, act conspicuous; if he is a playboy, play; if he is a steady provider, marry. Instead, we find the steady provider boring and marry the playboy. By exercising our freedom, we often increase the conflicts in our lives.

In the model built by the doctrines of original sin, conflict is a sign of bondage. In nature, conflict is a sign of freedom, with freer creatures being more conflicted. Freedom entails inner conflict because we must make choices. Freedom brings individuals into conflict because we can have different points of view, different values, and different goals. Freedom brings groups into conflict because it allows us to develop different cultures, increasing our sense of the distance between ourselves and others. Freedom brings spiritual conflicts, the ability to hate and reject God when our religion commands love and obedience.

In order to function effectively, we human beings with our great capacities and enhanced freedom need standards to help us make good choices, choices proven effective over time. Cultures provide standards. Every culture recognizes rules, rights, and obligations. Every culture distinguishes right from wrong and holds people responsible for their actions. Every culture applies sanctions when its rules are broken (Brown 1991, 138–39). In short, cultures provide us with *ethical rules,* systems of values. Ethical rules decrease our freedom. They make it manageable. They make our lives manageable.

As sociobiology correctly predicts, all cultures tell us which choices we should make in matters directly related to reproduction. Every culture has ethical rules regarding sexual modesty, marriage, and care of children. This is not to say that cultures have the same rules. Some cultures are monogamous, some polygamous, a few polyandrous. Some encourage prepubescent youth to experiment sexually; others discourage the same behavior. Most prohibit sexual liberty by wives; a few endorse it.

The different rules are not arbitrary. Some have an economic base, some a biological one, and some both. As we might anticipate, because rules governing sexual relations and childcare are central to reproduction, sociobiology almost always correctly predicts correlations among the rules. For example, in cultures where a man provides for his wife's children, he needs to be certain that her children are also his. In these cultures, wifely adultery is punished, often severely. In cultures endorsing sexual freedom for wives, a man cannot be certain that his wife's children are also his. In these cultures, a man does not provide for his wife's children but for those of his sisters, for his sisters' children are sure to be at least 25 percent related to him.

These examples demonstrate the falseness of genetic determinism while indicating some ways that biology and culture interact. If genetic determinism were true, all cultures would have the same rules, especially in areas close to biology and evolution. If genes had no influence on culture, sociobiology could neither correctly predict that all cultures have rules governing reproductive relationships nor correctly predict correlations among central rules. In matters closely related to evolution, genes influence culture without determining it. In areas far from biology, like mathematics and ballet, genetic influence on behavior weakens or ceases altogether.

Some individuals and subcultures resist even the siren call of resources and reproduction. Most monastic orders demand individual poverty and practice celibacy, rejecting individual possessions, sex, and reproduction. Some individuals and subcultures that are not monastic make similar choices. People stage hunger strikes or starve themselves to death for various causes. Even in matters deeply influenced by biology and evolution, genes do not dictate. They suggest, but we can say no.

Our freedom to make myriad choices is a precious gift. It provides much that makes us human. If we were not so free, we would not have elaborate and distinctive cultures. If we were not so free, we would never have become ethical creatures, for we would not have required rules other than those provided by the synergy of genes and environments to govern our behavior. If we were not so free, we would not be so inventive and creative.

Nonetheless, our extensive freedom has consequences many people decry. Because of our enormous freedom, we endure conflicts greater and more diverse than those other animals suffer, conflicts that often seem terrible to us. Due to our immense freedom and creativity, we invent innumerable ways to diminish our own welfare and that of others. Our extensive freedom is a source of sin.

Sin

The doctrines of original sin tell us about sin. Sin springs from *concupiscence.* In modern American usage, concupiscence is desire, especially strong desire. In Christian theology, concupiscence is the spontaneous desire for temporal goods (McBrien 1994, 187–91; *Catechism* 1994, 95–96; Cross 1958, 324). According to Orthodox and Catholic doctrine, concupiscence is natural, and it is neutral in regard to sin, being neither sinful nor good in itself. Only inordinate desires for temporal goods are sinful. Protestantism has a different view. It sees our desires themselves as sinful.

Sin is a theological term, and sociobiology cannot proffer a definition of it, but it paints a clear picture of our desire for temporal goods. We want them. If we are to survive and reproduce, we must want them. We must desire resources and reproduction because we are mortal. Without them we would die and our species would become extinct. Interestingly, Genesis 3 reveals a similar insight. Denied access to the tree of life, Adam and Eve must labor to live and beget children. For Adam and Eve not to desire temporal goods and labor for them would be simultaneously suicidal and genocidal.

For other human beings, too, not to desire temporal goods would be suicidal and genocidal. Because Christianity opposes suicide and genocide as sinful, it cannot view desires which save us from them as sinful without self-contradiction. Furthermore, Christianity claims that God is the giver and preserver of life. Without self-contradiction, Christianity cannot look upon our desires for the goods necessary to sustain life as sinful. On both these grounds, Orthodoxy and Catholicism are internally coherent, Protestantism incoherent. By the coherence test of truth, Protestantism must be wrong. Concupiscence itself cannot be sinful. When he claims it is, Augustine demonstrates "complete misunderstanding" of Genesis 3:1-6 (Westermann 1984, 249) and of the human situation. Concupiscence helps us survive and thrive, and a benevolent God must look favorably upon desires that help us do so.

Inordinate desires for temporal goods are a different matter, and sociobiology has something to say about them. Sociobiologists sometimes experiment by altering animals' natural world. Mary Midgley (1978, 262–63) relates some experiments reported by Niko Tinbergen, one of the founders of ethology (a precursor to sociobiology). My favorite is an experiment on birds called oyster catchers. The ethologists remove the birds' eggs from their nests and substitute larger and larger eggs. The birds choose to brood bigger and bigger eggs rather than eggs the appropriate size for their species. Finally, the birds sit brooding on huge artificial eggs, eggs bigger than the birds themselves. Thus, the ethologists demonstrate that natural selection does not supply the oyster catchers with a sense of proportionality. The birds have inordinate desires concerning egg brooding and have evolved no inhibitions to control them.

Midgley draws the moral. The oyster catcher is not the only species whose inordinate desires in artificial environments lack evolved controls. We stuff ourselves with sweets, swill alcohol, and gamble our homes away. The desires themselves are natural enough. A species whose ancestors' diet was rich in fruit inherited the desire for sweet tastes that led its ancestors to food, then steered them between the unripe and rotten; natural opiates in our brains help control pain; weighing and taking risks is part of daily life. But we live in a world far different from that of our ancestors, a world where candy racks line supermarket checkouts, liquor is available in the corner store, and gambling establishments dot the land.

There are three lessons here. First, genes and environments work in tandem. Our taste for sweets is genetic. In humanity's original environment of hunters and gatherers, it was an asset. In our present environment, it is a liability. We should equally blame our environment and our genes for our addiction to sweets—and we can control our environment.

Second, although natural selection provides no controls over desires that were helpful in our ancestors' environment, we know where following our inordinate desires leads because we possess reason and foresight. Usually we can control such desires rationally by rules. Wise people make rules for themselves about such temptations and obey them. We can either avoid places where liquor is served or we can make rules that prevent us from drinking too much, limiting ourselves to an amount our bodies can absorb. We can either avoid gambling or we can make rules that prevent us from losing too much, rules like quitting at a given loss or taking with us only what we can afford to lose.

Third, when dealing with inordinate desires, "know thyself" is an important precept. We may have similar desires, but they tempt us differently, and we find different rules work differently for each of us.

Attractions to sweets, alcohol, and gambling are natural desires without evolved controls. For desires our ancestors best used selectively, natural selection provides controls. Famous is brothers' and sisters' lack of sexual desire for each other. Experience in Israeli kibbutzim where unrelated children are reared together as if they were brothers and sisters has disclosed natural selection's strategy. Although encouraged to marry each other, children reared together rarely do so. Nor do they have extramarital sexual relations with each other. They simply do not find each other sexually attractive.

The normal pattern is for brothers and sisters to be reared together. When they are, they are not usually sexually attracted to each other. Natural selection has placed a barrier of childhood familiarity between brothers' and sisters' potential mutual sexual attraction. (For a more thorough review and answers to critics, see Brown 1991, 118–29).

Natural selection seems also to have selected people who have inhibitions against killing one another, for most people find killing other people repulsive. Notoriously, many soldiers deliberately trained to kill never fire their rifles in combat. Both westernized soldiers and tribal warriors suffer aversive psychological reactions to battle. Although successful warriors receive respect and high status, they also evoke repugnance. Tribal cultures believe killing contaminates warriors, and they must undergo ritual purification before rejoining their tribe. Furthermore, warriors typically do not attain the highest status in their society. Highest status falls on those skilled in the practices of peace (Keeley 1996, 144–46).

One sign of our freedom is that even where both nature and culture provide controls for inordinate desires, individuals can override the controls. Especially effective is brooding on a desire, nourishing it until it grows inordinate, then succumbing. Cultures sometimes do something similar. Midgley (1978, 264) mentions the ancient Chinese desire for small feet in females leading the Chinese to bind women's feet, crippling them, and the desire of some African tribes for copious mates leading some tribes to feed women until they are too obese to walk. Similarly, consumer capitalism tends to transmute our natural desire for resources into avarice.

Although sociobiology has no notion of sin, it helps clarify the theological concept. Natural desires in themselves cannot be sinful because they lead us to garner resources so we can live and reproduce, activities that help individuals thrive and our species survive. Only inordinate or inappropriate desires can be sinful. Inordinate and inappropriate desires spring from natural ones that become distended and distorted in various ways and for various reasons.

This insight from sociobiology appears to resemble the Orthodox and Catholic view of concupiscence that says spontaneous desires are natural and morally neutral; only inordinate desires are sinful. Historical Christianity has buttressed this view with the concept of natural law, claiming that natural laws are good because they are from God, and, therefore, to follow them is good, to break them, sinful.

Not only is this moralizing simplistic, science and sociobiology prove it false. First, the theory of evolution is not the only statistical theory in science. Almost all the laws of twentieth-century science are statistical, demonstrating that natural laws are typically statistical laws. Statistical laws apply only to groups, not to individuals. Therefore, to apply natural laws to individuals is usually to misuse the concept of natural law.

Second, various natural laws produce diverse results, some that Christianity judges good, some evil. For example, altruism is natural and law-like. It is good because it helps us rear our dependent children. It is evil because it leads us to advantage relatives unfairly, sometimes resulting in ethnocentricity, racism, and genocide.

Third, to follow natural laws sometimes means avoiding actions Christianity considers good and embracing those it calls sinful. Because human beings are sexually dimorphic, sociobiology predicts that we are naturally polygamous. The facts confirm this prediction. 93 percent of human societies allow some degree of polygamy and 70 percent approve and practice polygamous marriage (Clark 1998, 1047). Most societies that are legally monogamous and disallow polygamous marriage are polygamous in practice, the practices being concubinage and adultery. Both the theory of sociobiology and the facts of statistically normal practice lead to the conclusion that monogamy is unnatural. On the grounds that doing what is unnatural is sinful, monogamy is sinful.

But Christianity does not think monogamy sinful. Furthermore, monogamy cannot be sinful because monogamy helps people flourish. It distributes reproductive rights equally, allowing all to thrive reproductively. It tends to produce an egalitarian economy, helping all to thrive economically. And it breaks the ties of clan, thwarting nepotism and genocide.

Moreover, some people are naturally monogamous; that is, when they are attached to one partner, they spontaneously lose their sexual desire for other people. That individuals are sometimes naturally monogamous recalls the statistical nature of natural laws. Natural laws apply to groups, not to individuals. The fact that our species is naturally polygamous does not exclude the possibility that some individuals are naturally monogamous. Interestingly, monogamy and homosexuality are alike in these respects. Neither represents the norm, either theoretically or statistically. Yet some individuals spontaneously embrace one or the other or both.

I have now examined two central themes in the doctrines of original sin and two aspects of human nature, the concupiscence that helps us thrive and the freedom that helps make us human. Both are natural; both are good insofar as they help us flourish; yet both can be sources of sin. The third theme is different. It is love.

Love

Matthew (19:19; 22:39), Mark (12:31), Luke (10:27), and Paul (Rom. 13:8-9; Gal. 5:14) all comment that people who love their neighbors have fulfilled all the commandments. John calls loving one another a new commandment, and he clearly thinks it central to Jesus' message and life (John 13:34; 15:12, 17; 1 John 3:23; 2 John 5). Jesus' love is self-sacrificial (1 John 3:16), and ours should be the same (Rom 12:1). God is love (1 John 4:8, 16). Many sources and contexts in the New Testament say that Jesus called on us to love one another. The commendation of love must go back to the historical Jesus. Quoting Paul (1 Cor. 13:1) from the King James Version in chapter 8, I called this love by its theological name, *charity,* a usage I continue here. Charity is self-sacrificial behavior directed toward the benefit of others and motivated by concern for their welfare.

Sociobiology's nearest equivalent to charity is altruism, but altruism is silent about motives. Altruism refers only to behavior, only to activities by an organism that increase another's reproductive potential while decreasing its own. Altruistic behavior occurs repeatedly in nature, but almost exclusively among close kin.

In chapter 8, I argue that charitable motives may underlie our evolved altruism because natural selection is likely to have given us charitable motives to make us behave altruistically. If we have charitable motives, the laws and commandments of God are not essentially concerned with external behavior, but with fostering an inner attitude that is already part of our nature, fulfilling Deuteronomy 30:11, 14, "Surely, this commandment that I am commanding you today is not too hard for you, nor is it too far away. . . . No, the word is very near to you; it is in your mouth and in your heart for you to observe." Nonetheless, to get from altruism to charity as Christianity understands it is more difficult than the quotation from Deuteronomy and my explanation imply because Christian charity extends to all, not merely to close kin.

The Gospels make this vividly clear. When Jesus is asked to name the greatest commandment, Matthew (22:34-40) has him reply that we are to love God and neighbor. When asked who should be considered a neighbor, Luke (10:25-37) has Jesus respond with a narrative relating how two pious Jews ignore a man who has been robbed and beaten, whereas a Samaritan helps him. The story conveys a powerful message because Jesus and his listeners are Jews, and Jews despised Samaritans as people who are ethnically and religiously impure. Charity, the love Jesus commended, is to extend beyond racial and cultural kinship. Jesus' practice of keeping open table fellowship (Borg 1994b, 55–56; Crossan 1991, 263) in a culture where exclusive meals were the rule carries the same message.

Altruism is not charity because altruism is nepotistic and ethnic. Reciprocity is not charity because reciprocity is egocentric. Perhaps the doctrines of original sin are correct when they claim that human nature lacks charity.

For both theological and sociobiological reasons, I think the view that our nature lacks charity is too strong. The theological reason rests on Christological doctrine. As I mention in chapter 1, the Council of Chalcedon clarified questions about the personhood of Jesus Christ. It asserted that he has two natures, divine and human, but he is nonetheless one person, a single, integrated individual. Jesus remains fully human while being fully God, so there must be some connection between his nature and God's. It cannot be a substantial connection because humanity and God are different substances. The connection must lie in attributes, and because, according to 1 John 4:8, 16, God's primary attribute is charity, humanity must at least have some capacity for charity.

The sociobiological reason for thinking our nature has some capacity for charity is the existence of altruism. We already behave self-sacrificially for the benefit of our close kin. Our reason and symbolic language force us to extend our altruism to those in our group who are not close kin. As Peter Singer (1981, 87–124) argues at length, we must give reasons that satisfy everyone in our group. "I'm the best" or "she's my sister" are rarely reasons a group finds adequate for someone, or someone and her sister, to take all the beans. Eventually, Singer argues, reason leads us beyond the circle of kin, clan, and immediate group to charity toward all.

Moreover, the natural reciprocity that binds us to those who are not our kin supplements our altruism. Reciprocity is egalitarian. In reciprocal exchanges, each person's interests must be treated equally or the exchange falls apart. People who engage in reciprocal exchanges will perceive the other party's altruism as nepotism, the unfair favoring of relatives. Eventually, they must see their own altruistic behavior in the same light.

As I suggested in chapter 8, once we see the need for charity to non-kin, we inculcate it by manipulating symbols, referring to others who are not close kin as brothers, sisters, and parents. The New Testament is replete with the symbolic language of blood relationship. If we believe the language, it has power to transform.

One other capacity may underlie our charity—erotic love (Collier and Stingl 1993). Erotic love is not the same as *agape*. In Greek, it is *eros*. Erotic love can be lustful, egocentric, and jealous. It is not charity. Yet, like reciprocity, it brings into relationship two people who are not close kin. Moreover, at its best it is not egocentric but self-sacrificial, caring deeply for the beloved's welfare.

Supplemented by reason, reciprocity, symbolic language, and erotic love, altruism provides a natural capacity for charity, and actual charity may arise by naturalistic means. On the other hand, our charity is not natural in the sense altruism is. Nepotism must be fought, charity nurtured.

Samuel and Pearl Oliner (1988) demonstrate the existence in us of charity in its fullest sense. They show that rescuers of Jews in Nazi-occupied Europe fed and hid nonrelatives who were often aliens and strangers without hope or expectation of reward, frequently at considerable cost and risk to themselves and their relatives. The rescuers behaved like the Samaritan Jesus told about.

The Oliners offer diverse naturalistic explanations for the charity of the rescuers, then mention a common pattern of upbringing. Parents of the rescuers encouraged their children to give without expectation of reward and reasoned with them about their behavior.

Christian doctrine holds that God is *immanent*, existing in all things, and both the Orthodox and Catholic doctrines of original sin include the idea that nature is graced. Perhaps this kind of upbringing and its charitable results are examples of God's grace working through our nature. Perhaps the evolution of altruism and reciprocity are examples of God's grace permeating the natural world. There is no proof that this is so, but the natural existence of altruism, reason, reciprocity, and freedom appear to reflect God's wisdom and benevolence, not anger or punishment.

Punishment

All three doctrines of original sin hold that our present human nature is God's punishment for Adam and Eve's transgression. In their emphasis on punishment, the doctrines correspond closely with the text of Genesis 3. Having learned of the disobedience of the miscreant pair, God curses the ground so Adam must labor for his food until he dies. God curses the woman with increased pain in childbearing, yet with desire for her husband so she will bear his children and be subordinate to him. Finally, God removes Adam and Eve from the vicinity of the tree of life, confirming their mortality. Whether their mortality is one of the curses is ambiguous in the text. Returning to dust is Adam's curse, not Eve's, and even after cursing them, God still must remove Adam and Eve from the vicinity of the tree of life lest they become immortal like the gods. The clear curses are conflict, sexual desire, sexual inequality, and the need to work. Although not made explicit in the text, the egocentricity that makes the curses efficacious is an abiding part of the tradition.

The curses in Genesis 3 explain aspects of human life that sometimes feel cursed. However, the explanation is false and the feeling deceptive. The needs of sexually-reproducing, diploid organisms and the results of natural selection better explain such aspects of life. After all, this is how nature works. All organisms struggle for resources; all sexual organisms seek to reproduce, and all die; almost all diploid organisms have conflict. Nature began working this way since organisms came into existence more than 3 billion years before we evolved. Rather than being set apart as cursed, we are part of nature.

Furthermore, these aspects of our natural life may be blessings. Our penchant for conflict shows us to be the freest organisms on Earth. The fulfillment of sexual desire is one of our greatest pleasures. Sex meets our deep needs for intimacy and bonds people who are not kin. Work provides satisfaction as we accomplish our goals and, if we have chosen well, is an outlet for our creativity. It gives our lives stability and meaning.

Sexual inequality results from sexual dimorphism. Our ancestors were more sexually dimorphic than we and probably lacked male bonding and nuclear families. Our reduced sexual dimorphism allows for both. It provides a natural division of labor and therefore natural exchange between men and women, strengthening bonds. The fact that on average men are bigger and stronger than women means that they can give women the help women need to rear dependent children. There is no reason to assume that the small degree of sexual dimorphism in human beings entails male brutality.

Pain in human childbearing results from one of evolution's most famous compromises. In chapter 8, I mention that our infants are exceedingly dependent compared to the offspring of other primates. Their gestation period should be about ten months longer than it is, but later parturition would be lethal because the infant's head would be too large to pass through the mother's birth canal. The perfect answer seems to be bigger birth canals, but bigger birth canals would compromise our bipedal gait. Evolution's solution was a shortened gestation period, but not so short that it is fatal to the neonate. One result of the compromise is pain in childbirth. Another is the coalescence in us of efficient bipedalism and high intelligence.

In chapter 8, I comment on the advantages of egocentricity. Among other things, it helps us consider our own interests and thrive. Famous in the annals of psychology is the case of Phineas Gage, once an engaging and responsible man, who accidentally had a railroad spike driven through his frontal lobes. He survived, apparently mentally intact except that his decisions no longer seemed to take his best interests into account. After his wound healed, he drifted from job to job and place to place, dying years later down and out in San Francisco. (For this and other cases of the sad results of inability to correctly judge self-interest, see Damasio 1994.)

Christians should hardly view death as a curse, for Christianity views it as the gateway to a new and better life. Moreover, it is necessary from an evolutionary and ecological point of view. Without it, species could not evolve and Earth would be swiftly overrun with living organisms. Furthermore, it saves us from undergoing increasingly awful decrepitude with advancing age. Death, too, may be more blessing than curse.

The aspects of human life Genesis 3 presents as cursed are natural aspects of our evolutionary and primate heritage. They may be construed as blessings. They are not punishments for sin. With this realization, gone is the punitive God of Genesis 3 whose inexplicable ferocity has prompted such diverse and curious interpretations.

At the beginning of this book, I promise to retain six classical Christian doctrines. Among those retained, I list God's attributes of omniscience, omnipotence, omnibenevolence, and creativity. In ridding Christian theology of the punitive God of Genesis 3 and Noah's flood, this book supports God's benevolence. The vicious God who punishes people incommensurately, who castigates childishness and drowns creatures to no purpose, never existed. In presenting the diversity of life and the ingenuity of natural selection, this book defends God's creativity. From the Big Bang to the elements necessary for life to the evolution of humanity, the world is integrated and orderly. That human reason is capable of discovering the laws that integrate and order it may be a positive sign of God's benevolence and creativity.

This chapter is the culmination of the previous chapters of this book. It views human nature through the lens of evolution, focusing on four concerns central to Christianity in general and the doctrines of original sin in particular. The solutions to these concerns are salutary for Christian theology.

Freedom. We are remarkably free, far freer than any other animals on Earth, a liberty manifested in our proficiency with symbols, our creativity, and our diverse cultures. Our lives are guided and often circumscribed by our evolutionary inclinations to pursue resources and reproduction, but even those strong dispositions do not determine our actions.

Sin. We sin because we have natural, evolutionarily necessary desires that may become inordinate, especially in environments different from that in which our ancestors evolved. We sin greatly because we have great gifts, a matter pursued further in the next chapter.

Charity. Charity is not natural to us, although it can arise in us by naturalistic means. Natural to us are our sociality and altruism. These potential sources of charity may be supplemented by our reason, reciprocity, symbolic language, and erotic love. Charity is rooted in these natural abilities and inclinations, but to reach fruition, it must be nurtured.

Punishment. We do not suffer because God is punishing Adam and Eve's sin in us. Adam and Eve were never historical people, merely symbolic figures in a symbolic narrative. Moreover, Christian theology asserts that God is benevolent, not vindictive. Most aspects of human life that Genesis 2 and 3 presents as cursed may equally be construed as blessings.

These are evolution's resolutions of four concerns central to the doctrines of original sin. The resolutions have interesting consequences for the philosophical problem of evil.

Chapter 10

The Problem of Evil

The problem of evil asks why evil exists. The existence of evil is a problem for Christianity because Christianity considers God omnipotent, omniscient, omnibenevolent, and the creator of everything. Logically, a universe formed by such a God should contain no evil, for such a God is utterly good and has both the power and the knowledge to create a perfectly good universe. However, when we examine our lives, we conclude that they contain evil because our lives seem filled with undeserved suffering.

This chapter addresses the problem of evil because chapters 3, 4, and 5 negate Christianity's traditional solution to it, that evil came into the world with Adam and Eve's sin. Much of the answer given here relies on cosmology, sociobiology, and history. Such evidence is relevant because Christianity considers God the creator of the universe. Logic as well as ancient Christian tradition hold that the universe reflects its creator's plans and values. Moreover, we derive our knowledge of evil from our examination of the universe, especially our own place in it. Therefore, this chapter opens with *cosmology*. Cosmology studies the origin, processes, and structure of the universe. Contemporary cosmology reveals an expanding and developing universe.

A Developing Universe

The cosmology presented here is the standard model from contemporary science. Although it is a highly mathematized model, many books explain it without equations. A clear, interesting presentation is Joseph Silk, *The Big Bang* (1989). The figures I cite and my emphasis on structure and variety in the universe are from Lee Smolin (1997).

The Big Bang is Fred Hoyle's somewhat facetious but descriptive name for a model of the universe that begins in an unimaginably hot and powerful explosion. At that explosion, the basic matter-plus-law of the universe comes into being. The matter-plus-law is very peculiar, so to avoid confusion I will use *stuff* as a technical term in place of *matter*. The stuff is not like anything else we know; it is unimaginable; the law appears inseparable from it.

I emphasize that the stuff is unimaginable because most people taught high school chemistry are familiar with an imaginable model of matter as tiny, round, hard, separable bits of something-or-other, but the stuff is not at all like that. It is best described as fuzzy or foggy because we cannot locate it and tell its velocity at the same time, as we can for the things we use every day. Sometimes it acts like a wave, at other times, a particle. No single thing in our daily lives behaves in both these ways. The seemingly separate fuzzy fogs are mysteriously connected to each other so that one reacts to the state of another even when they are widely separated. Again, things in daily life never behave like this.

Furthermore, the law—usually considered immaterial—came into being with the stuff, and although cosmologists can separate the law from the stuff conceptually, the law may not exist apart from the stuff, except in cosmologists' heads and computers. At this original, fundamental level of existence, the classical distinction between material and immaterial may be meaningless.

The first stuff makes its appearance as radiation, then as electrons, protons, neutrons, and neutrinos. Each electron is alike, each proton like other protons, each neutron like the others, and neutrinos come in only a few varieties. At this early time in the developing universe, one law rules all. Movement is chaotic. The early universe has little variety and almost no structure.

This universe expands, cools, and becomes less dense. As it changes, the single law, which physicists have not completely reconstructed, splinters into four laws known to physics. Three make possible the chemical elements. They are the weak and strong nuclear forces and electromagnetism. At this point in the developing universe, electrons, protons, and neutrons interact, forming the lightest chemical elements, hydrogen and helium, today the most abundant elements in the universe. Movement begins to obey the fourth law, gravity, which is very weak but all-pervasive. These four laws are today the fundamental laws of the universe. Through the splintering of the law and the interactions of fundamental stuff, the universe develops more variety and structure.

Although weak, gravity pulls everything in the universe toward every other thing. As it tugs, the universe becomes a little clumpy, a little less uniform. Eventually, gravity nudges the clumps into galaxies and stars. Structure and variety in the universe escalate beyond imagination. Today, astronomers estimate that the universe has 100 billion galaxies, each about 100 thousand light years across, with more than 100 billion stars per galaxy. Although each galaxy and star is unique, astronomers are able to classify them according to their similarities. They find more than twenty-five types of galaxies and more than one hundred types of stars. After galaxies and stars form, the universe contains stupendous structure and variety.

Stars burn hydrogen and helium and explode to generate the other natural chemical elements, almost a hundred of them. The presence of new elements once more increases structure and variety in the universe. Because the elements can combine with one another, the potential for increased variety and structure accelerates. Exploding stars spew the new elements into the gaseous medium between the stars where gravity pulls the material into more clumps to form various structured arrays like our solar system, some containing planets like our Earth. By peculiar and intricate physical and chemical causes, stars create enormous amounts of carbon. Thus, stars create the amounts of carbon plus the nitrogen, oxygen, and trace elements necessary for life. Life is stardust. Our lives depend on the lives and deaths of stars.

For the universe to contain the chemical elements necessary for life and to be large enough and cool enough for planetary systems to form, it has to develop over 12 billion years. For life to exist, some twenty separate parameters must be exact, parameters like those of the nuclear forces, the charge on the electron, the masses of the proton, neutron, electron, and neutrino, and the range and force of gravity. The expansion speed of the universe and the density of matter that gravity pulls inward must be balanced to a precision of at least sixty decimal places. If these numbers were chosen randomly, the chance the universe would contain stars is 1 followed by 229 zeros. Rather than arising randomly, the parameters appear to have been selected by design.

In chapter 7, I discuss William Paley's argument for the existence of God from the apparent design of organisms. Paley says there are only two possibilities. Either random forces create organisms or they are designed. Because they are so intricate and complex, random forces could not have created them, therefore they must be designed. I show how Darwin's theory of natural selection offers a third choice and wrecks Paley's argument.

As far as we know, only one universe exists. Natural selection cannot operate on single things, so no Darwinian mechanism destroys cosmological arguments analogous to Paley's. The contemporary cosmological argument for the existence of God based on parameters like those listed above is called the *anthropic principle*. The classic work is John D. Barrow and Frank J. Tipler (1986). Shorter but less well organized is M. A. Correy (1993). Explanations other than design for the existence of the exact, unrelated parameters of the standard model have been proposed, including a modified form of natural selection requiring more than one universe, and the existence of an infinity of universes. Neither is impossible. An infinity of universes is one of the many interpretations of quantum theory. However, neither is testable, so, by a very common theory of science, not scientific. Because this book assumes God exists, we need not enter the fray.

Physical and chemical processes in Earth's atmosphere, ocean, and crust allow the first self-replicating entities to appear on Earth. Their appearance marks a new stage in the escalation of structure and variety in the universe. Driven by the fracturing of the tectonic plate, rising mountains, shifting oceans, vulcanism, climate change, the march of seasons, and competition, life on Earth evolves into five kingdoms (bacteria, protoctista like algae, fungi, plants, and animals), today estimated to contain as many as 50 million to 100 million separate species. Since biologists estimate that 99 percent of species once alive are now extinct, an unimaginable number of species has existed. Evolution continues to create more.

With the evolution of *Homo sapiens,* cultures proliferate, adding yet another means for the development of structure and variety in the universe. During a single century, anthropologists have studied and catalogued more than one thousand living cultures, and we know many have disappeared. Cultures develop everywhere people walk on Earth, all different, each varying over time. Each has its own structure, laws, and mores. Given the number of stars and the suitability of a carbon-rich universe for life, other planets probably have evolved living forms, and some may have produced cultures of their own.

This brief tour of the developing universe tells us at least two things about its creator. First, the creator seems to rejoice in development and the accelerating increase of variety and structure. In the universe, structure and variety escalate unimaginably over time and exist at many different levels, from atomic to galactic, from cellular to cultural.

Second, the creator seems to enjoy creating structures that are increasingly *autonomous.* Autonomous means self-ruled, governed by law. The developing physical and chemical universe seems to be inherent in the original stuff-plus-law, autonomous from God's transcendent intervention. Once it begins, God does not have to step in from outside to push, pull, and rearrange it. The expansion and the fundamental forces do these things without further guidance. The physical and chemical universe unfolds like a well-plotted novel. The autonomy of the universe explains why science has so successfully explored the universe without resort to a creator as an explanation of events.

With the beginning of life and the advent of the new law of natural selection, autonomy increases. Although natural selection must be consistent with the laws of physics and chemistry, it is not predictable from them, and it introduces an element of randomness above the level of the atom where randomness had not previously existed.

The evolution of human beings again increases autonomy in the universe. For the first time, entities in the universe create laws deliberately. Moreover, and again for the first time, some of the laws conflict with underlying ones; that is, some of the laws we create are inconsistent with the dispositions formed by natural selection. Furthermore, each human culture develops its own laws, its own ways of ruling itself. Using our autonomy, we add structure and variety to the universe.

The anthropic principle appears to offer a third insight into the plans of the creator, but this appearance is misleading. The strongest interpretation of the anthropic principle says God designed the universe to produce human life (*anthropos* is Greek for human). This chapter contradicts this interpretation. It notes that the universe has a vast quantity of stars likely to have other planets where other forms of life and intelligence evolve. God rejoices in variety, structure, and autonomy, and additional intelligent life would increase all three. The universe does not seem to be designed exclusively for our particular form of life.

Moreover, the universe is still developing. Our evolution is not the triumphant culmination of 12 billion years of cosmological expectancy. According to every viable cosmological theory, the universe will expand into the future for many billions of years, and our planet will be extinguished in the process.

Furthermore, cosmology suggests that God did not directly design the universe for life. Rather, God designed it to increase in variety, structure, and autonomy. Long before the beginning of life, all three increased enormously. The evolution of life and of our own species merely adds new levels of variety, structure, and autonomy to the universe. Apparently, we are an important part of God's plan, but not its goal.

This tour of the developing universe carries a final, portentous message. The classical philosophical distinction between material and immaterial may be crumbling. Four different areas of inquiry testify to this breakdown. First, cosmology indicates that immaterial law may be inseparable from the material universe. Second, quantum physics demonstrates that the stuff of the universe is not similar to classical material objects like rocks and trees. To refer to the stuff as *material* represents a lexical error stemming from a conceptual hangover. Third, in an area of science not covered in this book, neuropsychology suggests that immaterial mind and material brain are intimately related. Fourth, Christianity asserts that an immaterial God created the material universe, then became material flesh. Material and immaterial are strangely interrelated. Perhaps they are inseparable. Perhaps, like matter and energy, they are interchangeable. Perhaps they are different aspects of the same thing.

So far, I have tried to look at the developing universe as a whole. The discussion shows that, although we are not the culmination of the development of the universe, we are an important part of the creator's plan. In order to understand that plan more fully, it will be helpful to try locating ourselves in it more exactly.

Locating Ourselves

While God could have created many different universes, God chose to create one that increasingly develops variety, structure, and autonomy. Our evolution fits well into this plan because we bring additional structure, variety, and autonomy to the universe through at least five evolutionary innovations, innovations new in degree if not always in kind.

First is symbolic language. I mention in chapter 7 that symbolic language is probably our only unique contribution to evolution. Being varied and structured, symbolic language adds to the variety and structure of the universe. As a highly developed form of communication, it enhances our autonomy. Moreover, its evolution lays the foundation for the other four innovations.

Our second innovation is the self and, with it, the ability to self-reflect. The psychological self is a new type of existence in the universe. Work with living chimpanzees suggests that a sense of self probably began evolving in our ape or australopithecine ancestors, but the self seems to develop fully only in us. Since each self is different, the advent of the self increases variety. Each self is also structured, so structure increases. A sense of self and the ability to self-reflect help us achieve autonomy from our evolved dispositions, from others, and from our cultures. The existence of self and self-reflection lay the foundation for our third innovation, the ability to be moral creatures.

Of all species on Earth, ours seems to be the only one whose members are capable of reflecting on our own experiences, desires, and choices, evaluating them, codifying them, and altering our own behavior in accord with our reflective judgments. In other words, we are probably the only species whose members make fully developed moral decisions and follow moral rules.

Nonetheless, our moral capacities arise from our ancestors' social nature, as Darwin notes. "The following proposition seems to me in a high degree probable—namely, that any animal whatever, endowed with well-marked social instincts, would inevitably acquire a moral sense or conscience, as soon as its intellectual powers had become as well developed, or nearly as well developed, as in man" ([1871] 1981, 71–72).

With their intricate social lives, living apes have rudimentary moral dispositions. They show sympathy through their attachments and special treatment of the disabled. They regulate their social lives. They demonstrate reciprocity and moralistic aggression. They get along with others as they avoid conflict, negotiate, and actively make peace (de Waal 1996, 211). Because living apes have these dispositions, our primate ancestors probably had them as well.

Other living apes eat mostly vegetables and fruit. Despite having canine fighting teeth, they are not primarily predators and are often prey. Ancestral *Homo* lost their canines. Our ancestors must have been even less predatory and suffered more predation than living apes.

Barbara Ehrenreich argues that we are the only animals who have been both primarily prey and primarily predators, and that the transition comes with the invention of effective hunting tools (Ehrenreich 1997). She maintains that we retain our ancestral fear of being prey and, therefore, we have a deeply ingrained understanding of what it is like to be victims.

Her argument provides further insight into the evolution of our morality. Predators do not see suffering; they see meat. Victims see suffering. The empathetic, moral point of view is the victim's (Baumeister 1997, 1–2). The fear of victimization that haunted us when we were primarily prey may remain with us, enhancing our moral imagination and ability to empathize.

Furthermore, evil is largely a victim's problem. When we see ourselves as victims of evil, we ask, why us? Then, why evil? Had we always been predators, we might find it difficult to cross Baumeister's magnitude gap between the perpetrator's point of view and that of the victim and develop empathy for the victim's suffering. We might never have tried to solve the problem of evil.

Morality develops naturally. It arises from our ancestral heritage and our efforts to live together, not through an externally imposed set of rules. With our evolution, a remarkable capacity for morality enters the universe. Like God, we know good from evil. As God creates a moral universe, so do we.

Our fourth innovation is culture. Theologian Philip Hefner describes the evolution of cultural creatures as "a new stage of freedom" (Hefner 1993, 32). This is an apt description, but I need to add, "and autonomy," because I have used *freedom* to mean freedom of choice and *autonomy* to mean ruled by law. The evolution of culture marks new stages of both. Our cultures give us more choices than any other creatures, choices among such items as clothes, coiffures, cuisines, careers, and crimes. We structure cultures through the implicit and explicit laws we make. Moreover, our laws increase our autonomy because they help free us from servitude to immediate desires and from some of the dispositions of our evolved nature. With culture, new kinds of structure, variety, and autonomy enter the universe.

Hefner goes further. His central theme is that God creates us to be cocreators (Hefner 1993, 27). Although his arguments are different from mine, we come to the same conclusion. My argument is that God wants increasing structure, variety, and autonomy in the universe. As we create cultures, we construct new kinds of structure, variety, and autonomy. More importantly, for the first time in the universe, creatures exist who exercise autonomy similar to God's. We, like God, deliberately make laws, and our laws enhance structure, variety, and autonomy in the universe. As Scripture says, God made us in the divine image (Genesis 1:27). We, too, are creators.

My perspective and Hefner's together form a consilience that helps us locate our place in the universe. I have suggested that we are part of God's plan but not the goal, which is the increase of variety, structure, and autonomy. Because we ourselves bring increased variety, structure, and autonomy to the universe, we have an important role in it. Hefner makes our role explicit. It is to be cocreators with God.

If, as Christianity has thought, we are the goal or purpose of creation, we ourselves are left without a role, a goal, or a purpose in it, for we are its purpose and culmination. There is nothing left for us to do. The usual Christian answer to this conundrum is that we are here to serve God or to glorify God. But when asked why God, an all-sufficient being, needs our service or why God who is all glory needs glorification, no one can answer. In truth, under this scenario we have nothing worthwhile to do. On the other hand, if we are not the universe's goal, then we can be its workers, furthering God's purpose. And if God's purpose is increasing variety, structure, and autonomy in the universe, we fulfill that purpose naturally, by doing the things we do best. This looks like a remarkably good plan, one a benevolent and omniscient creator might have had.

The fifth innovation we bring to the universe is the ability to envision a future for ourselves. This is a concomitant of our symbolic language, sense of self, culture, and morality. It brings with it the possibility of envisioning a future self and working to bring it about, thus enabling us deliberately to develop our own selves or characters.

Another way to locate ourselves is to say that we are the only creatures on Earth who have individual biographies and collective histories. The physical and chemical universe has a history that unfolds according to the original laws and parameters given it. Life has a history because of the law of natural selection. But human beings have a history because we create it ourselves, almost as God does. We also create our own biographies through our activities, relationships, goals, moral decisions, and self-reflection. For other animals, survival and reproduction seem to be ends; for us, they are means. Our biological lives have an instrumental quality. They support our biographies. As James Rachels, one of the most interesting contemporary moral philosophers, notes, "being alive [biologically] is important to an individual because it enables him or her to have a [biographical] life" (Rachels 1991, 199).

In summary, our evolution brings new freedom and autonomy to the universe and a new kind of creativity. We are cocreators with God. All seems well until we remember the evil in our lives. In order to solve the problem it raises, we need to locate evil accurately.

Locating Evil

Chapter 3 notes that the Gnostics believed in a supreme, good God, but they thought an evil god created the material universe. Thus, they located evil in a second divine being and solved the problem of evil through polytheism. Polytheism is one of the traditional solutions to the problem of evil, a solution that places the blame for evil on a divine opponent of God.

By locating evil in Satan and emphasizing Satan as God's opponent, Christianity has flirted with this solution, too. However, the monotheism of orthodox Christianity seems to disallow such a solution, a position too complex to argue for here. In any case, this book need not invoke a separate, divine force to solve the problem of evil, for this chapter eliminates the reason for such an explanation.

However, there is a need to understand what evil is. Traditional philosophy has defined it from the point of view of the victim, thinking of evil as undeserved suffering. Evil is what happens to us; it is not something we do. Christian theology has blamed Adam and Eve for the existence of evil and made all suffering deserved. This took care of the problem.

Philosophers who have not invoked Adam and Eve have listed two causes of evil: *natural evils*, resulting from events like storms and earthquakes, and *moral evils*, caused by human beings. I believe that this book has shown the division to be mistaken. Because human beings and our morality are part of nature, all evils are natural. Philosophers have enumerated four basic evils. They are pain, disease, death, and natural disasters. While imperfect, this list provides a good place to start locating evil. I begin with death.

Our tour of the universe has shown death to be pervasive. Everything in the universe dies except the stuff. The original law splinters, chemical bonds break, molecules fragment, stars explode, species become extinct, organisms expire, and cultures perish. If death is evil, creation is evil.

But our tour has disclosed the value of death. God created a developing universe and death makes development possible, for death feeds the formation of variety, structure, and autonomy. When stars burn, explode, and die, the heavy elements are born and distributed, feeding life. When the first living organisms die, they make room for more complex ones and begin the process of natural selection. When organisms die, new life feeds on them. When we die, our bodies are recycled. The death of the old creates material for the new. In a developing universe, death is part of God's plan.

The eighteenth-century essayist and poet Jonathan Swift satirizes our longing for an end to death. In Part III of *Gulliver's Travels* ([1726] 1970, 181–84), he describes the region of Luggnagg where the Struldbruggs dwell. Unlike other Luggnaggians, the Struldbruggs are immortal. As they consider their immortality, they become increasingly depressed. Theirs is a future to dread. They grow older, more feeble, and diseased. Their mental faculties fail. Their families and friends die, and others in the region shun them. Luggnaggian culture changes, and they cannot keep up. The language shifts, but their language does not. They become more and more isolated. The other inhabitants of Luggnagg hate and despise the Struldbruggs, thinking of them as peculiarly cursed. Their immortality is a fate worse than death.

Swift makes us realize that, if we cannot have perpetual youth among others like ourselves, death is a blessing. Christianity, too, sees our death as a blessing, but for it, death offers greater benefits than mere release from isolation and suffering. In Christianity, death is the gateway to a new life, a life to be lived forever with the one whom the Christian loves most, Jesus Christ. For Christianity, death is betrothal portending eternal union. From all these perspectives, death is beneficent, not evil.

Yet, we see human death as evil and rightly condemn murder as sin. Death is evil for us because of our unique capacities. Unlike other creatures, we build selves, but death destroys what we have built, or might have built. We create our own biographies, with death as termination. We envision a future for ourselves, but death ends all our plans and hopes. Furthermore, the death of individuals means a loss to culture, morality, and history, to the structure, variety, and autonomy the dead might have added to the universe. For these reasons, killing unwilling people is murder, sinful except perhaps in self-defense and just wars.

Death is not an evil for other organisms because they do not have biographies or collectively make history and culture. Moreover, early death is one of the necessary steps in natural selection, the force in organic evolution adding variety and structure to the universe. For these reasons, killing other animals is not murder, although there are situations that make it wrong.

Furthermore, Swift vividly demonstrates that the death of human beings who are old and suffering is not a great evil. Their characters have grown and matured; they have contributed to culture, morality, and history; they are suffering, and in their suffering, they have ceased to make plans for the future. When pneumonia was lethal to the elderly, it was called the old person's friend, a saying that captures a common view. At the end of life, death is minimally evil and may represent a positive good. Because it saves us from suffering, premature death brings good as well as harm. In the vast universe, human death is a small evil. Nonetheless, in a discussion of the problem of evil, it must be justified.

Disease is the second evil on the list, but disease is not evil. Other living organisms cause most diseases, perhaps all. From a disease organism's perspective, its host provides food, shelter, and a place to reproduce. Hosts are necessary for them just as shelter and sustenance are for us. God creates structure and variety; disease-causing organisms add both to the universe.

Although there are indications that bacteria or viruses play a role in cancer, cancer is mostly a change in genes that control the systems causing cells to die, and so cells proliferate. Since cancer changes the systems that cause cells to die, then either we do not have cancer but our cells die and our bodies with them, or our cells proliferate and we die with cancer. In either case, death is the outcome, so it is difficult to ascertain exactly where the evil lies, except in death.

Moreover, inexact gene replication is a necessary part of our biology. If genes always replicated exactly, evolution could not have occurred and we would not be here. Inexact replication is part of God's plan for increasing variety, structure, and autonomy in the universe.

In the final analysis, we consider diseases evil not because they are bad in themselves, but because they cause pain and death. I have already shown that death is largely good. The same is true of pain.

Pain is necessary for mobile creatures because it warns of bodily injury and teaches avoidance of harmful situations. People born lacking the capacity for pain illustrate pain's importance. They damage their joints and ligaments by bending their limbs too far. They bleed from cuts and scrapes of which they are unaware. They burn their flesh terribly because pain does not warn them of their danger. Most die by age thirty (Sober and Wilson 1998, 316). Absence of pain is harmful.

Mobile creatures are sometimes subject to pain unnecessarily. Predators play with prey as cats do with mice, and many predators eat their prey without first killing them. We sometimes inflict unnecessary pain on other animals. Unfortunately, in a book primarily about human nature, I cannot treat the problem of animal pain in depth. A few remarks must suffice.

Two solutions to the problem of unnecessary animal pain are common. The first solution is that animal pain may not be an evil because the analyses of evil may have mistaken pain for suffering. Suffering entails a psychological component involving the self. *I* feel that pain is awful because *I* suffer when my leg is in pain. We have no way to know how pain feels to other animals, but because they lack selves, it does not entail suffering. Certain human experiences with drugs suggest that a person can feel pain but remain unbothered by it because, somehow, it does not hurt. I have had the experience myself. This experience is not directly analogous to animal pain because pain clearly bothers them. It would not do its protective job if it did not. Nonetheless, the drug experience suggests that pain can be experienced apart from suffering.

The second solution is that the problem of unnecessary animal pain is not a problem for animals because animals neither know that their pain is unnecessary nor that it raises existential questions. In other words, the problem may be a pseudo-problem because it does not afflict the victims. Although helpful, neither of these solutions to the problem of unnecessary animal pain is adequate. Moreover, even if pain is necessary, it hurts. Although animals would not live long without pain, while alive, they would feel better without it. It appears that both animal pain and human suffering must be accounted for if the problem of evil is to be solved.

Natural disasters like earthquakes and volcanoes are disasters from our point of view because they cause suffering and death. Many people see climate change and its concomitant ecological shifts as equally disastrous. However, earthquakes and volcanoes occur partly because Earth's original plate fractured and the separate plates began to move around, running into each other to build mountains and spreading apart to sink ocean trenches. Climatic and ecological change in Africa that destroyed the forests 5 to 6 million years ago also created the savannas on which bipedal apes evolved. Natural events like these drive evolution. They are a necessary part of a universe designed to increase structure, variety, and autonomy. Without them, we would not be here.

I have discussed the four basic evils as natural evils, although clearly any of them can be caused by human beings—one reason the traditional distinction between natural and moral evil is inadequate and confusing. Moral evil differs from natural evil because it invokes human agents, but the point of view remains the victim's. This leaves one of the most pressing questions about evil unanswered, the question of why we do evil or have the potential to do it. This question shifts perspective and sees evil through the eyes of the perpetrator. Traditionally, taking the perpetrator's perspective has been treated as a theological issue and turned into the problem of sin. If science (and philosophy!) and Christianity are to be reconciled, these divisions must cease. Surely, sin is evil. It is evil because it causes undeserved suffering and because it corrupts character, destroying the self of the sinner. Sin is a subset of evil, the problem of sin a subset of the problem of evil.

Sin itself may be divided into two categories, *personal sin* and *structural sin*. Personal sin arises when institutions are arranged so that individuals suffer by sinning and flourish by not sinning. Structural sin ensues when institutions are arranged so that individuals flourish by sinning and suffer by not sinning. An example of personal sin is a kindergarten teacher who secretly has sexual concourse with her students, is caught, prosecuted, incarcerated, and never allowed to work with young children again. An example of structural sin is a Nazi officer who is told to select prisoners for gassing and offered comfortable quarters, good pay, and rapid promotion if he does so. If he refuses, he is sent immediately to the Eastern Front, to terrible suffering and near-certain death. Structural sin has its roots in personal sin, for example, Hitler's thirst for power, his racism, and his scapegoating of Jews.

Genesis 2 and 3 have no room for the concept of structural sin. There are too few actors and no social institutions—no politics, no commerce, no banks, no schools, no libraries, no war, no prisons, no social workers, and no environmental polluters. Indeed, there is little scope for sin in Genesis 2 and 3 (Rauschenbusch 1919, 51). The doctrines of original sin ignore the social and institutional aspects of evil, which is another reason they are so inadequate as descriptions of our humanity, which is forged in culture and society (Rauschenbusch 1919).

Sociobiology suggests that personal sin is inherent in our good and necessary nature. In a familiar example, to rear dependent children successfully, we must favor our children. A strong bond between mother and child produces empathy, and empathy often leads people to help others, obeying the commandment to love our neighbor. But parental favoritism has a dark side. Because it lies deep in our evolved emotions, we do not suddenly cease to prefer our children when they achieve independence. Yet, certain kinds of favoritism to our adult children harm others, and the harm we cause is sinful. Favoritism has turned into nepotism. Nepotism can become tribalism, and tribalism can turn genocidal. Our good and necessary dispositions have a potentially sinful underside. We do not sin necessarily, however. Our freedom allows us to say no, and our culture helps us to do so when it discourages nepotism.

We are sexual beings, and sexual desire produces good, constructive results in our lives. Sex provides pleasure, knits powerful bonds between non-kin, enhances love, and produces children. Sexual desire can also turn destructive, becoming lustfulness willing to rape and jealousy capable of murder.

Our evolved nature gives us desires for resources, and resources help us flourish. However, these good desires may be twisted to produce greed, resulting in deceit, theft, and murder.

We evolved the capacity to develop selves. Having a self allows us to self-reflect, create morality, and control our undesirable impulses. Yet, having a self also means that we can be egocentric. Egocentricity lies at the root of sin. Egocentric people love themselves exclusively, caring for neither God nor neighbor.

One of our species' most remarkable traits is its creativity. Not only have we built thousands of different cultures, we have also created great art and intricate technology. We are cocreators with God. But even our creativity can turn to sin. A creative torturer tortures more horribly than an uncreative one. We can use our highest virtues to harmful ends. In considering the problem of evil, the existence of personal sin requires solution.

Structural sin seems even more destructive than personal sin because it can manipulate and corrupt the best in us against our better judgment. Moreover, good individuals caught in structural sin can do horrid deeds. Two examples will suffice.

In 1970, a court sentenced Franz Stangl to life imprisonment as the commandant of Treblinka, a Nazi extermination camp. After his trial, a journalist interviewed him extensively and turned the interviews into a book (Sereny 1974).

She discovered a remarkably talented administrator who kept order where others could not. As commandant, he did not use power to enrich himself, nor did he directly murder anyone. He was not sadistic toward the prisoners; he even protected some of them. His main reason for accepting the post of commandant was fear— fear he would be returned to a former, hated job, fear for his own life, and fear for the lives of his wife and children. His fears were well-founded. The Nazis controlled most of Europe, and their hands were wet with blood.

Stangl was unusually decent at a personal level. He was self-disciplined, faithful to his wife, kind to his children, untempted by greed and the common corruptions of the powerful, hardly given to anything we would consider personal sin. Yet, he was convicted of the murder of 900 thousand people.

The second case is that of a physician, Hans Delmotte, an idealist who found an outlet for his idealism among the elite of Nazi Germany, the SS. (His story is in Lifton 1986, 309–11, 436–37.) He was posted to Auschwitz where the doctors selected some prisoners to die in the gas chambers and others to live as slave laborers.

He could not do it. Instead, he hid in his quarters and drank. Finally, a fellow physician, Josef Mengele, talked to him, reminding him of his duty to the SS and to Germany. Delmotte protested that he would prefer the Eastern Front to the slaughterhouse at Auschwitz. Mengele then appealed to his idealism. He knew selecting prisoners was difficult, but the SS were to handle the difficult jobs. A good SS officer could stand the suffering. It was for Germany. The Jews had to be destroyed, and gassing was more merciful than disease and starvation. Delmotte succumbed. The institutional structures around him transformed his idealism into murder.

The Nazis murdered so effectively because Germany was the greatest scientific and technological nation of the mid-century, and the Germans were superb organizers. Germans held the patent on the pesticide Zyklon B, and the efficient German chemical industry manufactured it in quantity. The Nazis used it to gas everyone they hated—Jews, Slavs, Gypsies, homosexuals. With Nazis in power, the trains ran on time. Many carried Jews to the East, to the extermination camps at Auschwitz-Birkenau, Belez, Chelmno, Majdanek, Sobibor, and Treblinka. Germans could organize masses of people. The Nazis organized invading armies, killer police, slave labor brigades, and extermination camps.

Idealism, technology based on a long and proud cultural history, industrial organization, and creativity manufactured death. Hundreds of thousands of ordinary people participated. Where structural sin exists, ordinary people are caught in its nets and often cannot struggle free. (Browning 1992 offers a case study.)

Structural sin is a terrible evil. It turns God's cocreators into destroyers. It, too, requires solution.

In summary, the traditional analysis that locates evil in pain, disease, natural disaster, and death and divides evils into natural and moral is inadequate. All evil is natural. Most of it is ours. It is located in our suffering, death, personal sin, and structural sin. It is also found in animal pain, so its arrival on Earth preceded ours. Evil is not a product of the human imagination. It is real.

That evil is natural and real nullifies a second traditional solution to the problem of evil, the claim that evil is an illusion. Evil is not an illusion. It lies at the heart of nature—predominately at the heart of human nature. Locating evil accurately provides a new way of solving the problem of evil.

Solving the Problem

To solve the problem of evil, it is necessary to revisit the five evils located above. I begin with human suffering.

We suffer. By definition, suffering involves the self. Our suffering is a direct result of our having selves.

Selves enable us to self-reflect, and self-reflection in turn helps us be moral creatures, to create moral selves, laws, and cultures. Having a self is one of the attributes that enables us to be cocreators with God. One of the most comprehensive traditional answers to the evil of suffering has been that suffering enhances the self by building character (or soul). In building the self, suffering serves a good purpose.

The value of suffering as a solution to the problem of evil is particularly meritorious in the framework provided here because it involves a recycling mechanism analogous to those in the rest of the universe. Here, we recycle evil to build better characters. Knowledge of history also helps us recycle evil because we can repair some of the damage of the past and prevent recurrences in the future.

A traditional criticism of this solution is that suffering is not always recycled into good. Some suffering destroys. On the whole, labor and death camps were not places that built character. Inmates lost faith in God, in humanity, and in their own moral rectitude because of the things they saw, suffered, and performed. Whatever reparations and preventions have occurred, they do not alter the past. Thus, the character-building solution to the problem of evil can mitigate the evil of suffering, but it leaves a residue of evil to be explained.

This residue of evil leads us to ask which is better: to have a self and suffer or not to have a self and not to suffer. Would we rather be like bears, bats, and barn animals, or be persons? Would we rather be dead or unconscious and not suffer, or alive and conscious but suffering? The classic answer to this question comes from a famous quotation by moral philosopher John Stuart Mill in a different context, "Better Socrates unsatisfied than a pig satisfied." The central answer to the problem of suffering provided in this chapter is that having a self compensates for almost any suffering we might endure, whether it is eventually turned into good or not.

This solution to the problem of suffering is unusual. Because it establishes the pattern for the solution to the problem of evil in general as presented in this chapter, it is worth summarizing here.

The central solution to the problem of evil is that we have attributes that are marks of our humanity, attributes enabling us to be cocreators with God. These same attributes are the sources of our experience of evil. In the case of suffering, the attribute is the self. Without it, we would not suffer, but without it, we would not be human. Most of us choose to suffer rather than to eliminate the self. (That is, most of us do not commit suicide.) God, it appears, has made the same choice. In God's eyes, it must be better for human beings to exist—beings with selves, beings who suffer—than for us not to exist. Having the attributes more than compensates for the evils that come with having them. This is the only answer required to solve the problem of evil because it justifies the existence of evil.

Nonetheless, in addition to the central solution, the problem of evil has another, secondary solution. Frequently, good comes out of evil. In the case of suffering, suffering helps build the self, the very cause of suffering. Thus, the universe is a better place than it needs to be, morally. Our suffering is not only more than compensated—it is mitigated. It is compensated by our having a self, mitigated by being a source of good.

The solutions to the other evils follow the same general pattern.

Animals feel pain, a concomitant of their mobility. The central solution to the problem of animal pain is that their pain is more than compensated by their mobility. If asked, mobile creatures would reply that being mobile and subject to pain is far better than being painlessly affixed to one place throughout life, like potatoes. This intuition is captured in the medieval Great Chain of Being that makes animals more valuable than plants. Animals do not have greater value, but because they are mobile, they do have more extensive possibilities in life.

The secondary solution is that good comes from pain. It often saves mobile creatures from harm.

Human beings die. Death is an integral and necessary part of the recycling systems of the universe. As an integral and necessary part of a developing universe, our death is like any other.

However, it is also different. Human death is an evil. It is the end of the selves we have built or might have built. It is the conclusion of our biographies, the cessation of our plans. It is the limit to our ability to add history, culture, and morality, structure, variety, and autonomy, to the universe.

The central solution to the evil of our death is that the evil is more than compensated by our having the very attributes that make us experience death as an evil. Death is an evil to us because we have selves, create biographies, and plan for the future. Having these things and experiencing death as an evil is far better than not having these things.

The secondary solution to the evil of death is that good comes out of it. Death marks an end to our suffering. Premature death ends suffering early. Furthermore, death drives evolution, makes room for new children, and recycles nutrients. All these things mitigate the evil of our death.

We sin. We have within us the potential for personal sin, and all too frequently, we actualize it. Our personal sins cause suffering and death to ourselves and to others. We sin because we are free to sin, and we are free to sin because we make choices. We have an enormous range of choices, far more than other animals.

The central solution to the problem of personal sin is that personal sin is more than compensated by our capacity for freedom. Freedom of choice and the creativity that comes with it are major goods. We show that we believe our freedom is a great good whenever we fear that we are not free, but machines or robots, programmed to do what we do. Many movies, plays, and novels explore this common fear. We demonstrate how much we value freedom when we strive for it despite tremendous costs, as we have done throughout history. The American patriot Patrick Henry famously captured the value we place on freedom when he said, "Give me liberty or give me death."

The secondary solution is that good comes from our sins. Others recycle them by using our misdeeds to improve their characters. Realizing our deeds are evil and repenting helps our own characters mature. The personal sins we commit are mitigated evils.

We create structural sin. We build structures of sin that ensnare even idealistic and personally decent individuals into committing horrid deeds. We are able to build structures of sin because we have autonomy. Autonomy gives us the ability to make laws for ourselves, to build intellectual and cultural structures, adding variety and structure to the universe and creating even more autonomy in it.

The central solution to the problem of structural sin is that our attribute of autonomy and all it brings with it more than compensate for the evil caused by structural sin. It is better to have these things and to have structural sin than not to have them.

The secondary solution is that we mitigate the evil that comes with our autonomy by creating structural goodness. We create institutions that punish personal sin and reward personal decency. Awareness of the errors of history helps us build such structures and, in doing so, enables us to bring good out of the evils of the past. Moreover, being caught in structural sin may help us build character.

The answer to the problem of evil presented here has not been traditional, yet it has left untouched only one of the traditional philosophical solutions to the problem of evil, namely, to weaken one of God's attributes, making God either not powerful or knowledgeable enough to build a good universe or not good enough to create one. The answer to the problem of evil presented here obviates the need to resort to this solution.

This chapter has attempted to solve the problem of evil arising in Christianity, a monotheistic religion whose God is omnipotent, omniscient, and omnibenevolent, and created the universe. It has shown that things traditionally thought evil are not, that the true evils are animal pain, human suffering and death, and human sin, both personal and structural.

The source of evil is not some divine opponent of God. The source of evil is not even human sin. Rather, the sources of evil lie in attributes so valuable that we would not even consider eliminating them in order to eradicate evil. Presumably, neither would God. If the universe is to have the goods it does, evil cannot be abolished. God has structured the universe so that these greater goods more than compensate for evil. The fact that evil is more than compensated is enough to justify its existence.

Being benevolent, God has structured the universe so that the evil in it is also mitigated. Good comes out of evil. Thus, by the argument presented here, the universe contains far more good than evil. In so constructing the universe, God has provided a natural solution to the problem of evil. By gratuitous grace, God has added to that arrangement another, special solution—the atonement.

Chapter 11

The Atonement

The previous chapter solves the problem of evil logically by showing that the good attributes making us human are also at play when we commit sin, experience suffering, and know death as harmful. It argues that having these good attributes is more than sufficient compensation for the evils we commit and suffer. Moreover, good often arises out of the evils themselves so that the universe contains a large surplus of good. This seems to be God's natural solution to the problem of evil.

Because evil has a natural solution, God might have left us to pursue our lives without any self-revelation to us. However, our evolved dispositions can lead us to be mistaken about God and to confuse good and evil. The book of Joshua in the Hebrew Scriptures demonstrates our potential for confusion. It relates how the Hebrew people, claiming to be one kinship group, believed God told them to murder every man, woman, and child in a locale where no Hebrews lived, raze their cities, plunder their gold and silver, then occupy their land as if it were God's gift to the Hebrews. Sociobiology shows the Hebrews mistook their evolved dispositions for God's will. Their evolved dispositions, not God, told them their kin group was special and that resources should be garnered for its benefit. Because murder and pillage are often easier than building, sowing, and reaping for oneself, murder and pillage make economic sense. But they are not godly.

In part because we often become confused about God's will and convince ourselves that evil is good, God provides a second, special solution to the problem of evil. The special solution is the *atonement*. The word *atonement* has two meanings that are often conflated. First, it means at-one-ment, unity between human beings and God, a meaning the word itself highlights. However, the concept of atonement also includes actions performed to bring about that unity, actions involving reconciliation, expiation, and purification (Yerkes 1952, 178–82). Medieval and Reformation Christianity emphasized expiation and purification, making atonement center on the forgiveness of sin with Jesus as a sacrifice who, somehow, brought about reconciliation between God and humanity. Theologians differ as to how. This chapter moves the concept of unity back to its rightful place as the center of the atonement.

In Jesus, God reveals deity to us in a way we can understand, for Jesus is a human being like us. In living a fully human life, Jesus reveals how human beings can and should live, shedding divine illumination on good and evil. By raising Jesus from the dead, God shows us that death is not our end. Jesus' life and resurrection also show us that divine power is available to us to transform our lives.

Moreover, by manifesting divinity through Jesus, God preserves the autonomy of the universe. Jesus follows its laws by entering fully into human life, following the laws of growth and maturation as well as the laws of physics, as every human being must. By being revealed through Jesus, God also preserves human freedom. In Jesus, God does not overwhelm us, robbing us of our freedom. In fact, the Gospels report that a number of people disapproved of Jesus and wanted him removed from their lives. The same is true today. God leaves us free to accept or refuse unity with the divine.

Coinage of the word *atonement* about 1517, the year Luther posted his ninety-five theses on the door of the church in Wittenberg, added little to existing theology. Theologians had already developed a plethora of conflicting atonement doctrines. The Reformation added to the chaos, and the divisions within Christianity have kept anyone from resolving the issues. Current doctrines of the atonement fail the correspondence, consilience, and coherence tests of truth. There are four principle difficulties.

Four Difficulties

The first difficulty with almost all doctrines of the atonement is their dependence on the historicity of Adam and Eve. For Paul, Adam's sin is disobedience; Jesus atones for Adam's sin through obedience (Rom. 5:19). That is, he performs certain actions that bring about unity between humanity and God. Adam's sin brings death; Jesus' resurrection brings life (1 Cor. 15:22-34).

Later interpretations also depend on a historical fall and emphasize the atonement as an action. Chrysostom thinks Adam's sin angers God; Jesus propitiates God's wrath. Origen, Tertullian, and Augustine claim Adam's sin sold us to Satan; Jesus pays the ransom. Luther and Calvin maintain Adam's sin deserves a penalty; Jesus pays it. Anselm thinks Adam's sin puts us in debt to God's justice; Jesus pays the debt. Aquinas adds technical details to Anselm's solution, details some other theologians alter or reject.

All these doctrines depend on the historical existence of Adam and Eve. However, the historicity of Adam and Eve fails all three tests of truth. Realizing this, liberal theologians retain the story but call it a myth and reconceptualize the fall as metaphor. They ruin Paul's neat equations. Adam and Eve's mythological disobedience cannot be atoned by Jesus' historical actions, nor can Adam and Eve's mythological sin be responsible for our sinful nature or our death.

The best liberal theology can do is to read the narrative as a story about the human condition. However, as discussed in chapter 6, the conditions Adam and Eve represent are the social and economic situations of peasants on the one hand and the biological circumstances of all organisms on the other. The narrative does not apply to all human beings or only to human beings. Of course, it is possible to interpret the narrative generally and say that Adam and Eve's sinfulness shows us our own sinfulness, from which Jesus saves us. Why we need this particular narrative (or any narrative at all) to tell us we are sinful is difficult to say. Moreover, if Adam and Eve are not historical, the historical Jesus has no work to do under existing atonement doctrines that treat the atonement as a deed. Realizing this, the Catholic Church and conservative Protestantism insist on the historicity of Adam and Eve.

The second difficulty with almost all the doctrines is that they fail the coherence test of truth both together and separately. They cannot be combined into one coherent doctrine because they were largely written as corrections of one another. Even if they could be reconciled in broad outline, separately none of the doctrines make sense. Linwood Urban (1986, 101–24) examines them in hopes of overcoming this difficulty, but in the end, he cannot. To provide a taste of the chaos he encounters, I quote:

The difficulty with Anselm's proposal lies . . . in his calculation that the voluntary offering of Christ's life is of incalculable worth and thus capable of making just reparation. Abelard was troubled over just this point. If the life of Christ was of infinite value, surely his execution was of infinite disvalue. . . .

The infinite value of Christ's self-oblation is further called into question if death is viewed as natural. . . . If [Christ] must die, then his dying is robbed of its special value. . . .

This question is addressed by St. Thomas Aquinas, who modifies Anselm by proposing a different satisfaction or payment. Where Anselm spoke of the life of Christ, St. Thomas speaks of his suffering. . . . [However,] calculations designed to support the inestimable worth of Christ's suffering become even more difficult. For example, Christ's sufferings do not seem more acute than those of many others who have been tortured and killed. . . .

The Protestant Reformer, John Calvin, . . . proposed that Christ satisfies God's justice by being punished in our place, but this only seems to make matters worse. How can God's justice be satisfied when the wrong person is punished? . . . It seems but an act of God's mercy to accept the death of Christ or his suffering in lieu of something owed by human beings. If it is after all really a matter of mercy, why cannot God simply forgive us without any reparation? (Urban 1986, 118–19)

The more detailed the examination of atonement doctrines, the less credible each becomes. To try combining them into a single, coherent doctrine merely multiplies the confusion.

The third difficulty is the lack of correspondence between Scripture and atonement doctrines. With a copy of Mark in front of him and knowing Paul's theology, the author of the Gospel according to Luke deliberately eschews their interpretations of Jesus' life and death as atoning (Ehrman 1993, 199–204). This is not surprising because all the Gospels attest that Jesus and his mentor, John the Baptist, reject the need for atonement. Both ignore the method of atonement practiced by first-century Jews (and Gentiles), animal sacrifice by a priest in the Temple (or temples). According to all the Gospels, John the Baptist proclaims God's forgiveness outside the Temple, baptizing the penitent in the cleansing waters of the Jordan. Jesus pronounces forgiveness without resorting to any rituals. All the

Gospels show John the Baptist and Jesus disdaining atoning sacrifices for the forgiveness of sins. For Christians, the fact that Jesus dismisses the need for atoning sacrifices should reveal that atoning sacrifices are unnecessary.

The fourth difficulty, then, is the idea that God requires actions of a certain kind before divine and human can be united. More narrowly, the difficulty is that people think the deity(s) requires sacrifice for atonement. For Jews and Gentiles alike in the first century, atonement meant sacrifice. Everyone sacrificed animals at altars in temples for atonement. Therefore, both Gentile and Jewish followers of Jesus would have inevitably interpreted Jesus' unexpected and puzzling crucifixion as sacrificial.

We no longer think this way. The idea that God commands us to kill an animal and drain its blood properly before forgiving us boggles the modern mind. Puzzle as we may, we can find no connection between slaughter and forgiveness. Furthermore, we are not the only ones puzzled, for long before the death of Jesus, Jewish prophets cry that the blood of sacrifices avails us nothing (Isa. 1:11; Jer. 6:20; Amos 5:21-24). Jesus stands in the mainstream of a long and powerful Jewish tradition. Why, then, does almost everyone in the ancient world think God demands animal sacrifice for salvation from sin, suffering, and death?

One answer is that God demands animal sacrifice because deities can suffer hunger, and they like meat. Often in the ancient world, gods eat human flesh, especially relishing tender young children. Remnants of practices of human sacrifice remain in the Hebrew Scriptures (Gen. 22:1-14; 1 Kings 16:34; 2 Kings 16:3, 17:17, 21:6; Jer. 7:31), but by the time of Jesus, Judaism had repudiated human sacrifice. Nonetheless, their God retains some attributes of carnivores. Several passages in the Hebrew Scriptures depict God savoring the sweet smell of cooking meat (Gen. 8:20-21; Exod. 29:18, 1:19; Num. 15:14). Moreover, the Torah is filled with God's detailed requirements for animal and agricultural sacrifices.

That ancient religions treat God as a carnivore is a typical interpretation (Burkert 1996; Ehrenreich 1997). The origin of the idea lies in our heritage. When large carnivores roamed places human beings inhabited and we were their prey, throwing meat to a hungry carnivore or having it devour a companion rather than oneself literally and immediately saved a person from suffering and death. The living had every reason to offer meat to carnivores and to glorify with heartfelt gratitude the salvific sacrifices of dead companions. The ritualization of suffering, death, and sacrifice mirrored reality.

The great world religions repudiate the ancient concept of God as a carnivore. Because we do not think God savors flesh, and both John the Baptist and Jesus ignored sacrifice, there is no reason for us to think of Jesus' death as a sacrifice. As I explain below, his death occurs because his behavior threatens the power and prerogatives of those in authority, not because God demands it to satisfy divine hunger, even hunger for justice. If God hungered for justice, the torture and death of an innocent man would sicken, not satisfy. Jesus' death does not bring about justice, but judgment—God's judgment on the powers that murder Jesus in every age.

As I note at the beginning of chapter 3, during the long history of atonement doctrines, the Interpreter has been working on intractable material. In order to understand the atonement, we must jettison most of the old interpretations and conceive of the atonement in a new way.

The remainder of this chapter depends on understanding the historical Jesus portrayed in the Gospels. Contemporary scholarship such as I present in chapter 6 has profoundly influenced my interpretation. The deeds and sayings I present as Jesus' are those that scholars consider most likely to have been his; others, I disregard. I follow no particular scholar but present my own summary of the scholarly consensus. The first problem I address is Jesus and sin.

Jesus and Sin

[Major influences on the following section are Borg (1994a, b), Borg and Wright (1999), Chilton (1992), Crossan (1991, 1993), Dulles (1987), Dunn (1988), Ehrman (1993), Eisenman (1997), Funk, Hoover, and the Jesus Seminar (1993), Funk and the Jesus Seminar (1998), Grant (1977), Helms (1988), Hurtado (1988), Josephus ([77–100] 1981), Ludemann (1996), Meier (1991, 1994), Murphy (1991), Sanders (1985, 1993), Schmidt (1997), Shanks (1993), Vermes (1973), Wise, Abegg, and Cook (1996), Wright (1996), Young (1975), and Biblical Archaeology Society seminars held annually in Greensboro, North Carolina.]

In chapter 10, I divide sin into two categories: personal sin and structural sin. I begin the discussion here with personal sin.

Personal sin is sin that stems from our good and necessary nature. Because sin is part of our nature, we cannot ever rightly think of ourselves as free of sin, but we can make choices about our behavior and influence our dispositions. Christians ask Jesus to guide our choices and help us overcome our sinful inclinations. Because God raised him from the dead and he lives, he can help us do these things here and now. Because he is fully human and lived an earthly life, he understands our plight, for he had to make such choices himself.

The Gospels relate some of the choices Jesus made. His choices are of two types: choices influenced by evolved human dispositions and choices conventionally available in Jesus' own culture.

Evolution has given us a robust propensity to survive that leads us to want to garner resources for ourselves, to acquire wealth and power. It has also given us a strong partiality for family. We want to have sex and reproduce, then protect and promote our children, extended families, and clans. Does Jesus follow evolution's lead, making sex, kinship, wealth, and power central to his life?

The Gospels say no. They say that when Jesus chooses, he chooses a celibate life without spouse or child. Moreover, when he is with his disciples and his mother and siblings ask to see him, Mark (3:31-35) says he replies, "Whoever does the will of God is my brother and sister and mother." Jesus rejects his kin in favor of his circle of friends and followers. He seems remarkably lacking in family values.

Jesus chooses a life of relative poverty and recommends a similar life to his disciples. According to Luke (12:22-34), Jesus thinks the God who clothes the lilies and feeds the birds will take care of us, that we need not worry about what we eat or wear. Jesus often castigates the wealthy, saying they are unlikely to find God. Approached by a rich man who has assiduously followed the Torah, Mark (10:21) has Jesus tell him, "Sell what you own, and give the money to the poor, and you will have treasure in heaven."

Nonetheless, Jesus is not an ascetic. He does not demand celibacy; Peter, his leading disciple, is married. He does not require separation of the sexes; many of his followers are women. He does not insist on conventional chastity; some of his woman followers have dubious reputations, and Jesus forgives adultery. Jesus takes no Nazarite vows; he drinks wine. The Gospel of John portrays him as miraculously transforming some 150 gallons of water into wine at a wedding after the guests had already drunk all the wine the host provided (John 2:3-10), which indicates something of Jesus' reputation, even if the story itself is allegorical. As the gallonage suggests, Jesus had a reputation as a drunkard and a glutton (Matt. 11:19; Luke 7:34), not labels an ascetic is likely to acquire. Taken together, the Gospels portray Jesus as well-balanced, not filled with inordinate desires for temporal goods and therefore avoiding the extremes of asceticism on the one hand and rapaciousness on the other. The best word to describe Jesus is *free,* free to make his own choices without being captivated by his natural dispositions.

According to the Gospels, Jesus rejects power as one of the three great temptations in the wilderness (Matt. 4:8-10; Luke 4:5-8). Instead, he makes friends with the powerless and the outcasts and invites them to eat with him. At the end of his life, he again rejects power, choosing to die helpless on a cross rather than escaping, fighting, or calling down angels. In rejecting power, Jesus sides with the God who creates an autonomous universe.

Jesus asks us to minimize the dispositions evolution encourages us to augment, but not to reject them outright unless they interfere with our perception or acceptance of the present and coming reign of God. His minimization of them helps liberate us from bondage to our dark side and free us to follow him into the light that is God.

More strongly, Jesus repudiates the conventional choices available in his culture. In the first century, many Jews long for holiness. To find it, some separate themselves from contact with Gentiles; many of these also separate themselves from less devout Jews. Pharisees and Essenes do both. Although not priests, the Pharisees seek holiness by keeping Torah laws applicable to priests, laws more stringent than those for lay people. They segregate themselves from the less devout, but they continue to worship in the Temple and teach in the synagogues. The Essenes are more extreme. They also want to keep the Torah laws applicable to priests, but they establish separated communities. They reject worship in the Temple because they consider it contaminated.

Jesus chooses neither path. Instead, he joins the upstart John the Baptist. Once baptized, he disappears into the wilderness alone, seeking God in his own way, and filled with the Holy Spirit, returns to found his own movement. Although his movement focuses on the present and coming reign of God, neither he nor his followers seek conventional holiness. On the contrary, the conventionally holy castigate them for feasting on fast days, working on God's day of rest, consorting with unsavory characters, and eating with sinners.

Conventionally religious Jews respected the Temple and supported it financially. They went to Jerusalem for the great festivals and bought unblemished animals in the Temple for sacrifice. The Gospels never show Jesus or his followers participating in Temple sacrifices. Rather, Jesus famously overturns the tables of the moneychangers whose work made Temple sacrifice possible. Jesus angers Temple authorities rather than supporting and respecting them.

Jesus seems firmly to repudiate another possibility many Jews favored, assimilation to Roman society. Rather than assimilating, Jesus threatens Roman power in such a way that the Romans execute him.

Thus, Jesus says no to the conventional choices available in his culture. His doing so helps free Christians to examine and reject the conventions in our own culture that lead us toward sin and away from Jesus and the reign of God in our midst.

Jesus' choices are not merely negative, however. His minimal acceptance of natural dispositions and outright rejection of conventional holiness arise from his positive choice to love God and neighbor.

Most characteristic of Jesus' relationship to God is its immediacy. For many in the first century, God seems to have been a distant figure, a king enthroned in heaven surrounded by choirs of angels or hidden in the Temple's inner sanctum, inaccessible as the emperor in Rome, approachable only in fear through intermediaries. Most people seem to have learned about God secondhand, from Temple and Torah.

The result is that most first-century Jews loved Temple and Torah. Some loved them enough to torture, murder, and die for them. The Temple became the focus of vicious civil wars. Some deeply religious Jews felt the need to be certain that Temple worship was done the right way, their way, according to their group's reading of Torah. Only then, they thought, would God continue to dwell in the Temple and, so, remain with them.

Characteristically, Jesus does not seek Temple, Torah, or priest. For him, God is here unmediated, reigning now. He sees himself as God's beloved and calls God *Abba*, our equivalent of Daddy, a word of intimate and trustful relationship. When he preaches, the Gospels depict him as speaking with authority from a firsthand knowledge of God's continuing presence and care. Jesus does not need mediators between him and his beloved Abba, and he never makes the mistake of loving Temple and Torah more than, or instead of, God.

Most characteristic of Jesus' charity toward his neighbor is its inclusiveness. He dines with all sorts of people, a shocking practice in a hierarchical culture in which a man dined with equals and sought to dine with superiors. In contrast, Jesus opens his table to outcasts. He invites himself to dinner with tax collectors, hated traitors to their nation who squeezed the conqueror's booty out of their own kin.

Jesus preaches inclusiveness as well. By word and action, he breaks down the barriers his culture erects to separate the holy from the profane, the sinless from the sinful. Some scholars think he offers inclusion in the reign of God to the wicked without demanding repentance (Crossan 1991, 263; Sanders 1985, 271).

Jesus actively demonstrates the depth of his love for God and neighbor. When asked how many times one person should forgive another, in Matthew he offers the impossible figure of 490 (Matt. 18:22), presumably meaning infinitely. So far does God's forgiveness extend. Jesus does not stop preaching about the present and coming reign of God, he does not cease publicly healing and forgiving his neighbors, yet he must have foreseen where his words and actions would lead, for he knew the fate of John the Baptist and the fate of others who had gathered eager crowds around them. He is warned repeatedly. Yet he continues his behavior until execution silences him. For him, personal sin would have been to love his life more than God and neighbor.

The structures of sin kill him, structures about which Genesis 2 and 3 are silent. Power in Rome and religion and wealth in Jerusalem kill Jesus. In Rome and Jerusalem, the structures of power, wealth, and religion center in an aristocracy of kinship, money, and land that enhances its domination through a culture where advancement depends on patronage rather than merit. The huge majority of the population is poor and many are slaves. Rome has conquered and rules. To maintain their own preeminence, the powerful in the provinces strive to retain the Roman prerogative, by whatever means.

At the time of Jesus, Galilee is a hotbed of radicalism. Galileans are suspect; a Galilean with a following is dangerous. Jesus is a Galilean with a following who sparks rumors, or makes claims, of being Messiah-king. Rome was quick to execute such men, and Pilate notoriously brutal. In Pilate, personal sin and structural sin combine. Jesus does not need to be violent or to threaten violence to find himself on a Roman cross.

Jesus asks people to follow him. After his death, theirs is a stark choice. One interpretation of Mark's passion narrative highlights the radical choice Jesus' followers face by asking, whom shall I worship as Lord, Jesus or Caesar? The interpretation is Thomas Schmidt's (1997).

Mark's narrative (Mark 15:16-39) has a whole cohort of soldiers (at least two hundred men!) in the palace courtyard (*praetorium*) clothe Jesus in purple, crown him, kneel before him, and hail him as king. They then lead him in procession through Jerusalem as Simon of Cyrene carries his cross. He is crucified at the place of the skull (or head) between two bandits, with a sign proclaiming him "King of the Jews."

Schmidt compares this account with narratives of the triumphal entry into Rome of a victorious general made divine emperor. The victor begins in the *praetorium,* dressed in the purple array of the god Jupiter Capitolinus, crowned with laurels, and acclaimed king and god by soldiers. The procession then winds through Rome to the Capitoline (head) hill accompanied by a sacrificial bull with its executioner carrying a two-headed (cross-shaped) axe. The climax of the procession comes at the moment of sacrifice and enthronement. Near the time of Mark's Gospel, emperors chose to be enthroned flanked by two other people, Claudius by his two sons-in-law (44 C.E.) and Vitellius by two generals (68 C.E.). According to Schmidt, in Mark's narrative, Jesus has all the marks of a divine Roman ruler in victorious procession.

Schmidt's interpretation reflects Paul's exclamation, "But thanks be to God, who in Christ always leads us in triumphal procession" (2 Cor. 2:14a). Jesus' triumphal passion procession must have been a common Christian idea.

Mark, of course, has the soldiers mock Jesus. Schmidt suggests that Mark is mocking the emperors' self-deification and emphasizing Jesus' triumph and God's sovereign rule over all. Through Jesus, God says yes to humility and peace and no to the sinful structures of power and violence in Rome.

All the Gospels maintain that Rome crucifies Jesus at the behest of Jewish leaders connected to the Temple. The Temple is the largest and wealthiest in the ancient world. Not only does it represent the Jewish aristocracy and monopolize Jewish sacrifice, making it the center of Jewish national religious power, it is the Jews' central bank, recipient of the Temple tax paid by almost every Jew. The Temple's power and wealth exist in a world where most Jews are powerless and terribly poor. In that world, the Temple is one of the principal structures of sinful exploitation.

During most of his ministry, Jesus ignores the Temple. His mentor John the Baptist did the same. Both forgive sins outside the traditional structures of sacrifice and finance. By doing so, both men must have angered Temple authorities. Each person accepting forgiveness outside the Temple is one less person purchasing animals from the Temple's flocks and herds and giving a portion of the sacrificial meat to Temple priests. By ignoring the Temple, John the Baptist and Jesus undermine the structures of religious power and wealth in first-century Judaism.

Then, during Passover in about 33, Jesus brings judgment to the Temple. In a symbolic gesture reminiscent of the prophets, he overturns the tables of the moneychangers. (Had Jesus' actions threatened real violence, he would have been killed immediately.) How much the moneychangers were exploiting the people, no one knows. But the Temple system needed them. To buy animals for sacrifice, Jews from throughout the Diaspora not only needed to use a common currency, they had to convert Roman coins with their image of the divine Caesar into coinage acceptable to a religion that repudiated idols.

Again, Jesus' response to structural sin is not merely negative. He builds alternatives. When he calls twelve disciples, he symbolically begins a new Israel with twelve new tribes. His new Israel is not a kinship system like the old, but a fellowship of charitable followers. Jesus' alternative lifestyle embraces itinerancy, rejecting the earlier Jewish search for a land of one's own and the first-century desire of pagan and Jew alike for landed wealth. Unlike ancient Jewish kings and aspiring Jewish messiahs, Jesus' alternative is nonviolent. Jesus' way liberates from structural sin. It offers a new, inclusive way of life, building new structures. It offers new varieties for living, increased choices, and enhanced autonomy. Jesus' way reflects God's plan for increasing structure, variety, and autonomy in the universe as well as God's commandment that we love one another.

God deals with sin through Jesus in yet another way. In becoming fully united with a human being, God identifies with us completely. God knows from the inside what it is like to be human, to have one's best virtues and talents always ready to turn toward sin. Jesus consorts with some of the worst characters in first-century Judaism. He dies a criminal and an outcast. He knows what evil is like. Yet, knowing this,

Jesus forgives sins without demanding sacrifice. From this, we may be sure that God understands the worst of us, yet forgives us without requiring payment. Atonement doctrines based on restitution misunderstand God's free acceptance of us.

Sociobiology makes sense of God's readiness to accept and forgive, for it says the very capacities and talents that make us human are the capacities and talents that enable us to be evil. If God loves us, it cannot be merely our good part, because there is no good part. We are whole beings, good-and-evil beings, not good beings who became evil, as the doctrines of original sin declare. God loves the whole person and, so, forgives. The problem of sin is not so much whether God forgives us but whether we are too proud to accept unmerited pardon.

God deals with sin through Jesus. Jesus' person reveals a God who understands and forgives us. Jesus' example shows us how to manage our freedom, avoiding personal and structural sin while acting with charity and compassion. Jesus' Holy Spirit gives us strength to overcome the dark side of our natural inclinations. God also deals with our suffering and death through Jesus.

Suffering and Death

The Gospels depict Jesus as enduring almost every human suffering. He grieves when others die and mourns the evils in his society. He suffers unfair criticism and misunderstanding, being rebuffed at home and spurned by the powerful. During his passion, he is betrayed, rejected, humiliated, mocked, and abandoned. On the cross, he endures thirst, humiliation, suffering, suffocation, and death. Because he is fully human, we can be certain he really suffered.

Because Jesus is also filled with God, he shows us who God is. Contrary to a strand of Christian theology borrowed from Greek philosophy that says God is *impassible,* meaning not subject to suffering or pain and therefore not able to suffer with us, Jesus' suffering demonstrates that God identifies with our suffering, particularly with the suffering of those who are poor, marginalized, and powerless. Jesus reveals that God willingly assumes our suffering, even though not subject to it (for God is sovereign and subject to nothing).

God could intervene in the universe to stop suffering. However, in the last chapter, I argue that God designed the universe to become increasingly autonomous, and our arrival marks a new stage in its autonomy. Moreover, I argue, our suffering is more than compensated by our having selves and mitigated by helping us create better selves. For God to intervene in this system would be to interfere with its laws, to decrease or defeat the autonomy we bring to the universe, and to stop good from arising through human self-discovery and character building. Rather than interfere, God acts with extraordinary charity by suffering with us so we do not suffer alone.

Jesus not only suffers, he dies. Yet, Jesus is said to be without sin. One possible interpretation of these statements is that sin is not the cause of suffering and death. This book has reached this same conclusion from several different perspectives: from cosmology, evolution, the literary rather than historical character of Genesis 2 and 3, and now, theology. Suffering and death are natural. Both are part of what it is to be human in this universe.

I think Jesus' death says something more, something like God loves us enough to die for us if dying for us were possible, but it is not, for God is eternal. Because God cannot die for us, Jesus dies. God's response is to resurrect him.

In raising Jesus from the dead, God tells us at least three things. First, the resurrection vindicates Jesus. Jesus' way of seeing and living is God's way, the right way, and should be our way. The ways of kin, clan, and tribe; of power, wealth, and property; of exploitation, violence, and separatist, exclusive holiness are wrong.

Second, Jesus' resurrection indicates that death is a door through which we enter a new form of life newly embodied. I think contemporary science allows us to say something about this new form of embodiment and perhaps something additional about structure and variety in the universe.

I note in the last chapter that everything in the universe dies except the stuff. The stuff has properties unlike those of matter. The changing material world we know arises from the stuff, arises as the stuff retains its properties but reorganizes itself.

As far as we know, the stuff came into existence at the Big Bang. Because this book assumes that God exists, it is reasonable to say that before the Big Bang, only God existed, and God is Spirit. According to Paul and Luke, God is also "all in all" (1 Cor. 15:28), the one "in whom we live and move and have our being" (Acts 17:28), or, according to Paul Tillich, "the ground of being." God is not merely the transcendent deity but the immanent Spirit. This is standard Christian theology.

I want to develop a model of the immanence and transcendence of God based on an analogy with the transition of stuff to matter—with a strong caveat that models are schemas, not replicas. Here it is.

Before the Big Bang occurs, Spirit exists. At the Big Bang, Spirit reorganizes itself (whatever that means) as stuff. But this does not mean Spirit ceases to exist as Spirit. Just as the stuff continues to exist without changing its properties after it organizes itself into matter, so Spirit exists without changing its properties after it organizes itself into stuff.

At the stuff-matter transition, stuff reorganizes itself as matter without either losing its stuff properties and ceasing to be stuff or losing its Spirit properties and ceasing to be Spirit. This model tends to spiritualize matter and therefore is far different from the model *vitalism* constructs. Vitalism's model conceptualizes matter as inert, then claims that inert matter could never be alive, that living entities require something additional in order live, something not obeying the laws of physics and chemistry. That is, the vitalistic model requires a separate, vitalizing Spirit. In the model presented here and in modern physics, matter is not inert, but self-organizing. It does not need an extra-added ingredient to live. The material and immaterial, matter and Spirit, are not separable in this way.

To extend the analogy, at the resurrection matter reorganizes itself as resurrected body. Whatever resurrected body is, it has several properties. First, it is made of Spirit-stuff-matter, reorganized. Second, the biblical accounts say that sometimes it is solid enough to be touched, while at other times it passes through doors or simply vanishes. Third, Scripture says it can retain personality or personhood or individual identity or mind or soul. (In this philosophical and theological minefield, I will not quibble over words.) Presumably, retention of individual identity is how the disciples recognize Jesus, although his body is transformed. That resurrected body can retain personality is no more mysterious than brain being the source and location of mind—which, of course, is both completely mysterious and a familiar fact.

Argument by analogy here seems appropriate because it produces results consilient with our prior knowledge. We already know God's universe is filled with the recycled and transformed. Stuff recycles to matter, hydrogen and helium recycle to heavier elements, heavier elements recycle to living creatures, living creatures recycle as nutrients. The argument by analogy simply says that the recycling and transformation with which we are already familiar continue to work in areas beyond our current knowledge. The idea that known processes have been at work in the past and will continue to operate in the future is called *uniformitarianism.* James Hutton introduced uniformitarianism as a geological concept in the late eighteenth century, and Darwin later applied it to biology. In its most general form, it is one of the pillars of science.

The third thing God tells us is related in metaphor. As Christians, our lives here and now are to be lives of death and resurrection, of continuing transformation. We, like Jesus, are to be filled with the Holy Spirit. Paul captures the Christian sense of life transformed when he exclaims, "I have been crucified with Christ; and it is no longer I who live, but it is Christ who lives in me" (Gal. 2:19b-20a) and "So if anyone is in Christ, there is a new creation: everything old has passed away; see, everything has become new!" (2 Cor. 5:17).

The metaphor has substance for Paul. Jesus is alive, and that makes Paul a new creature. Yet Paul remains recognizably Paul. In this life, the Christian undergoes a transformation like the transformations occurring in the rest of the universe, a recycling of the old person into a new person, a transformation of personality that somehow leaves the person recognizable. It is this transformed person who is resurrected, given a new body and a new form of life, a form of life that adds structure, variety, and autonomy to the universe.

Something can even be said about the enhanced autonomy of our new lives. In our mortal lives, we enhance autonomy in the universe not only because we have more choices than other creatures and make our own laws, but also because we can free ourselves from some of our evolved dispositions. Yet we are always subject to physical and chemical laws. The biblical portrayal of the resurrected Jesus suggests that his transformed body is no longer subject to these laws. Neither will ours be. The person with a resurrected body is more autonomous, freer from external laws, than the person with a mortal one. The cocreator acquires new scope for creativity.

This new interpretation of the atonement involves both revelation and transformation. The atonement as revelation is an old idea, articulated most clearly by Peter Abelard who extols Jesus as an example for humanity to emulate. Athanasius, whose views on original sin I examine in chapter 4, celebrates the atonement as transformation, believing it changes human nature. The ideas of these two venerable Christian theologians best capture how scientifically educated people can most plausibly interpret the atonement now.

Atonement Now

Genesis 3 portrays God as angered because Adam and Eve have gained knowledge and become more like gods. God exiles them from Eden, placing angelic watchers and a flaming sword between them and the tree of life so they cannot become immortal.

Leviticus 16 has a similar flavor. Leviticus 16 describes the requirements for the annual Day of Atonement. The day is dangerous. On pain of death, no one may enter the Holy of Holies except the high priest who must be a descendant of Aaron. He may enter only that one day. To approach God safely, he must purify himself and wear the prescribed clothes. On pain of death, he must hide the mercy seat of God from sight in a cloud of incense. The point of the Day of Atonement is to cleanse the mercy seat and the altars from the people's sin so God will remain with the people. It appears that God can be contaminated by people's sin. To approach safely, the priest must be genetically correct and ritually pure. Many are the barriers erected between God and humanity.

Traditional Christianity reverses these ideas. At Jesus' death, Mark 15:38 says the curtain dividing the Holy of Holies from the rest of the Temple is torn in two from top to bottom. In Mark's symbolism, the barriers dividing God from humanity cease to exist. In Christianity, Jesus is united with God, living in the most intimate relationship with God imaginable. Then God raises Jesus to an unimaginably intimate relationship beyond the grave. Because Jesus is human, we know God is doing the same for us. God reaches toward us through the barriers between the divine and the human.

The scientific approach taken in this book reinforces the Christian perspective. Human beings evolved. Our characteristics and talents evolved. As we evolved into *Homo sapiens,* we acquired enhanced choices, autonomy, and creativity. We became more like God, cocreators. God does not resent our similarity to deity; our similarity is part of the divine plan.

At the same time, we become subject to and capable of evil because our evolved characteristics make us into creatures for whom suffering and death are evils and whose choices result in sin. That we have these evolved characteristics is not our doing. We did not choose them. As we merit no praise for them, so we deserve no blame. Nor can we cure ourselves of them. Indeed, we do not want to, for these characteristics mark who we are and constitute our good.

God's response to our situation is not to destroy the good characteristics that are also the sources of our suffering and sin. Rather, God shows complete understanding of us and, through that understanding, forgiveness. God becomes one with Jesus. In doing so, deity humbly establishes a kind of reciprocity with humanity. We evolved to be cocreators with God. In turn, God becomes a co-sufferer with us, in Jesus becoming subject to death and capable of sin. Thus, God initiates the most intimate relationship with us.

The Gospels reveal our typical response to God's compassionate charity and offer of intimacy. We reject them. We reject them just as Jesus' contemporaries rejected him. When Jesus preaches in his home synagogue, Luke says his hearers respond by trying to throw him over a cliff (Luke 4:28-29). Mark says his family thinks he is crazy (Mark 3:21). The religious authorities consider him blasphemous, deserving death (Mark 14:63-64). The Romans judge him dangerous to the state and kill him. All these people represent us, fleeing from God's presence and call. God's response to our rejection is to seek unity—at-one-ment—with us. One way God does this is to show what the at-one-ment of God and humanity looks like through showing us Jesus. The atonement is not an action Jesus performs. It is the message Jesus incarnates and enacts.

Jesus has power to transform our lives. Because he is human, he is like us, setting an example we can emulate. We can cease our misuse of sex and resources, wealth and power. We can reject exploitation and sin. Building on our evolved altruism and our capacity to use symbols, with the help of the Holy Spirit, we can overcome our egocentricity and love God and neighbor as Jesus did.

Jesus forgives the sins of the wicked without mediation or sacrifice. He invites them to dinner. Because Jesus reveals who God is, he shows us that God forgives our wickedness and wants to dine with us now and always. Accepting this is life transforming.

Jesus is more than a revelation in history. God raised him from the dead. Today, he seeks intimacy with us with the compassion and charity of God. Through the Holy Spirit, he wants to transform us from evolved creatures who suffer, sin, and die. Being divine and human, he is a bridge between us and God, a mediator and a liberator. His presence with us here and now helps us overcome our evolved bondage to sin and death. His power is power to transform.

Jesus shows us our salvation from death. He shows us that our earthly lives do not end but recycle into new lives, lives filled with new variety, structure, autonomy, and cocreativity.

This new interpretation of at-one-ment rejects the doctrine of the atonement as an action Jesus performs so that God becomes able to forgives us. Rather, Jesus' words and deeds show us that God is always forgiving us. This new interpretation of the atonement retains the message underlying the metaphors for atonement in the New Testament. It speaks of forgiveness and liberation. Atonement does not depend on us or bind us to perform certain actions. It is God's gift to us, freely given here and now.

Unless we refuse.

Conclusion

This book has searched for truth in the two sources of revelation traditional Christianity has claimed come directly from God, Scripture and nature, in order to unite science and Christianity. The search has employed the standard, positive philosophical tests of truth and the unique, negative test of canalization. Together, these tests of truth have undermined the scriptural basis of Christian doctrines of original sin and, then, the inerrant authority of Scripture. The results can be summarized in a phrase: the demise of Adam and Eve. Both the literal and liberal interpretations of the narrative of Adam and Eve have collapsed.

Science has demolished them by showing that Adam and Eve are not historical figures. Their reputed historicity conflicts with well-established scientific theories, the same theories that have created the technological revolution we confront each day as we drive to work, consult physicians, watch television, and access the Internet. Eden is nowhere. The labor with which Genesis says God cursed Adam is a passing phase of human history. Effective birth control and pain medications have mitigated Eve's alleged punishment. God has not cursed us. We are blessed to have evolved from creatures with fewer capabilities, even though our enhanced capacities increase our ability to choose, do, and suffer evil.

Science says the claim liberal theology has retained from literalism, that we are alienated and exiled, is false. Humanity evolved here on Earth. This is our native habitation. The elements in our bodies originate in the stars that light our way home. Our blood comes from the salt seas that stroke our shores. We are related to all other organisms. Every cell in our bodies contains information gleaned from 3 billion years of survival and reproduction by organisms on this planet. We know how to live here, and we have done so with remarkable success. We have inhabited every continent, traversed the seas, and walked on the moon. Our numbers are legion.

Moreover, the concept of alienation is recent. It arrived with agricultural surpluses and class divisions, about ten thousand years ago. When we are divided into rich and poor, we suffer alienation because we live with systematic structural injustice. The narrative of Adam and Eve is a product of one period of human history. Rather than being a broad myth full of truths about human nature, it is a narrow one about the human condition in peasant states.

Sociobiology tells us we are remarkably flexible and free. It tells us our self-interest is a natural product of evolution without which we would fail to flourish, but self-interest also leads us into fear and egocentricity. Sociobiology tells us we naturally love our kin. This natural love may be extended by reason and symbol beyond the circle of kin and clan, but it may also involve us in nepotism, murder, and genocide. Indeed, we have too many conflicting desires and too many choices. When we make wrong ones, evil comes into our lives. We need guidance from ethical rules and role models to realize how to live.

Jesus, too, has destroyed the literal and liberal interpretations of Adam and Eve, even while he has also resolved our ethical confusion. Jesus tells us that the labor of Adam's curse is not the human lot, that we are overly concerned with sustenance and apparel. Jesus shows us that our lives are not confined by Eve's curse, and that we can forgo sex and childbearing, for he chose celibacy. By charity toward his neighbor and his rejection of kin and clan, he shows us that egocentricity, nepotism, and fear need not rule us. By revealing the reign of God in our midst, he demonstrates God's parental love and care for us, God's will for an intimacy with us whose outcome, if we are willing, is at-one-ment, unity.

Thus, Jesus shows us that we are not alienated from God, but live in God's presence. God does not run away when we approach or haughtily withdraw from sinners to dwell only with the righteous. Rather, God embraces sinners as the father of the prodigal son embraces his own.

By consenting to suffering and death, Jesus asks us not to dread them. Jesus' resurrection tells us that we have dodged the flaming sword at the entrance to Eden, eaten of the tree of life, and live beyond the grave. His resurrection suggests ultimate union with God awaits us after death—a final at-one-ment.

Together, Jesus and science disclose an error in Christian theology that stretches back two thousand years. For two thousand years, Christian theology has hearkened to the myth of Adam and Eve and turned its back on Jesus. Ironically, science—Christianity's purported enemy—has freed it from falsehood. Because science has a model of human nature to substitute for that in the Christian doctrines of original sin, it finally enables Christianity to turn away from Adam and Eve and come face to face with Jesus. When Christian theology searches for truth rather than assuming it knows the truth, when it accepts the demise of Adam and Eve and discovers human nature, instead, in sociobiology, when it turns to Jesus to learn how to manage our remarkably complex nature, Christianity will heed Jesus' message and also embrace the unification of science and Christianity. But Christianity can embrace this important new consilience only if it consents to doing without Adam and Eve.

Glossary

agape. Self-denying, other-directed love; the charity of 1 Corinthians 13.

altruism. In biology, behavior that enhances another organism's prospects for reproduction while diminishing the altruist's own reproductive potential. The technical, biological term has nothing to say about motives.

anthropic principle. The contemporary design argument for the existence of God, which says that important yet minute details of the universe must have been designed for human beings to have evolved.

Archaeopteryx. A famous fossil found in the nineteenth century that looks like a dinosaur but has feathers. One of the first single fossils to imply that species evolved into one another.

artificial selection. Darwin's term for human intervention in plant and animal reproduction to enhance desirable attributes in domestic stocks.

atonement. Both unity with God and the action(s) performed to bring about that unity.

autonomous. Self-ruled; governed by one's own laws.

Big Bang. Theory that the universe began in a sudden, violent explosion approximately 12 billion years ago. Compare steady state.

biogeography. The study of the distribution of living and fossilized organisms on Earth.

canalization. In biology, the idea that some thoughts and behaviors are stereotypical. Canalization constitutes a negative test of truth. If ideas are canalized, we should be especially skeptical of them.

canonists. Scholars of the Hebrew Scriptures who consider the canonical text the appropriate source for theological reflection and reject the search for sources behind the text.

Catholic. Both the western church under Rome and the universal church.

charity. In this book, a technical term. Charity is self-sacrificial behavior directed toward the benefit of others and motivated by concern for their welfare.

coherence test of truth. If statements are logically consistent, they are true.

concupiscence. Desire, especially the desire for temporal goods.

conscious literalism. Interpreting the Bible literally or considering it inerrant or infallible while knowing that the results of this method of interpretation contravene modern understanding of science and history.

consilience test of truth. Usually restricted to scientific theories, it says scientific theories must fit together in such a manner that the coherence and correspondence tests of truth are satisfied.

correspondence test of truth. If statements correspond to the way the world is or, more accurately, to a model of the world, they are true. The test may also apply to literary texts.

cosmology. The study of the origin, processes, and structure of the universe.

D. The Torah document found in the book of Deuteronomy. It is one of the four sources of the Torah.

documentary hypothesis. The theory that the Torah is not a single document but is composed of at least four documents, designated by the initials J, E, P, and D.

E. The Torah document in which God is called *Elohim.* It is one of the four sources of the Torah.

egocentric. The modern term for the ancient term, pride; to put one's self at the center of one's attention and concern.

endemic species. Species that developed in one locale and are found nowhere else.

environmental determinism. The false idea that environment exclusively determines behavior.

exaptation. *See* preadaptation.

fall. The doctrine that Adam and Eve's sin brought about a degenerate change in human nature.

feminist scholars. Scriptural scholars whose work aims to counteract patriarchal ideology in Scripture.

Five Books of Moses. *See* Torah.

four-source hypothesis. The idea that the sources for the Synoptic Gospels are Mark and Q plus the materials special to Matthew and Luke, designated M and L, respectively.

freedom. The ability to make choices that affect our lives and the lives of others. This definition contrasts with that of western Christianity, which defines freedom as necessary obedience to God.

game theory. A branch of mathematics concerned with conflicts. It has been influential in the study of reciprocity.

gene pool. The collective genes of a designated biological group.

genetic determinism. The false idea that genes exclusively determine behavior.

genus. In biology, the level of hierarchy above a species. A genus contains several species. Plural, genera.

gnosticism. A religious movement that thought knowledge leads to salvation, the material world is evil, an evil god created it, but a good God reigns supreme. Christian Gnostics saw Jesus as Savior because he brought saving knowledge to humanity.

God of the gaps. Wherever scientific explanations fail, God becomes the explanatory hypothesis to salvage the failure.

group selection. Natural selection acting on a group composed of individuals not closely related to each other.

haplodiploid. Organisms in which the females share three-quarters of the copies of their genes with their sisters, half with their own offspring, and one-quarter with their brothers. Species with these features tend to form colonies with highly cooperative females and uncooperative males.

Hymenoptera. The most famous haplodiploid order in biology, which includes bees, wasps, and ants.

immanent. Existing in all things; said of God in classical Christian theology.

impassible. Not subject to suffering and pain; said of God in classical Christian theology. The idea comes from Greek philosophy, not from Scripture.

imprinting. The almost instant process in which, for example, an infant animal becomes attached to its primary caregiver. Imprinting is an example of a highly canalized process.

Interpreter. An element of brain and mind that insistently invents explanations of events, even if lacking the relevant data.

J. The Torah document in which God is called Yahweh (German: Jehovah). It is one of the four sources of the Torah.

kin selection. A form of natural selection in which close kin help one another. It underlies the evolution of altruism.

magnitude gap. The psychological disjunction between victim and perpetrator. Victims get more pain from their victimization than perpetrators receive pleasure from their vicious acts.

mitochondrial DNA. DNA that occurs outside the nucleus, in the mitochondria. It does not undergo recombination because it passes only from female to female, making it very useful for studies of evolution.

mitochondrial Eve hypothesis. A hypothesis that has nothing to do with Eve. Using mitochondrial DNA, it traces the first human beings to a relatively small group, numbering about ten thousand individuals, living about two hundred thousand years ago.

moral evils. Evils springing from wrong moral choices, such as revenge.

natural evils. Evils having natural causes, such as earthquakes.

naturalistic explanations. Explanations limited to science or common sense, excluding miracles and acts of divine or demonic beings.

neo-Darwinism. *See* New Synthesis.

nepotism. Favoring one's own relatives unfairly.

New Synthesis. In biology, the synthesis of genetics and Darwin's theory of evolution by natural selection.

original sin. Both the first sin committed by Adam and Eve and a model of human nature that sees us as corrupt and inclined to sin.

orthodox. Both Christians who believe central doctrines of the Christian church and the Greek-influenced churches of the Christian East.

P. The Torah document concerned with priestly matters. It is one of the four sources of the Torah.

Pentateuch. *See* Torah.

personal causal agents. Agents thought to cause natural events. To think personal causal agents cause natural events, rather than or in addition to natural forces, is a canalized response in human beings.

personal sin. Sin arising when institutions reward good and punish evil. There is no institutional social pressure to do wrong, yet a person does wrong anyway.

philosophical materialism. The view that nothing exists but matter; mistakenly thought to underlie or support science.

plate tectonics. The theory that continents move because hot magma wells up between them, creating sea trenches and mountain ranges.

population. In biology, a subset of a species; typical unit of speciation.

pragmatic test of truth. "If it works, it's true" is the pragmatic slogan. The test applies to science and technology. If a particular technology works, the scientific theory underlying it is said to be true. Often used as one component of the correspondence test of truth.

preadaptation. A feature that serves one purpose during evolution but a different purpose later. Sometimes called exaptation.

Q. From *Quelle*, the German word for *source*. Q is the hypothetical source for the material common to Matthew and Luke not found in Mark.

reciprocal altruism. Reciprocity, mutual exchange.

recombination. The mixing of genes in every generation because of sexual reproduction.

redactor. Editor.

regulative genes. Genes that regulate other genes. A change in a regulative gene can affect many genes and therefore produce large evolutionary changes suddenly.

reproductive isolation. Populations do not interbreed in the wild even if they inhabit the same locale.

sexual dimorphism. A difference in size between male and female. It can have profound effects on behavior.

sexual selection. In biology, mate choice based on attributes. Sexual selection may pick out different traits from natural selection and conflict with it.

sin. Disobeying the known will of God, failing to love God and neighbor.

sociobiology. The study of animal social behavior based on genetics.

species. Groups of actually or potentially interbreeding natural populations that are reproductively isolated from other such groups.

split-brain patients. People in whom the two halves of the brain have been severed surgically, disrupting communication between the halves.

steady state theory. Theory that the universe is eternal and that matter is continuously created to balance the universe's expansion. Compare to Big Bang.

structural sin. The idea that sin arises from the fact that institutions may reward evil and punish good. Institutions apply social pressure to encourage people to do wrong, often by saying that evil is right and good.

structuralists. Scholars of the Hebrew Scriptures who analyze the literary structure of the text.

stuff. In this book, a technical term used for the fuzzy, foggy, strangely behaving, indefinable whatever underlying all material things. Stuff does not resemble classical matter and its existence calls philosophical materialism into question.

Synoptic Gospels. The Gospels of Mark, Matthew, and Luke. They are alike. *Synoptic* means *see together.*

Synoptic problem. The problem posed by the fact that the Synoptic Gospels are so much alike.

theory. In this book, anything that can be tested for truth.

Torah. The first five books of the Hebrew Scriptures. Also known as the Pentateuch and the Five Books of Moses.

transcendent. Beyond and independent of the material universe; said of God in classical Christian theology.

two-source hypothesis. The idea that the Synoptic Gospels have two main sources, Mark and Q.

uniformitarianism. An assumption in science that the natural processes seen today operated in the past and will continue to operate in the future.

vitalism. The false idea that matter is inert and therefore organisms need some kind of special something added to them to make them live.

References

Ackerman, Jennifer. 1998. Dinosaurs Take Wing. *National Geographic* 194, no. 1:74–99.

Alcock, John. 1989. *Animal Behavior: An Evolutionary Approach.* Massachusetts: Sinauer.

Alter, Robert. 1981. *The Art of Biblical Narrative.* New York: Basic Books.

Anderson, Bernhard W. 1987. *Creation versus Chaos: The Reinterpretation of Mythical Symbolism in the Bible.* Philadelphia: Fortress Press.

Aquinas, Thomas. [1265–1271] 1964. *Summa Theologicae.* Vol. 26, *Original Sin.* Translated by T. C. O'Brien, O. P. London: Blackfriars.

Aristotle. [c. 320 B.C.E.] 1989. *The Nicomachean Ethics.* Translated by David Ross. New York: Oxford Univ. Press.

Athanasius. [c. 318] 1997. *St. Athanasius on the Incarnation: The Treatise de Incarnatione Verbi Dei.* Translated by a C.S.M.V. Crestwood, N.Y.: St. Vladimir's Orthodox Theological Seminary.

Augustine. [397] 1961. *Confessions.* Translated by R. S. Pine-Coffin. London: Penguin.

———. [413–426] 1984. *Concerning the City of God against the Pagans.* Translated by Henry Bettenson. London: Penguin.

Balaban, Evan, Marie-Aimee Teillet, and Nicole Le Douarin. 1988. Application of the Quail-Chick Chimera System to the Study of Brain Development and Behavior. *Science* 241:1339–42.

Barr, James. 1983. *Holy Scripture: Canon, Authority, Criticism.* Oxford: Clarendon.

———. 1993. *The Garden of Eden and the Hope of Immortality.* Minneapolis: Fortress Press.

Barrow, John D. and Frank J. Tipler. 1986. *The Anthropic Cosmological Principle.* Oxford: Oxford Univ. Press.

Batson, C. Daniel. 1991. *The Altruism Question: Toward a Social-Psychological Answer.* Hillsdale, N.J.: Erlbaum.

Baumeister, Roy F. 1997. *Evil: Inside Human Cruelty and Violence.* New York: Freeman.

Blenkinsopp, Joseph. 1994. The Documentary Hypothesis in Trouble. In *Approaches to the Bible: The Best of Bible Review.* Vol. 1, *Composition, Transmission and Language,* edited by Harvey Minkoff. Washington, D.C.: Biblical Archaeology Society.

Bloom, Harold. 1990. *The Book of J.* New York: Vintage.

Borg, Marcus J. 1994a. *Jesus in Contemporary Scholarship.* Valley Forge, Pa.: Trinity Press International.

———. 1994b. *Meeting Jesus Again for the First Time: The Historical Jesus and the Heart of Contemporary Faith.* San Francisco: HarperSanFrancisco.

Borg, Marcus J. and N. T. Wright. 1999. *The Meaning of Jesus: Two Visions.* San Francisco: HarperSanFrancisco.

Bowlby, John. 1990. *Charles Darwin: A New Life.* New York: Norton.

Bowler, Peter J. 1988. *The Non-Darwinian Revolution: Reinterpreting a Historical Myth.* Baltimore: Johns Hopkins Univ. Press.

———. 1989. *Evolution: The History of an Idea.* Rev. ed. Berkeley: Univ. of California Press.

Brown, Donald E. 1991. *Human Universals.* Philadelphia: Temple Univ. Press.

Brown, Peter. 1967. *Augustine of Hippo: A Biography.* Berkeley: Univ. of California Press.

Browning, Christopher R., 1992. *Ordinary Men: Reserve Police Battalion 101 and the Final Solution in Poland.* New York: HarperCollins.

Burkert, Walter. 1996. *Creation of the Sacred: Tracks of Biology in Early Religions.* Cambridge, Mass.: Harvard Univ. Press.

Calvin, John. [1559] 1995. *Institutes of the Christian Religion.* Translated by Henry Beveridge. Grand Rapids, Mich.: Eerdmans.

Carson, Hampton L. 1982. Evolution of Drosophila on the Newer Hawaiian Volcanoes. *Heredity* 48, no. 1:3–25.

Cartwright, Nancy. 1983. *How the Laws of Physics Lie.* Oxford: Clarendon Press.

Catechism of the Catholic Church. 1994. Mahwah, N.J.: Paulist.

Chilton, Bruce. 1992. *The Temple of Jesus: His Sacrificial Program within a Cultural History of Sacrifice.* University Park: Pennsylvania State Univ. Press.

Clark, Geoffrey A. 1998. Human Monogamy. *Science* 282:1047.

Clutton-Brock, T. H. 1991. *The Evolution of Parental Care.* Princeton, N.J.: Princeton Univ. Press.

Collier, John and Michael Stingl. 1993. Evolutionary Naturalism and the Objectivity of Morality. *Biology and Philosophy* 8:47–60.

Corey, M. A. 1993. *God and the New Cosmology: The Anthropic Design Argument.* Lanham, Md.: Rowman & Littlefield.

Cross, F. L., ed. 1958. *The Oxford Dictionary of the Christian Church.* London: Oxford Univ. Press.

Crossan, John Dominic. 1991. *The Historical Jesus: The Life of a Mediterranean Peasant.* San Francisco: HarperSanFrancisco.

———. 1993. The Passion, Crucifixion and Resurrection. In *The Search for Jesus: Modern Scholarship Looks at the Gospels,* edited by Hershel Shanks. Washington, D.C.: Biblical Archaeology Society.

Damasio, Antonio R. 1994. *Descartes' Error: Emotion, Reason, and the Human Brain.* New York: Putnam.

Darwin, Charles. [1859] 1964. *On the Origin of Species,* Cambridge, Mass.: Harvard Univ. Press.

———. [1871] 1981. *The Descent of Man, and Selection in Relation to Sex.* Princeton, N.J.: Princeton Univ. Press.

Dawkins, Richard. 1976. *The Selfish Gene.* New York: Oxford Univ. Press.

de Waal, Frans. 1996. *Good Natured: The Origins of Right and Wrong in Humans and Other Animals.* Cambridge, Mass.: Harvard Univ. Press.

Deacon, Terrence W. 1997. *The Symbolic Species: The Co-Evolution of Language and the Brain.* New York: Norton.

Degler, Carl N. 1991. *In Search of Human Nature: The Decline and Revival of Darwinism in American Social Thought.* New York: Oxford Univ. Press.

Dennett, Daniel C. 1995. *Darwin's Dangerous Idea: Evolution and the Meanings of Life.* New York: Simon & Schuster.

Dobzhansky, Theodosius. 1937. *Genetics and the Origin of Species.* New York: Columbia Univ. Press.

Duffy, J. Emmett. 1996. Eusociality in a Coral-Reef Shrimp. *Nature* 381:512–14.

Dulles, Avery. 1987. *Models of the Church.* New York: Doubleday.

Dunbar, Robin. 1996. *Grooming, Gossip, and the Evolution of Language.* Cambridge, Mass.: Harvard Univ. Press.

Dunn, James D. G. 1988. Pharisees, Sinners, and Jesus. In *The Social World of Formative Christianity and Judaism,* edited by Jacob Neusner, Peder Borgen, Ernest S. Frefichs, and Richard Horsley. Philadelphia: Fortress Press.

Ehrenreich, Barbara. 1997. *Blood Rites: Origins and History of the Passions of War.* New York: Holt.

Ehrman, Bart D. 1993. *The Orthodox Corruption of Scripture: The Effect of Early Christological Controversies on the Text of the New Testament.* New York: Oxford Univ. Press.

Eisenman, Robert. 1997. *James the Brother of Jesus: The Key to Unlocking the Secrets of Early Christianity and the Dead Sea Scrolls.* New York: Viking.

Fackelmann, Kathy A. 1989. Avian Altruism: African Birds Sacrifice Self-Interest to Help Their Kin. *Science News* 135, no. 23: 364–65.

Fisher, R. A. 1930. *The Genetical Theory of Natural Selection.* Oxford: Clarendon.

Friedman, Richard Elliott. 1987. *Who Wrote the Bible?* New York: Harper & Row.

———. 1995. The Cycle of Deception in the Jacob Tradition. In *Approaches to the Bible: The Best of Bible Review.* Vol. 2, *A Multitude of Perspectives,* edited by Harvey Minkoff. Washington, D.C.: Biblical Archaeology Society.

Funk, Robert W., Roy W. Hoover, and the Jesus Seminar. 1993. *The Five Gospels: The Search for the Authentic Words of Jesus.* San Francisco: HarperSanFrancisco.

Funk, Robert W. and the Jesus Seminar. 1998. *The Acts of Jesus: The Search for the Authentic Deeds of Jesus.* San Francisco: HarperSanFrancisco.

Gazzaniga, Michael S. 1992. *Nature's Mind: The Biological Roots of Thinking, Emotions, Sexuality, Language, and Intelligence.* New York: Basic.

Gerstner, John. 1982. A Protestant View of Biblical Authority. In *Scripture in the Jewish and Christian Traditions: Authority, Interpretation, Relevance,* edited by Frederick E. Greenspahn. Nashville: Abingdon.

Giere, Ronald N. 1988. *Explaining Science: A Cognitive Approach.* Chicago: Univ. of Chicago Press.

Gilby, Thomas, ed. and trans. 1955. *St. Thomas Aquinas, Theological Texts.* London: Oxford Univ. Press.

Gilligan, Carol. 1982. *In a Different Voice.* Cambridge, Mass.: Harvard Univ. Press.

Gnuse, Robert. 1985. *The Authority of the Bible: Theories of Inspiration, Revelation and the Canon of Scripture.* New York: Paulist.

Goldsmith, Timothy H. 1991. *The Biological Roots of Human Nature: Forging Links between Evolution and Behavior.* New York: Oxford Univ. Press.

Grant, Michael. 1977. *Jesus: An Historian's Review of the Gospels.* New York: MacMillan.

Greene, Erick. 1989. A Diet-Induced Developmental Polymorphism in a Caterpillar. *Science* 243: 643–46.

Hamilton, W. D. 1964. The Genetical Evolution of Social Behaviour I and II. *Journal of Theoretical Biology* 7:1–51.

Hefner, Philip. 1993. *The Human Factor: Evolution, Culture, and Religion.* Minneapolis: Fortress Press.

Helms, Randel. 1988. *Gospel Fictions.* Buffalo, N.Y.: Prometheus.

Helmuth, Laura. 1999. Spider Solidarity Forever: Social Spiders Create the Communes of the Arachnid World. *Science News* 155: 300–2.

Hunt, Morton. 1990. *The Compassionate Beast: What Science Is Discovering about the Humane Side of Humankind.* New York: Morrow.

Hurtado, Larry W. 1988. *One God, One Lord: Early Christian Devotion and Ancient Jewish Monotheism.* Philadelphia: Fortress Press.

Huxley, Julian S. 1942. *Evolution, the Modern Synthesis.* London: Allen & Unwin.

Jacob, F. 1977. Evolution and Tinkering. *Science* 196: 1161–67.

Josephus, Flavius. [77–100] 1981. *The Complete Works of Josephus.* Grand Rapids, Mich.: Kregel Publications.

Kagan, Jerome. 1984. *The Nature of the Child.* New York: Basic.

Keeley, Lawrence H. 1996. *War Before Civilization.* New York: Oxford Univ. Press.

Kelly, J. N. D. 1960. *Early Christian Doctrines.* New York: Harper & Row.

Kikawada, Isaac M., and Arthur Quinn. 1985. *Before Abraham Was: The Unity of Genesis 1–11.* Nashville: Abingdon.

Kohlberg, Lawrence. 1981. *Essays in Moral Development*. Vol. 1, *The Philosophy of Moral Development*. San Francisco: Harper & Row.

———. 1984. *Essays in Moral Development*. Vol. 2. *The Psychology of Moral Development*. San Francisco: Harper & Row.

Kohn, Alfie. 1990. *The Brighter Side of Human Nature: Altruism and Empathy in Everyday Life*. New York: Basic.

Kugel, James L. 1998. *Traditions of the Bible: A Guide to the Bible As It Was at the Start of the Common Era*. Cambridge, Mass.: Harvard Univ. Press.

Leakey, Richard. 1994. *The Origin of Humankind*. New York: Basic Books.

Leakey, Richard, and Roger Lewin. 1992. *Origins Reconsidered: In Search of What Makes Us Human*. New York: Doubleday.

Lewin, Roger. 1998. *Principles of Human Evolution: A Core Textbook*. Oxford: Blackwell.

Lifton, Robert J. 1986. *The Nazi Doctors: Medical Killing and the Psychology of Genocide*. New York: Basic.

Lorenz, Konrad. 1979. *The Year of the Greylag Goose*. Translated by Robert Martin. New York: Harcourt Brace Jovanovich.

Ludemann, Gerd. 1996. *Heretics: The Other Side of Early Christianity*. Louisville, Ky.: Westminster John Knox.

Mann, Janet. 1992. Nurturance or Negligence: Maternal Psychology and Behavioral Preference among Preterm Twins. In *The Adapted Mind: Evolutionary Psychology and the Generation of Culture*, edited by Jerome H. Barkow, Leda Cosmides, and John Tooby. New York: Oxford Univ. Press.

Margulis, Lynn, and Rene Fester, eds. 1991. *Symbiosis as a Source of Evolutionary Innovation: Speciation and Morphogenesis*. Cambridge, Mass.: MIT Press.

Mauss, Marcell. 1967. *The Gift: Forms and Functions of Exchange in Archaic Societies*. New York: Norton.

Maxwell, Mary. 1990. *Morality among Nations: An Evolutionary View*. New York: State Univ. of New York Press.

Mayr, Ernst. 1942. *Systematics and the Origin of Species*. New York: Columbia Univ. Press.

———. 1982. *The Growth of Biological Thought: Diversity, Evolution, and Inheritance*. Cambridge, Mass.: Harvard Univ. Press.

McAllister, Murdoch K., and Bernard D. Roitberg. 1987. Adaptive Suicidal Behavior in the Pea Aphids. *Nature* 328 , no. 6133:797–99.

McBrien, Richard P. 1994. *Catholicism*. San Francisco: HarperSan-Francisco.

McCarter, P. Kyle, Jr. 1994. A New Challenge to the Documentary Hypothesis. In *Approaches to the Bible: The Best of Bible Review.* Vol. 1, *Composition, Transmission and Language,* edited by Harvey Minkoff. Washington, D.C.: Biblical Archaeology Society.

Meier, John P. 1991. *A Marginal Jew: Rethinking the Historical Jesus.* Vol. 1, *Roots of the Problem and the Person.* New York: Doubleday.

————. 1994. *A Marginal Jew: Rethinking the Historical Jesus.* Vol. 2, *Mentor, Message, and Miracles.* New York: Doubleday.

Midgley, Mary. 1978. *Beast and Man: The Roots of Human Nature.* Ithaca, N.Y.: Cornell Univ. Press.

————. 1983. Selfish Genes and Social Darwinism. *Philosophy,* 58:365–77.

Milne, Pamela J. 1995. Eve and Adam: A Feminist Reading. In *Approaches to the Bible: The Best of Bible Review.* Vol. 2, *A Multitude of Perspectives,* edited by Harvey Minkoff. Washington, D.C.: Biblical Archaeology Society.

Milton, John. [1667] 1966. *Paradise Lost.* In *Milton: Poetical Works,* edited by Douglas Bush. London: Oxford Univ. Press.

Moses, Phyllis B., and Nam-Hai Chua. 1988. Light Switches for Plant Genes. *Scientific American* 258:88–94.

Murphy, Frederick J. 1991. *The Religious World of Jesus: An Introduction to Second Temple Palestinian Judaism.* Nashville: Abingdon.

Newton, Isaac. [1687] 1946. *Mathematical Principles of Natural Philosophy.* Translated by Andrew Motte. Berkeley: Univ. of California Press.

O'Brien, T. C. 1964. Appendices. In *St. Thomas Aquinas Summa Theologicae.* Translated by T. C. O'Brien. London: Blackfriars.

Oliner, Samuel P., and Pearl M. Oliner. 1988. *The Altruistic Personality: Rescuers of Jews in Nazi Europe.* New York: Free Press.

Pagels, Elaine. 1989. *Adam, Eve, and the Serpent.* New York: Vintage.

Paley, William. [1802] 1970. *Natural Theology: Or Evidences of the Existence and Attributes of the Deity Collected from the Appearances of Nature.* London: Farnborough, Gregg.

Pelikan, Jaroslav. 1971. *The Christian Tradition: A History of the Development of Doctrine.* Vol. 1, *The Emergence of the Catholic Tradition 100–600.* Chicago: Univ. of Chicago Press.

Pennisi, Elizabeth. 1999. Genomes Reveal Kin Connections for Whales and Pumas. *Science* 284: 2081.

Piaget, Jean. 1967. *Six Psychological Studies.* New York: Random House.

Pius XII [1950] 1956. *Human Generis.* Translated by Ronald A. Knox. In *The Papal Encyclicals in Their Historical Context,* edited by Anne Fremantle. New York: New American Library.

Powell, Jeffrey R. 1997. *Progress and Prospects in Evolutionary Biology: The Drosophila Model.* New York: Oxford Univ. Press.

Rachels, James. 1991. *Created from Animals: The Moral Implications of Darwinism.* New York: Oxford Univ. Press.

Rauschenbusch, Walter. 1919. *A Theology for the Social Gospel.* New York: MacMillan.

Ricklefs, Robert E. 1973. *Ecology.* Newton, Mass.: Chiron.

Ridley, Matt. 1996. *The Origins of Virtue: Human Instincts and the Evolution of Cooperation.* New York: Penguin.

Ruse, Michael. 1986. *Taking Darwin Seriously: A Naturalistic Approach to Philosophy.* Oxford: Basil Blackwell.

———. 1989. *The Darwinian Paradigm: Essays on its History, Philosophy, and Religious Implications.* London: Routledge.

———. 1994. Evolutionary Theory and Christian Ethics. *Zygon: Journal of Religion and Science* 29:5–24.

Sacks, Oliver. 1989. *Seeing Voices: A Journey into the World of the Deaf.* Berkeley: Univ. of California Press.

Sanders, E. P. 1985. *Jesus and Judaism.* London: SCM.

———. 1993. *The Historical Figure of Jesus.* London: Penguin.

Schmidt, Thomas. 1997. Jesus' Triumphal March to Crucifixion: The Sacred Way as Roman Procession. *Bible Review* 13:30–37.

Schüssler Fiorenza, Elisabeth. 1993. *Searching the Scriptures.* New York: Crossroads.

———. 1994. *Bread Not Stone: The Challenge of Feminist Biblical Interpretation.* Boston: Beacon.

———. 1998. *Sharing Her Word: Feminist Biblical Interpretations in Context.* Boston: Beacon.

Schwartz, Mark W., and Jason D. Hoeksema. 1998. Specialization and Resource Trade: Biological Markets as a Model of Mutualisms. *Ecology* 79:1029–38.

Sereny, Gitta. 1974. *Into that Darkness: An Examination of Conscience.* New York: Vintage.

Shanks, Hershel, ed. 1993. *The Search for Jesus: Modern Scholarship Looks at the Gospels.* Washington, D.C.: Biblical Archaeology Society.

Sheu, Fwu-Shan, Brian J. McCabe, Gabriel Horn, and Aryeh Routtenberg. 1993. Learning Selectively Increases Protein Kinase C Substrate Phosphorylation in Specific Regions of the Chick Brain. In *Proceedings of the National Academy of Sciences* 90:2705–9.

Shipman, Pat. 1999. *Taking Wing: Archaeopteryx and the Evolution of Bird Flight.* New York: Touchstone.

Silk, Joseph. 1989. *The Big Bang.* Rev. ed. New York: Freeman.

Simpson, George Gaylord. 1944. *Tempo and Mode in Evolution.* New York: Columbia Univ. Press.

Singer, Peter. 1981. *The Expanding Circle: Ethics and Sociobiology.* New York: Farrar, Straus & Giroux.

Smolin, Lee. 1997. *The Life of the Cosmos.* New York: Oxford Univ. Press.

Sober, Elliott, and David Sloan Wilson. 1998. *Unto Others: The Evolution and Psychology of Unselfish Behavior.* Cambridge, Mass.: Harvard Univ. Press.

Spong, John Shelby. 1994. *Resurrection, Myth or Reality? A Bishop's Search for the Origins of Christianity.* San Francisco: HarperSanFrancisco.

Sproul, R. C. 1996. *Explaining Inerrancy.* Orlando, Fla.: Ligonier Ministries.

Stebbins, G. Ledyard. 1950. *Variation and Evolution in Plants.* New York: Columbia Univ. Press.

Suppe, Frederick. 1989. *The Semantic Conception of Theories and Scientific Realism.* Urbana, Ill.: Univ. of Illinois Press.

Swift, Jonathan. [1726] 1970. *Gulliver's Travels.* Edited by Robert A. Greenberg. New York: Norton.

Tattersall, Ian. 1995. *The Fossil Trail: How We Know What We Think We Know about Human Evolution.* New York: Oxford Univ. Press.

Tennant, Fredrick R. [1903] 1968. *Sources of the Doctrines of the Fall and Original Sin.* New York: Schocken.

Thewissen, J. G. M., ed. 1998. *The Emergence of Whales: Evolutionary Patterns in the Origin of Cetacea.* New York: Plenum.

Tillich, Paul. 1951–1963. *Systematic Theology.* 3 vols. Chicago: Univ. of Chicago Press.

Treseder, Kathleen K., Diane W. Davidson, and James R. Ehleringer. 1995. Absorption of Ant-Provided Carbon Dioxide and Nitrogen by a Tropical Epiphyte. *Nature* 375:137–39.

Trible, Phyllis. 1973. Eve and Adam: Genesis 2–3 Reread. *Andover Newton Quarterly* 13:251–58.

———. 1978. A Love Story Gone Awry. In *God and the Rhetoric of Sexuality*, edited by Walter Brueggemann and John R. Donahue. Philadelphia: Fortress Press.

———. 1984. *Texts of Terror: Literary Feminist Readings of Biblical Narrative.* Philadelphia: Fortress Press.

Trivers, Robert L. 1971. The Evolution of Reciprocal Altruism. *The Quarterly Review of Biology* 46:35–57.

———. 1974. Parent-Offspring Conflict. *American Zoologist* 14:249–64.

Urban, Linwood. 1986. *A Short History of Christian Thought.* New York: Oxford Univ. Press.

van den Berghe, Pierre L. 1981. *The Ethnic Phenomenon.* New York: Elsevier.

———. 1990. *Human Family Systems: An Evolutionary View.* Prospect Heights, Ill.: Waveland.

Vandervelde, George. 1981. *Original Sin: Two Major Trends in Contemporary Roman Catholic Reinterpretation.* Washington, D.C.: Univ. Press of America.

Vermes, Geza. 1993. *Jesus the Jew: A Historian's Reading of the Gospels.* London: Collins.

von Rad, Gerhard. 1961. *Genesis: A Commentary.* Translated by John H. Marks. Philadelphia: Westminster.

Walsh, Jerome T. 1977. Genesis 2:4b—3:24: A Synchronic Approach. *Journal of Biblical Literature* 96:161–77.

Ware, Timothy. 1993. *The Orthodox Church.* London: Penguin.

Wenegrat, Brant. 1995. Belief in Unseen Beings: Its Evolutionary Basis and its Effects on Morality. In *Evolution and Human Values*, edited by Robert Wesson and Patricia A. Williams. Amsterdam: Rodopi.

Westermann, Claus. 1984. *Genesis 1–11: A Commentary.* Translated by John J. Scullion. London: SPCK.

Wevers, John William. 1993. *Notes on the Greek Text of Genesis.* Atlanta, Ga.: Scholars.

Williams, Patricia A. 1992. Review of *The Biological Roots of Human Nature: Forging Links between Evolution and Behavior* by T. H. Goldsmith. *The Quarterly Review of Biology* 67:562.

———. 1995. The Implications of Biology for Liberalism and Conservatism. In *Evolution and Human Values*, edited by Robert Wesson and Patricia A. Williams. Amsterdam: Rodopi.

———. 1996a: Christianity and Evolutionary Ethics: Sketch toward a Reconciliation. *Zygon: Journal of Religion and Science,* 31:253–68.

———.1996b. Sociobiology and Philosophy of Science. *Biology and Philosophy* 11, no. 2:271–78.

Williams, Patricia A. and R. G. Wesson, eds. 1995. *Evolution and Human Values.* Amsterdam: Rodopi.

Wilson, Edward O. 1975. *Sociobiology: The New Synthesis.* Cambridge, Mass.: Belknap.

Wise, Michael, Martin Abegg, Jr., and Edward Cook. 1996. *Dead Sea Scrolls: A New Translation.* San Francisco: HarperSanFrancisco.

Wright, N. T. 1996. How Jesus Saw Himself. *Bible Review* 12:21–29.

Yerkes, Royden Keith. 1952. *Sacrifice in Greek and Roman Religions and Early Judaism.* New York: Scribner's.

Young, Frances M. 1975. *Sacrifice and the Death of Christ.* London: SPCK.

Zimmer, Carl. 1998. *At the Water's Edge: Macroevolution and the Transformation of Life.* New York: Free Press.

Index

Deacon, Terrence W., 138
Dead Sea Scrolls, 11, 86
Degler, Carl N., 125
Deists, 3
Dennett, Daniel C., 103
determinism, 143, 144, 147
Devonian, 114
dinosaur, 112, 113
diploid, 127–29, 133, 143
DNA, 7, 75, 77, 120, 121, 129
Dobzhansky, Theodosius, 29, 73, 74
documentary hypothesis, 84, 85, 87
Drosophila, 110, 111
Duffy, J. Emmett, 127
Dulles, Avery, 185
Dunbar, Robin, 108

E, 2, 16, 17, 66, 69, 85, 92, 97, 124, 129, 133, 160, 163, 165, 191
Eden, 1, 35–39, 61, 68, 86, 196, 199, 200
egocentricity, 11, 53, 54, 132, 133, 137, 141, 145, 155, 156, 197, 200
Egypt, 2, 3, 41, 60, 87
Ehrenreich, Barbara, 136, 166, 184
Ehrman, Bart D., 183, 185
Einstein, Albert, 27, 79
Eisenman, Robert, 185
Elohim, 85
endemic species, 109, 111
environmental determinism, 144
erectus, 119, 120, 121
ergaster, 119, 121
eros, 154
Essenes, 187
ether, 27
Ethiopia, 118
ethology, 77, 149
Eucharist, 10
Euphrates, 65, 67, 79
Europe, 10, 58, 69, 117, 119, 154, 174

Evil: Inside Human Cruelty and Violence, 52
evolutionary psychology, xiii
Ezekiel, 59

Fackelmann, Kathy A., 128
fall, ix, xiv, 2, 3, 4, 20, 21, 28, 29, 30, 32, 37, 38, 40, 42, 44, 45, 46, 47, 49, 50, 53, 54, 55, 56, 57, 58, 60, 61, 80, 86, 87, 129, 142, 143, 145, 182, 186
feminist scholars, 98
Fester, Rene, 134
Fisher, R. A., 73
Five Books of Moses, 84, 85
fossils, 63, 64, 67, 68, 69, 72, 74, 75, 108, 111–19, 121, 122
four source hypothesis, 92, 93
freedom, 11, 45, 46, 47, 49, 56, 61, 80, 90, 142–48, 150, 152, 155, 157, 166, 168, 173, 178, 181, 192
Freud, Sigmund, 131
Friedman, Richard Elliott, 65, 79, 85, 87, 98
Funk, Robert W., 7, 12, 93, 94, 95, 185

Gage, Phineas, 156
Galapagos, 70, 74, 108
Galilee, 5, 13, 95, 189
Galileo, 2
game theory, 136
Gamow, George, 76
Gazzaniga, Michael S., 15, 16
gene pool, 109
genetic determinism, 143, 144, 147
genetics, xiii, 29, 72, 73, 74, 77, 78, 109, 121, 124
Gentiles, 12, 31
genus, 108, 111, 118
geology, xiii, 29, 75, 76, 122, 123
Germany, 34, 174, 175
Gerstner, John, 82

Giere, Ronald N., 24, 27
Gilby, Thomas, 57
Gilligan, Carol, 18
Glashow, Sheldon, 29
Gnuse, Robert, 6, 96
God of the gaps, 3
Gold, Thomas, 76
Goldsmith, Timothy H., 125, 144, 145
gophers, 114
gorillas, 116
Gospel of Thomas, 12, 92, 100
Gould, John, 70
grace, 55, 56, 60, 61, 62, 80, 155
Grant, Michael, 185
Great Chain of Being, 117, 177
Greene, Erick, 144
group selection, 128–30, 133, 134
groupishness, 129, 130, 140

habilis, 118–20
Hadar, 118
Hagar, 7
Haldane, J. B. S., 73
Hamilton, W. D., 124
haplodiploid, 127, 128
Hawaiian Islands, 110
Hebrew scriptures, xii, 2, 7, 38, 44, 59, 83, 84, 89, 90, 98, 180, 184
Hebrews, 8, 33, 38, 41, 90, 99, 180
Hefner, Philip, 144, 166, 167
heidelbergensis, 119
Helms, Randel, 185
Helmuth, Laura, 127
Henry, Patrick, 178
Hoeksema, Jason D., 135
Holy Spirit, xiii, 6, 8, 187, 192, 193, 195, 197
Homo, 78, 118–20, 124, 128, 137, 162, 166, 196
homosexuality, 152
Hoyle, Fred, 76, 160
Hunt, Morton, 132
Hurtado, Larry W., 5, 185

Hutton, James, 195
Huxley, Julian, 29, 73
Huxley, Thomas Henry, 112
Hymenoptera, 126, 127, 129

Ichthyostega, 121
immanence, 79, 194
impassible, 192
imprinting, 16, 17
Indonesia, 67
inerrancy, 2, 4, 80, 82
Institutes of the Christian Religion, 49
Interpreter, 14, 15, 16, 30, 31, 46, 76, 116, 131, 185
Isaac, 3, 85, 87
Islam, 4, 63, 99
Israel, 11, 84, 191

J, 73, 85, 86, 87, 92, 97, 98, 162
Jacob, 3, 87, 107
Jeremiah, 59, 60
Jerusalem, 2, 3, 8, 92, 188, 189, 190
Jesus Seminar, 7, 12, 92, 93, 94, 95, 185
Job, 59
Johanson, Donald, 118
John, Gospel of, 8, 90, 91, 92, 93, 95, 99, 152, 154, 186
John the Baptist, 60, 93, 183, 185, 187, 189, 191
Josephus, 185
Joshua, 180
Judah, 84, 85, 87
Judaism, 4, 33, 40, 63, 184, 191, 192

Kagan, Jerome, 17
Keeley, Lawrence H., 136, 137, 140, 150
Kenya, 118, 119
Kidron valley, 93
Kikawada, Isaac M., 85
killdeer, 145, 146

Rome, xvii, 3, 34, 58, 91, 188–90
rudolfensis, 118
Ruse, Michael, x, xi, 28, 29

Sacks, Oliver, 17
sacrifice, 11, 20, 33, 131, 132, 181, 183, 184, 185, 188, 190, 191, 192, 197
Salam, 29
Samaritan, 86, 93, 153, 155
Samaritan Torah, 86
Samuel, 59, 86, 93
sanctifying grace, 55, 56
Sanders, E. P., 5, 185, 189
Sarah, 7
Satan, 40, 54, 168, 182
Schmidt, Thomas, 92, 185, 190
Schüssler Fiorenza, Elisabeth, 88
Schwartz, Mark W., 135
selection pressure, 110
selective breeding, 104, 105
Septuagint, 59, 92, 94
Sereny, Gitta, 174
sexual dimorphism, 119, 156
sexual selection, 107, 111
Shanks, Hershel, 185
Sheu, Fwu-Shan, 17
Shipman, Pat, 112
shrimp, 127
Sihetun, 112
Silk, Joseph, 159
silvestrus, 110, 111
Simon of Cyrene, 190
Simpson, George Gaylord, 29, 74
sin, xiii, xiv, xv, 4, 10, 11, 20, 33, 41, 42–51, 54–58, 61, 62, 80, 81, 86, 100, 142, 143, 148, 151, 152, 157, 158, 159, 170, 172–75, 178, 179, 180, 181, 182, 184, 185, 186, 188, 189, 191, 192, 193, 196, 197
Singer, Peter, 154
Sinosauropteryx, 112
Smith, Adam, 135

Smolin, Lee, 160
Sober, Elliott, 128, 129, 132, 171
Sociobiology, The New Synthesis, 77, 124
Socrates, 176
South America, 69, 70
speciation, 70, 73, 74, 108, 110, 111, 115, 120
species, 1, 3, 21, 30, 67, 68, 69, 70, 71, 72, 74, 75, 76, 78, 105, 106, 108–15, 116, 117, 118, 119, 120, 122, 124, 125, 126, 127, 128, 129, 134, 137, 138, 145, 148, 149, 151, 152, 157, 162, 164, 165, 169, 174
split-brain, 15, 16
Spong, John Shelby, 6
Sproul, R. C., 82, 83
SS, 174, 175
Stangl, Franz, 174
steady-state, 76
Stebbins, G. Ledyard, 74
structural sin, 172–75, 178–79, 185, 189, 191, 192
stuff, 149, 160, 161, 164, 169, 193, 194
substance, 9, 27, 195
Summa Theologicae, 55, 57
Suppe, Frederick, 24
Swift, Jonathan, 169, 170
synoptic Gospels, 91, 92, 95
Syria, 68

Tamar, 87
Tattersall, Ian, 115, 118
Temple, 94, 183, 187, 188, 190, 191, 196
termites, 126, 127, 128
Tertullian, 182
Tethys Sea, 113
theory of everything, 28, 123
Thomas, Gospel of, 12, 92, 100
Tigris, 65, 67, 79
Tillich, Paul, 79, 193